Selina of Sussex

With best wishes

Leonard Holder

Selina of Sussex
1818 – 1886

*Family life in Sussex, southern England,
seen through the eyes of Selina, the wife of
Eli Page, farmer and Baptist minister*

Leonard Holder

Copyright © 2014 by Leonard Holder.

ISBN:	Hardcover	978-1-4990-9092-5
	Softcover	978-1-4990-9091-8
	eBook	978-1-4990-9093-2

All rights reserved. No part of this book may be reproduced or transmitted in any form or by any means, electronic or mechanical, including photocopying, recording, or by any information storage and retrieval system, without permission in writing from the copyright owner.

Any people depicted in stock imagery provided by Thinkstock are models, and such images are being used for illustrative purposes only.
Certain stock imagery © Thinkstock.

Scripture quotations marked KJV are from the Holy Bible, King James Version (Authorized Version). First published in 1611. Quoted from the KJV Classic Reference Bible, Copyright © 1983 by The Zondervan Corporation

This book was printed in the United States of America.

Rev. date: 10/27/2014

To order additional copies of this book, contact:
Xlibris
0-800-056-3182
www.xlibrispublishing.co.uk
Orders@xlibrispublishing.co.uk
636196

Selina of Sussex
Order copies from author online:
www.holderfamilyheritage.de
or by email: orders@lenandphylsbook.de

Contents

PART 1

My Early Life
1818–1838

Chapter 1	My Home and Family	17
Chapter 2	Selina—Countess of Huntingdon	21
Chapter 3	Uncle George Gilbert of Heathfield	29
Chapter 4	Learning without School	35
Chapter 5	Eli Asks Me Out	41
Chapter 6	Courtship and Death of Eli's Father	49
Chapter 7	Eli's Conversion and Our Marriage	55

PART 2

Clifton Farm, Arlington
1838–1842

Chapter 1	Our Early Home and Daily Routine	61
Chapter 2	Sundays at Lower Dicker	67
Chapter 3	Our Household Increases	71
Chapter 4	The Gruesome Side of Farming	75
Chapter 5	An Additional Challenge	79
Chapter 6	Eli's First Sermon	85
Chapter 7	Springtime in Sussex	89
Chapter 8	A Distressing Family Incident	93
Chapter 9	Another Baby and the Birth of a Plan	97
Chapter 10	Man Sows, God Gives the Increase	101
Chapter 11	Harvest and Winter	107
Chapter 12	A Bigger Farm	115

PART 3
Limden Farm
1842–1856

Chapter 1	The Move	121
Chapter 2	A New Location with New Experiences	123
Chapter 3	A New Crop	127
Chapter 4	New Neighbours	129
Chapter 5	Finding a New Church	135
Chapter 6	New Challenges	139
Chapter 7	Charcoal Burning	145
Chapter 8	Grain Harvest	153
Chapter 9	Harvesting Our Hops	157
Chapter 10	Years Roll By	161
Chapter 11	New Friendships	165
Chapter 12	Bringing Up the Children at Limden Farm	171
Chapter 13	Beekeeping	177
Chapter 14	Eli Unsettled	183

PART 4
Perching Manor Farm, Fulking
1856 onwards

Chapter 1	A New Challenge	191
Chapter 2	Exploring Our South Downs	197
Chapter 3	Sheep Farming on the South Downs	201
Chapter 4	Family Readjustments	205
Chapter 5	The Family Grows Up	209
Chapter 6	Man Shall Not Live by Bread Alone	215
Chapter 7	Sheep Washing and Shearing	221
Chapter 8	Marriages	227
Chapter 9	Eli as Itinerant Preacher	235
Chapter 10	More Changes	241
Chapter 11	Ruth's Wedding	245

Chapter 12	John and Mary Ann	251
Chapter 13	Mayfield	257
Chapter 14	A Sunday Evening Service at Mayfield Chapel	269
Chapter 15	Spiritual Conversation	275
Chapter 16	The Lord Gives and the Lord Takes Away	283
Chapter 17	Two Contrasting Weddings	287
Chapter 18	'A Faithful God'—But Is He?	295
Chapter 19	Page in History	303
Chapter 20	Ebenezer Dan Holder	307
Chapter 21	My Epilogue	309
Postscript		313
Appendix 1	Eli's Own Testimony of His Conversion	315
Appendix 2		319
Appendix 3	Sussex Windmills	323
Appendix 4		325
Index		327

Dedicated to Selina's great-great-great-great-grandchildren:

Barnaby, Sophia, Timothy, David, Beatrice, Benedict, and John Holder
whose lives in Switzerland in the twenty-first century are so very, very different from hers.

Family Tree
Simplified to show the author's side of Selina's and Eli's large family

Eli Page - Selina Westgate
b. 11 Oct. 1817 *b. 17 Aug. 1818*
Married 12 Feb. 1838

|

Ruth Page - Dan Holder
b. 2 July 1841 *b. 9 Jan. 1844*
Married 13 April 1868

|

Ebenezer Dan Holder - Mary Gertrude White
b. 3 April 1877 *b. 31 Dec. 1883*
Married 13 Sept. 1908

|

Edgar Ebenezer Holder - Ellen Rachel Wilkins
b. 15 July 1909 *b. 28 July 1908*
Married 16 Jan. 1937

|

Leonard Edgar Holder - Phyllis Mary Pittwell
b. 3 April 1946 *b. 22 Nov. 1946*
Married 3 June 1967

|

Geoffrey Leonard Holder | Daniel Francis Holder
b. 5 April 1968 | *b. 5 May 1970*
and Ruth Anne Leyshon | *and* Martina Franz
Married 30 Dec. 1995 | *Married 12 Sept. 1993*

| | |

Barnaby John Holder | Sophia Evangeline Holder
b. 30 Oct. 1997 | *b. 23 Jan. 1998*
Timothy Dafydd Leonard Holder | David Gregory Holder
b. 12 Feb. 1999 | *b. 28 Jan. 2000*
Beatrice Ellen Holder | Benedict Francis Holder
b. 13 July 2000 | *b. 16 Oct. 2001*
  | John Michael Holder
  | *b. 2 Feb. 2008*

Selina's Introduction
(imagined by the author)

Hello, I'm Selina, and I want to tell you all about myself, my husband, and my family. We have had a very challenging life, and I want to share something of it with you and to acknowledge God's help and blessing from the day of my birth and throughout it all.

My grandson's grandson is writing this as a diary of my life, and because he never knew me and can have no personal contact with me, he is using a lot of imagination. I'm sure you would find it very boring if he were to merely list the bare facts he's found out about me and Eli! He's done a lot of research to find out how life was in Sussex in the nineteenth century and, through census information, who our neighbours were, so I think the story that comes over isn't far from the truth. However, he has been very kind in not imagining and mentioning many of our serious failings! One of the wonderful things about being a Christian is that God has forgiven our sins and, in the words of the Bible, 'cast them into the depths of the sea'. As someone once said, he's also put up a sign saying, 'No fishing'. I'm sure, however, you will find enough humanity in this story to realise that we were far from perfect. On the other hand, one of the main purposes of us sharing these details is to glorify God and his grace towards us, and I think you will find this comes across strongly.

I'm now in the place that the Bible calls 'glory', and it's far more wonderful than you could ever imagine. Please, please take the Bible and spiritual things seriously. There is most certainly life after death, and you each need to be prepared for it. Maybe this book will help you find the way. I hope so and that, through our Saviour Jesus Christ, you will one day come and find me in heaven!

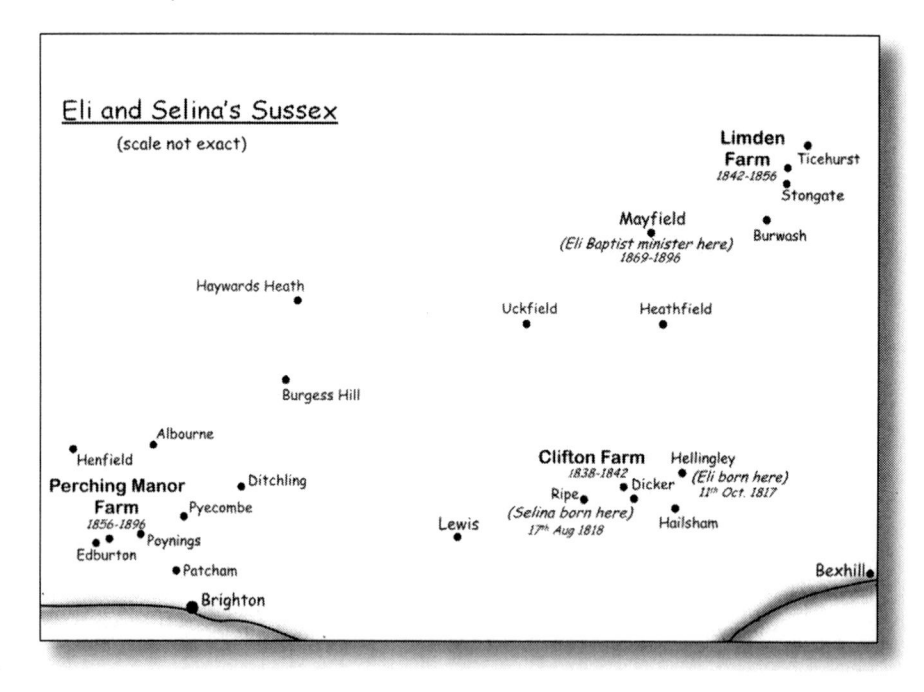

Eli and Selina's Sussex
(scale not exact)

- Limden Farm *1842-1856*
- Ticehurst
- Stongate
- Mayfield *(Eli Baptist minister here) 1869-1896*
- Burwash
- Haywards Heath
- Uckfield
- Heathfield
- Burgess Hill
- Albourne
- Henfield
- Perching Manor Farm *1856-1896*
- Ditchling
- Pyecombe
- Poynings
- Edburton
- Patcham
- Brighton
- Lewis
- Clifton Farm *1838-1842*
- Ripe
- Dicker
- *(Selina born here) 17th Aug 1818*
- Hellingley *(Eli born here) 11th Oct. 1817*
- Hailsham
- Bexhill

Eli and Selina's Sussex

Part 1

My Early Life
1818–1838

Chapter 1

My Home and Family

I was born on the 17 August 1818 in the little village of Ripe in Sussex in southern England. If you look for Ripe on a map, you'll find that as the crow flies it's about five miles due west of the town of Hailsham and about six miles due east of Lewis. Of course by the winding country lanes, it's quite a bit further, and when I was a girl, these lanes were really atrocious. They had deep ruts from the wheels of the farm wagons and the hoofs of cattle and oxen, and after rain, the mud was terrible and the ruts filled up with water which made travelling extremely difficult and also dangerous. There used to be a riddle going around which the village boys really loved: 'Why are the legs of oxen, swine, women, and other animals so much longer in Sussex?' Answer: 'Because they get stretched being pulled out of so much mud!'[1]

Having said that, I'm very proud to be a true Sussex girl from a village that was once part of the estate of Earl Harold. This was the same Harold who became king of England in 1066 and, in fact, was our last Anglo-Saxon king. Sadly, he only reigned just over ten months

---

[1] Elizabeth Mararetta Bell-Irving, *Mayfield: Story of an Old Wealden Village* (William Clowes & Sons, 1903) 11. Quoted from the journal for year 1751 by Dr Burton of Cambridge.

and died in battle that same year, trying unsuccessfully to defend our country from the Norman invaders led by William the Conqueror.

Our family name is Westgate, and my parents ran a market garden in Ripe. My mum, Ann, and we children had to do a lot of the field work, growing vegetables and fruit, and my dad, Samuel Westgate, sold the produce. He had a good number of local clients and also a stall which he used to take around to markets in our local villages. He would also buy-in other produce to sell. We children had to help a lot both in the house and on the land. Mum is Dad's second wife. Barbara, whom we didn't hear much about, died in 1804. She had one son, Richard, who was quite a lot older than us and was already living away from home when we were children. Funnily, his surname wasn't Westgate, and we often wondered about this but it was never explained to us. Dad married my mum in 1805. Mum's quite a bit younger than Dad and gave him eight children, and I'm one of the youngest. I'm hoping you'll get to know me quite well as you read on, but I just want to say that as a girl I was quite slight and not tall and my light-brown hair was naturally a bit wavy, which I was pleased about. We children didn't get a lot of chance of using a mirror, but when I did see my reflection, I used to thank God I wasn't like Dorcas on the farm down the lane. I was happy with my light-blue eyes, even that greenish tinge which I could see if I looked carefully. However, as I grew older I did fear my nose was growing a bit big!

As a little girl, I really hated my name Selina because my brothers often called me Silly. But I must say, by the time I was a teenager, I really loved it. The main reason was the connection. Selina, countess of Huntingdon, had had a strong influence on our family, which was why I was called Selina, and as I got to know about her, I was proud to share the name with her.

I shall need to tell you about my namesake soon, but first I want you to be able to picture our family life a bit better as I'm sure you will find it very different from yours.

Our family home was a four-roomed cottage on the outskirts of the village. There were two rooms upstairs and two rooms downstairs, one of which was our kitchen and living room. Mum and Dad slept in the other downstairs room, and we children slept upstairs. We girls had one room, and my brothers had the other. A door from the kitchen led into our backyard where we had a pump which drew water from a well in the ground. Dad was very proud of our well, and I was really sorry for families who didn't have one because they had to walk much further to get water from either a stream or the main village pump.

In many ways our lives revolved around our water pump. Each morning we children would pump water over our heads to wake us up and give us a bit of a wash, and a least once a week Mum would insist that we stripped and had a good dowsing all over. In the summer we would run around to dry off, and when it was colder, we would rub ourselves hard with a cloth and sit by the fire in the kitchen for a while. I know Mum and Dad did something similar, but this must have been either early in the morning or later at night when we children weren't about. Very occasionally in winter, we were allowed a hot wash in the kitchen, but Dad always maintained that cold water was better for us.

All water for the kitchen had to be drawn up out of the well, and it was one of my brothers' jobs to make sure the big water bucket next to the sink in the kitchen was always full. We burnt wood on the kitchen fire, and all our food was cooked on this. Near the pump in the yard was an outhouse. It wasn't very big but big enough to store wood for the fire and also a supply of sand. This was used on the kitchen floor which was simply earth, and Mum would sweep it each day and scatter a fresh supply of sand as necessary to keep everything fresh. Mum often used to quote the saying 'Cleanliness is next to godliness', and she also impressed on us that homes that neglected cleanliness got far more illness. We were all very familiar with family tragedies when children in the village became ill and died.

Next to the outhouse was our privy, which was a simple wooden shed with a bucket under a wooden seat with a hole in it. You can guess what this was for! It had to be emptied every day, and Dad had this well organised in order to use its contents to best advantage to help our vegetables to grow well. I remember hearing him say jokingly that it was our privy that made the difference between profit and loss in our market garden business! All our other waste and rubbish was either burnt on the kitchen fire or, if it wasn't going to attract vermin, thrown on a compost and manure heap, which later also helped to enrich our soil.

In the winter evenings, we had an oil lamp in the kitchen which made it very cosy, and when it was time for bed, we went upstairs with a candle. These we made ourselves out of tallow, which is animal fat purified by melting and straining it through cheesecloth. Of course we had to use them sparingly. One of our earliest lessons as children was how to use candles safely. I remember really looking forward to my sixth birthday because I was then allowed to carry my own candle!

A large table filled most of the kitchen, and for meals Dad had his special armed chair at the head. Mum had her chair at the other end, and we children sat along two long benches.

As I think back on my childhood, I realise there were many very happy times which could never be enjoyed again in the same way once I grew up. One special memory was sitting on the floor with straw to make us comfortable around the kitchen fire while Mum or Dad told us stories. We had no books to read. The only books I remember in the house were a Bible and a book called the *Pilgrim's Progress*, and most of the stories we heard came out of these two books.

God was a very important person in our home. We couldn't see him but we thanked him for each meal, and Dad would often talk to him and ask him to look after us all and help with the business. Then there would often come a funny phrase which it took me a long time to understand. Dad would pray that God would put his grace into each of our hearts!

I was never frightened of God because Dad had explained to us children that although God is very powerful and very holy, he loves us. He wants us to be kind and good, and we each had to learn and repeat the Ten Commandments in order to understand what being good meant. But Dad also told us about God's Son, Jesus, who died on a cross to forgive the sins of all his people. Anyway one winter's evening, we had a different story which I want to share with you because I never forgot it, and it made me very proud to have the name Selina.

Chapter 2

Selina—Countess of Huntingdon

It was a wild and stormy evening in late November. We'd had supper early—one of Mum's delicious vegetable stews with chunks of homemade bread. Mum mostly baked bread herself. We had to really use our teeth to get into it, but once through the crust, the steaming warm bread was something special and certainly soon filled us up. That suppertime with the wind howling outside and the flame of the lamp jumping up and down and casting moving shadows all around the room, Dad read the verses in the Psalms about 'those that go down to the sea in ships'. It goes on to describe a stormy wind which lifts up the waves and the poor sailors mount up to the heavens and then drop back into the depths. It was so descriptive, and I began to imagine it all happening. Wonderfully, the passage finishes with the verse that Dad got us all to repeat together. 'Then they cry unto the Lord in their trouble and He bringeth them out of their distresses.' In his prayer that evening, Dad especially prayed for sailors and anyone else who might be frightened because of the weather that we all might know God's deep peace inside us.

It was quite an emotional evening for me, and so I listened with special attention when Mum later sat with us around the fire, with blankets around us, and told us a wonderful story.

'Not long ago', she began, 'there lived a very important lady named Selina. She was born into a rich family in a very big house, with lots of servants, and there was always plenty of lovely food to eat and beautiful clothes to wear. She wasn't actually a princess, but her family was related to the king of England. Anyway, although you would think there was every reason for her to be happy, she wasn't. Her father was a very difficult man, and there were always rows and arguments, and she would hear the servants complaining and saying dreadful things about her family. Sometimes relatives came to visit and then almost invariably there were more rows.

'When Selina grew up, she married an earl, which meant she became a countess. She was very happy with her husband and grateful to have escaped from her own family home. God gave her several children, and although she was often unwell, her husband loved her, and she always tried to do her best and to live a worthwhile life.

'Then something happened which eventually changed her life completely. One of her sisters got enthusiastic about the Bible. The family blamed the preachers, who at that time were roaming the country and attracting large crowds of people. Although most of these preachers were ordained ministers, the bishops and vicars who controlled the churches were very suspicious of them, and many banned them from preaching in their buildings. This of course made them even more popular as lots of people were fed up with organised religion and thought most ministers were hypocrites who claimed to represent God and yet lived lives as bad, if not worse, than normal people. Selina had, of course, heard about these preachers, the most famous being John Wesley and his brother Charles and another man named George Whitefield, who were all then regularly preaching on common land and village greens and even in churchyards with the people standing and sitting around the gravestones. Although she had read many different views about them, the fact that they were ordained Church of England ministers and, as most fair critics agreed, were only preaching doctrine based on the official Thirty-Nine Articles of the Church, Selina's private opinion was that if their preaching helped the common people, then let them preach and God bless them! However, for royalty, and particularly her own family, to support these men openly was going too far. She went to stay with her sister and had lots of conversations about the Bible and heard how these men explained it and was introduced personally to Benjamin Ingram, a follower of Wesley. The end result of this was that she too was converted to this evangelical faith.[2]

'The whole emphasis of Selina's life changed. Her husband was sympathetic to her new views and encouraged her in her efforts to teach her children about Jesus. Sadly, he died at quite a young age, and although Selina struggled for a while as a widow, she now found she had complete freedom to use her extensive wealth as she wanted. She began to use her money almost exclusively to enable as many people as possible to hear the good news that Jesus came into the world to be our Saviour.

'One day in the spring of 1757, about seventy years ago, Selina, countess of Huntingdon, came to Sussex. Her youngest son was ill, and the doctors had advised her that the sea air and salt water of Brighthelmstone, as Brighton was then called, could help him. Soon after arriving, she was walking along the seafront when a woman came up to her with a beaming face.

'"Madam," she said, "you've come at last!"'

Mum paused to let this poor Sussex woman's astonishing exclamation sink in.

'Did she know her?' asked Sam, my brother.

'No,' answered Mum with a little smile. 'Selina had never been to Brighton before, and the woman knew nothing about royalty.'

'But she must have been expecting her,' retorted Sam.

'Selina was a kind lady,' continued Mum, 'and, although it caused a bit of consternation from passers-by, she sat down on a bench and invited the woman to sit next to her and explain her remark. At first she had difficulty in understanding the broad Sussex language, but eventually she gathered the following facts. Three years previously, the woman had had a very vivid dream. She had seen someone who, because of her unusual clothes, she now recognised to be Selina, coming to Brighton with a very important message. The dream had not said

---

[2] Faith Cook, *Selina, Countess of Huntingdon* (Banner of Truth) 36.

what this message was, but since then the woman had been watching and waiting for this lady to come. [3]

'Selina arranged a time to meet the woman again, and when this happened, she was able to tell her about Jesus and especially the fact that he is the Saviour of sinners. She explained that nobody can get to heaven by simply going to church or giving money to charity and that whether a woman was a fisherman's wife or a daughter of royalty it made no difference to God. "All have sinned and come short of the glory of God", says the Bible and only Jesus has the authority to say "Your sins are forgiven" and this he does willingly to all who are sorry for the wrong things in the their lives and ask him for mercy. The woman accepted the gospel with faith and joy, and Selina knew that God had been preparing her for this message which he had told her in the dream was coming.'

This story gave me a wonderful warm feeling inside, and I couldn't wait to hear more about my namesake. All of us children looked at Mum, hoping there was more to come before she sent us up to bed, and we weren't disappointed because it was clear that Mum loved the story as much as we did.

'That was just the beginning,' continued Mum. 'Soon after this, Selina visited a soldier's wife who had just had twin babies and was dangerously ill. The mother knew she was dying and realised she was not prepared to meet God. Selina's message brought tears to her eyes, and she begged her to come back and tell her more. The news got around, and when Selina returned, the woman had several friends waiting around her bed to hear the wonderful gospel of God's love, which sadly had never been explained to them in their churches. But wonderfully, and surely this was part of God's plan, the woman's bedroom was next to a public bakehouse where poorer people who had no oven in their homes could bring their dough and bake their bread.

---

[3] This incident was recorded by Augustus Montague Toplady (1740–1778) who was told it by the countess on 30 August 1776, *Works*, 509—see Faith Cook, op. cit., 175.

There was a crack in the wall, and unknown to Selina, as she shared the stories of Jesus with those in the bedroom, several women waiting for their bread to bake were listening on the other side of the crack.'

'I wonder whether the crack was big enough to peep through,' commented my brother.

'That's not the sort of question to ask,' I couldn't help saying. 'Did they become believers too, Mummy?'

Mum continued with the story.

'Selina came regularly to talk to the dying woman, and the little group around her bed seemed to get bigger every time she came. The room was dark and dismal, and one day Selina noticed there was a man sitting quietly on the floor in the shadows in the corner of the room. At first she wondered whether she should challenge him and ask him to leave, but then something seemed to tell her to ignore him and to act as though she hadn't seen him. She told the women another story about Jesus. How Nicodemus came to Jesus by night and how Jesus told him, although he was an important Jewish leader, that he needed to be born again. It was clear to her that like Nicodemus, none of the women had any idea what this meant, and she went on to describe to them Jesus' explanation. That as Moses had lifted up a bronze serpent in the wilderness when the people were dying of snakebite and all who looked at the serpent on the pole had lived, so Jesus was going to be lifted up on the cross and everyone who looked to him for salvation would have new life—eternal life. We must all die physically, but all those who have looked to Jesus on the cross and trusted him to be their Saviour would go to live with him forever.

'This really touched many of the women's hearts, and in tears, several of them were truly converted. The man listening in the corner was a local blacksmith named Joseph Wall. It was well known that he was a wicked man, but God's Word pieced his conscience, and he too became a believer and a changed person.[4]

---

[4] Faith Cook, op. cit. 175–177.

'Dad knew someone who had met Joseph Wall, and he said that Joseph would often talk about that day he had listened to the gospel from Selina, sitting in the corner of the bedroom next to the bakehouse. He would tell everyone that Jesus had made him so happy and content that he wouldn't change places with anyone, not even the king of England.

'Selina stayed in Brighton as long as she could, and when other duties called her away, she would come back regularly, partly for the sake of her son's health and partly to meet with the small but growing group of women believers and to teach them more about God. She was later able to arrange for her friend George Whitefield, the famous preacher, to come to Brighton, and then through him, thousands of Sussex people heard for the first time they needed to be born again and that the only way to God was through Jesus Christ. God touched many lives, and this was really the beginning of an evangelical revival in Sussex.'

'Please tell us more about Selina,' I said. 'Did her son get better?'

'Sadly, not,' Mum said, 'in fact, Selina had quite a sad life, two of her sons had already died and just to show how important Selina and her husband were, these two boys had been pupils at the famous boys' school at Westminster, London, and when they died, they were buried in Westminster Abbey, which is probably the most important church in England.'

'What happened next in Brighton?' asked Sam.

'Selina, because of her influence, was beginning to organise a preaching rota for her evangelical minister friends over a wide area of Britain. Although, most of these were ordained ministers of the Church of England, they were rarely welcome in Anglican churches but were preaching widely in the open air and wherever God gave them the opportunity. Because of her social position, Selina was entitled to appoint one or more chaplains for her spiritual well-being and that of her family. It was a recognised custom for royalty to arrange for their chaplains to preach and then to invite family and friends to come and hear and to benefit from the sermon. Selina was already taking advantage of this in her Chelsea mansion in London. Around 1750 she had appointed George Whitefield as one of her chaplains, and whenever he was in London, he had a standing invitation to preach for her on Tuesdays and Thursdays. On these occasions, Selina would invite as many of her friends and acquaintances as she could gather, and the majority invited seemed willing to come. Many came out of curiosity. The preacher's name was now well known, and here was an opportunity to hear him in an environment which suited their social position. Celebrities from many walks of life crowded into Selina's drawing room to hear George Whitefield preach. Lords and ladies, dukes and duchesses, even Frederick, the Prince of Wales, came from time to time, and famous politicians like William Pitt, who later became secretary of state. With so many coming regularly, Selina decided to lease another home near Hyde Park and to double the opportunity for those from her social class to hear the gospel. Although there was no evidence that many were converted, there were a significant minority whose hearts God touched and who came to know and love Jesus. When Whitefield was travelling away, his place was sometimes taken by John Wesley and other preachers of reputation.

'When Selina saw the spiritual need of Sussex and also the eager response to gospel preaching, she was determined to provide a regular opportunity for people of all walks of life to hear about Jesus there too. The situation was very different from that in London. But as Selina thought and prayed about this, the idea came to her to build herself a big chapel which would include, as part of the building, living rooms for herself and her servants. This could then be considered as one of her homes, and she would be entitled to invite her Anglican chaplains to preach there as often as they could, without needing the permission of the bishop.

'But where could she get the money to do this? All her money was tied up in property and investments and very little was immediately available. After asking around her relatives, she found she could borrow £500. But although this is an enormous amount of money to us, it was not enough to build the sort of chapel she had in mind which would be worthy of God and to be part of the home of a countess! She really was a lady of great faith and of great love for Jesus, for his gospel, and the souls of the people of Sussex. She prayed further, and God challenged her to sell her jewellery to get the added needed finance. Her jewellery fetched nearly £700 when sold! Can you imagine that? She then had enough money to proceed and built the large chapel in North Street in Brighton. Dad and I'll take you there one day. It's a lovely building with galleries all round. When it was finished, Selina arranged for her minister friends to come and preach there regularly.

'Since then the preaching of God's Word in Brighton has influenced most of the villages around us in remarkable ways, and another evening I've got another story for you which shows how God converted and inspired another man who has personally blessed our own family here in Ripe.'

Mum sent us all up to bed after that, and as I followed my brothers and sisters up the creaky stairs with the flame of the candle making dancing shadows on the wall, I remember being very thoughtful and that, with a real sense of pride, I too was a Selina. Perhaps God had something special for me to do for him too. I said my prayers silently and asked God to truly make me his child and to use me too to bless others.

Chapter 3

Uncle George Gilbert of Heathfield

It was some days before Mum could carry on with the story she had begun. But one Sunday evening as we were sitting around the open wood fire toasting chunks of bread for our supper, Mum seemed relaxed and happy, and I asked her whether she could tell us a bit more about Lady Selina.

That morning we had all tumbled into our pony and trap. Dad and Mum at the front with Balaam, our pony, and we children on benches along both sides of the wagon which Dad used for taking his goods to market. We were off to chapel in Heathfield. We mostly go to the chapel in our little village of Ripe, but Heathfield is our main chapel, where I had been baptised as a baby, and today Mum and Dad had wanted to go and hear Uncle George preach. George Gilbert was then an old man in his eighties, and he died soon after this. I remember his funeral well as it was an extraordinary day when hundreds of people came to Heathfield to celebrate the life of this man of God. I was nine at the time, and it made a great impression on me. Uncle George only preached occasionally now, and John Press was the usual minister, and it was always a special Sunday for us when we could take Balaam and the trap to jog along the country lanes into Heathfield. It was a frosty morning, and this meant that the muddy lanes were a bit more solid than sometimes. When after rain the mud is really soft, Dad has to use Bullinger, our ox, to pull the trap, and then it takes a lot longer to get anywhere. Thankfully today Balaam could cope fine.

Mum began her story by telling us about Uncle George. He's not our real uncle of course, and to us children at church, he was really more like a granddad.

'As a young man, George Gilbert had been a soldier,' she began, as we huddled around the fire. 'He was under the command of an important man, General Elliott, who later became Lord Heathfield, and for several years, he experienced all the horrors of battle. Sometimes when he's preaching, he's mentioned things that happened when he was fighting the French in Germany and then later when he was with General Elliott in Havana.'

'Where's Havana, Mummy?' asked Sarah.

'Uncle George said it's the main city of an island called Cuba, a long way away over the sea, and they were fighting the Spanish there,' said Mum. 'Anyway Uncle George saw a lot of horrible things which changed him completely. He used to say that being a soldier made him feel and act like the devil. His home was Rotherfield, so he eventually came back to Sussex. Once home, it wasn't long before someone challenged him about his immoral way of life and told him about this new preaching and how it was possible to be born again and to have a living experience of God. Uncle George decided he must hear this preaching for himself, so his friend suggested he go to Ote Hall near Wivelsfield. You see many people from the villages of Sussex, including farmers had been going to Brighton to hear Selina's preachers and some of them begged her to open another preaching centre nearer to them in the countryside. Countess Selina prayed earnestly for a way of making it possible for the people in the villages of Sussex to hear Bible preaching, and God provided her with a big stately home, Ote Hall.

Great Ote Hall, Wivelsfield, Sussex
Picture from: www.greatotehall.co.uk by kind permission.

'Ote Hall belonged to Selina's relatives, the Shirley family, and the owner at that time offered to lease it to her. She saw this as God's answer. So in 1761 she adapted the house for herself, her servants, and her guests and converted one of the big rooms into a chapel. She had contact with Anglican ministers who loved the Bible, including John and Charles Wesley and George Whitefield and others like them, who the Holy Spirit was using in the revival that was then happening, and she would invite them to come to her house in Wivelsfield and preach in her chapel. She would then advertise services and open her private chapel to the public.[5]

'George came to these preachings, and God began to move in his soul. When soon afterwards he was moved on to Nottingham with his army duties, he looked around for evangelical believers there and found some of John Wesley's converts and was soon thoroughly converted himself. His Christian friends encouraged him to hold services in the

---

[5] Faith Cook, op. cit.

barracks, and this gave him valuable experience and helped to establish him in his personal faith and trust in Jesus and gave him confidence to talk to others about it.

'In 1765 his boss was promoted to the office of lieutenant general and rewarded with a considerable sum of prize money for his part in the Havana expedition with which he purchased a stately home, Bayley Park near Heathfield, which has recently been renamed Heathfield Park. Lieutenant General Elliott employed Uncle George on Heathfield Park estate, and eventually, he became an estate manager.

'So that's how Uncle George came to Heathfield,' continued Mum. 'He now saw life very differently because when anyone is converted, the life of God comes into them and they begin to see things through the eyes of God. He was alarmed at the godlessness of most people around him and their sinful living, and he began to talk to them about Jesus. This aroused a lot of anger and gave him many enemies who threatened his home and possessions and also his life. But gradually some of his neighbours came to him with serious questions, and he began to hold a service in his cottage. Soon his cottage was too small, and in 1767 he hired a barn. When this became overcrowded, he preached in the open air. Then in 1770 his supporters built a chapel for him to use, and together they formed a church membership. This chapel, however, soon proved to be too small, and seven years later, they built a bigger one. This too became too small, so in 1807 they built him the chapel we went to this morning.

'But in those early days, Uncle George was also challenged by the godlessness in many other villages around us in Sussex, and he has often told us stories about his visits to places like Rotherfield, where he was born, Crowborough, Ticehurst, and Bexhill, and people say he's preached in more than forty villages! He often preached in the open air or explained the Bible in isolated farm cottages. Wonderful things were happening for God in Sussex on those days, and one of the major factors that started it all off under God's influence was Countess Selina's first visit to Brighton.'[6]

I used to really love these stories about real people, and somehow they made the Bible stories come alive and helped me to realise that God is the same today as he was long ago.

---

[6] Ralph Chambers, 'A Voice in the Wilderness', *The Strict Baptist Chapels of England*, vol. 2, Sussex (published by author, date unknown) 59–66.

Chapter 4

Learning without School

It wasn't until my grandchildren's time that the state was legally obliged to provide schools for children and all children were compelled to attend. When I was young, schools for village children were few and far between, and it was only the very fortunate boys and even more fortunate girls who had any formal education. In my family, we children all learnt at home.

The main things we were taught related to practical everyday living. Because babies kept arriving, my older sisters soon learnt to look after little children, and this obviously gave them confidence to look after their own babies later. We girls also learnt from Mum how to look after the house, do cooking, and to care for the menfolk. My brothers learnt from Dad how to do practical things outside. They sawed and chopped wood for the fire, they learnt how to plough our fields with Bullinger the ox, and then how to cultivate, sow seeds, and plant our vegetables. Mum and us girls were also very much involved in the market garden, weeding and then picking and packing the produce for market. I must say that I enjoyed the work outside better than housework, although when things were busy we got very tired.

At least living in the country with our own nice little cottage and our own family business, we were with Mum and Dad all the time. We often heard about children who were much less fortunate and whose parents send them out to work for other people, and some had to work for long hours for quite cruel masters and mistresses who only paid them a few pennies, which they had to give to their mums and dads anyway. When the boys were twelve or so, Dad used to take them with him to the village markets, and soon they were doing some of the rounds taking Balaam, our pony, and the trap to our regular customers around the villages.

But Mum and Dad also knew it was important for us to learn to read and write. The main book we had in the house was the Bible. Dad, and sometimes Mum, would read a few verses from these scriptures most evenings after supper, and they encouraged us to look at the words and to repeat them after them. We learnt verses by heart, and then when we looked at the printed words, we could begin to identify letters and sounds. Later I realised what a privilege and blessing it was to have a mum and dad like ours. Many village children never learnt to read or write at all often because their parents couldn't read themselves. In many homes, the Bible wasn't read at all, and their dads often spent more money than the family could afford on drink at the village pub. Dad and Mum often told us that it was through the influence of Lady Selina's preachers that their lives had changed. Knowing God and having a relationship with him through faith in Jesus Christ had made a radical difference in their home and in the homes of many other families in Sussex.

The village of Ripe lies on the lower slopes of the South Downs in the area known as the Weald, which lies between the South Downs and North Downs of southern England. I think it must be typical English humour to call hills 'downs', but there you go! Anyway the uplands, which are called Downs, are made of chalk, hence the White Cliffs of Dover. What this meant to us as children was that there were bits of chalk everywhere. We found it in the garden, and after Dad or my brothers had been ploughing our field with Bullinger, bits of chalk came to the surface. We children loved to find good bits of chalk because we could draw with them. We loved to draw shapes and pictures on bits of wood and the trunks of trees and then Mum encouraged us to draw letters. She found us pieces of slate which had come from an old roof, and we soon learnt to write our own names on them.

Learning to count also came naturally. One incident I remember which helped in this was the day that Dad came home with a broody hen and ten eggs. He explained to us that the eggs should produce baby chicks.

'Not all hens' eggs will hatch,' Dad said, 'but these were laid by hens that are part of a family with a cockerel as a big daddy figure, so these eggs should have both a mother and a father.'

The hen sat on the eggs to keep them warm, and Mummy helped us to count the days. We used one of the slates and put a mark for each day. Mum explained that the hen will need to keep the eggs warm for about three weeks, which she said was twenty-one days. Every five days, we put a line across our marks, and we soon realised that we needed four lots of five days to give us twenty days. When we had reached this, we got really excited and could hardly wait for it to get light the next day before we rushed out to see our mother hen. Sure enough, something had happened. We could hear cheeping, and the mother hen was sitting in a very protective manner with her feathers fluffed out. Then as we watched, two or three little heads poked out from among her feathers, and there were some gorgeous little chicks. Later Mum showed us how to count them using our fingers. We counted five fingers on one hand and three on the other.

'That makes eight,' said my older brother proudly.

'But we wanted ten,' I said.

And then we realised that two eggs hadn't hatched, and we saw in a visual way that ten minus two leaves eight.

Dad later explained that probably those two eggs hadn't been fertile because what he called sperm cells from the cockerel hadn't reached them. I asked whether we could eat them.

'No, no,' he said, 'I've already thrown them on the compost heap. After three weeks, they'll be addled, which is the word we use for eggs when they've become spoiled and inedible.'

I know now that not all children had such helpful parents as we did and that some mums and dads explained hardly anything to their children.

Dad loved nature, and we often went for a walk with him on a Sunday afternoon, and he would explain all sorts of things to us and tell us the names of the flowers and birds and butterflies we saw. I learnt to really love the springtime. I decided that yellow was one of God's favourite colours to welcome spring. It is so bright and contrasts amazingly with the wonderful shades of fresh green growth. The yellow celandine is one of the earliest flowers you see in the hedgerows when the days begin to get warmer and then comes the yellow primrose. This is one of my favourite flowers, and we used to find great clumps of them flowering in the little copse behind our field. There were so many that Mum was happy for us to pick some for her. They looked really lovely on our kitchen window ledge in a little pot. Then one of the earliest butterflies is also yellow, the brimstone. The male is a very bright yellow, and Dad reckons that it's because of this that the name *butter*fly originated. Then very soon come the blue colours. Bluebells grow in great profusion in our copses; in fact, for two weeks or so, it looks as though God has placed a blue carpet amongst the trees to cover all the dead leaves of the previous autumn.

But of course, all the other colours are growing as well. In the fields amongst the fresh green grass and along the edge of the hedges, the red campion and ragged robin add beautiful shades of red amongst the yellow buttercups, the white cow parsley, and the lovely mauve of the lady's smock. Sometimes this latter flower, with its clusters of purple, is called the cuckooflower as it often flowers just when the cuckoo has arrived back from Africa and the unmistakable cuckoo call of the male bird is echoing around the fields. Some people blame the cuckoo for the white spittle-type fluid you often find amongst the blades of grass in the fields at this time of year, but Dad says although it's commonly called cuckoo spit, this frothy liquid is actually secreted by an insect, which lives inside it. He tried to show us the insect one Sunday afternoon, but it's very difficult to see as it's a creamy whitish colour inside this gooey stuff and less than a quarter of an inch long. It develops into a froghopper, a small brownish insect, which as its name suggests, jumps around in the grass.

We learnt a great deal as country children living close to nature, but I must say I wasn't prepared for the emotional changes that occurred once I got into my teens.

Chapter 5

Eli Asks Me Out

Our family business kept us very busy, so I had lots to occupy my mind. We worked six days a week, and Dad insisted that Sunday was a day for God. I must say we enjoyed our Sundays. Our village church dates back to the thirteenth century and was dedicated to St John the Baptist. However, Mum and Dad told us that, like many Anglican parish churches, it had lost its way somehow. The preachers, whom Selina had arranged to preach in Sussex during the eighteenth century, were also Anglican, but they had brought a different message—a Bible-based message which came across as the voice of God. People have described this as the evangelical awakening and have recognised it as a movement of the Holy Spirit.

Anyway the effect on many of those who were touched by this preaching, like Mum and Dad, was to make them dissatisfied with the ministry of their local vicars. They came to the conclusion that many of the clergy were more interested in fox hunting and social activities than the souls of their parishioners. The new preaching made the point that being a Christian didn't come through being baptised as a baby but through God planting his new life in a person's heart. The Word of God, the Holy Bible, is the seed which, through the Holy Spirit, creates this new life, and it makes people aware of sin in their life and then directs them to God's love in Jesus. 'Believe on the Lord Jesus Christ and you shall be saved' is the message of the Good News.

Those who were converted through the preaching of this gospel were encouraged to meet together in societies, and out of these societies often developed the so-called dissenting congregations. These were groups of people who had chosen to leave the state church for a form of service in which the preaching was more Bible-orientated and the necessity of a personal experience of the Holy Spirit emphasised. Those groups which we knew still accepted the doctrinal position of the Thirty-Nine Articles of the Church of England but felt they needed spiritual food from the Word of God for their souls which they couldn't get from their vicars.

We had such a group in Ripe. One of our landowner farmers, Mr Mannington, had become respected as a preacher and Bible teacher and, with the support and encouragement of local Christian believers, had begun to hold Sunday services in his farmhouse. Later when a regular and growing group was attending each Sunday, he built a small chapel. We've been going there most Sundays for as long as I can remember. I never knew the first Mr Mannington, as he died in 1801. I know this because there is a plaque to him on the wall of the chapel, but his son and now his grandson have continued to lead the fellowship and worship each Sunday. Some of the people also meet during the week to pray. There's never been a formal membership of our fellowship in Ripe, and many of the villagers who come regularly have connections with other larger chapels; some at the independent chapel at Lower Dicker, others at Lewis, and some like us at Heathfield. Others are still officially members of the Church of England.[7]

This link with Christian groups in other villages gave us youngsters contact with other children, and as we progressed into our teenage years, we began to think about more serious relationships. It was difficult for us girls to get to know the boys at a casual level because once we got old enough to appreciate them, our parents seemed to do their utmost to stop us spending time together! Church anniversary services were good

---

[7] Ralph Chambers, 'Ripe Chapel' op cit. vol. 2, 93.

times to mix, as it was usual to have an afternoon preaching service and then a couple of hours when we all sat down at long trestle tables and ate thick slices of bread baked by the ladies of the host chapel, with local cheeses and other produce from the farms, eggs and smoked ham and pickles. An evening service with an extended preaching session then followed. The time between the services was the time to get to know each other. The grown-ups chatted happily, and it was a natural thing for us youngsters to sit together without the parents getting suspicious.

It was this type of special service at the little chapel in Hellingly which, although I didn't realise it at the time, began the change which affected the rest of my life.

Hellingly is a small village not so far from Ripe. A village blacksmith, Thomas Pitcher, had been converted through the influence of Selina's preachers, had committed his life to God, and had begun to spread the Good News in Hellingly that we are justified and made right with God through Jesus Christ and not by our own works. Soon the believers wanted to have somewhere to meet, and with the support of Jenkins Jenkins of Lewis and the Independent Chapel of which he was then pastor, they built a small chapel. Thomas Pitcher was appointed preacher, and like the fellowship, in Ripe it never had a formal church membership and was seen as a daughter fellowship of the Independent Church in Lewis.[8]

Once a year Hellingly had a pastor's anniversary service. This gave believers from other villages the chance to show their support for Thomas Pitcher through attending the services and contributing to his financial support through a special collection. Of course it also gave opportunity for fellowship and to benefit from two preaching sessions. A farmer named Richard Page who had a farm in Hellingly and was a keen supporter of Thomas Pitcher had roped in his son Eli to help with practical arrangements for the service and tea. Eli sat next to me at tea and casually asked me whether I would walk out with him. This

---

[8] Ralph Chambers, 'Hellingly', op cit. vol. 2, 127.

was the phrase then used when asking for a date. I must say I was a bit shocked and didn't give him a clear answer.

The preacher was John Vinall, who was now minister in Lewis after the home call of Jenkins Jenkins. He was a very influential minister and a popular preacher. The little chapel was full to overflowing, but I must say I couldn't concentrate on that evening service. No boy had ever asked me to walk out with him before, and I didn't know what my parents would say about Eli Page.

Why did it have to be Eli? I thought. *Everyone knows he's not the best of boys.*

And yet I was fascinated by him.

A week or so later when I was weeding carrots, someone called my name from the other side of the hedge, and there, sitting on a pony, was Eli. I looked around to see if anyone else was watching, but in fact, everyone else was doing other things that afternoon, so I went across to him.

'I mean it,' said Eli with a smile. 'And I'm not taking no for an answer! I know I've been a bit wild, but I want a serious girl. I find you very attractive, and I think if I could get to know you a bit better, I could really love you. How about it? Will you give me a chance?'

'I'll have to talk to Mum and Dad first,' I said. 'We talk about everything, and I couldn't do this behind their backs.'

'I'll be back,' said Eli and with that cantered up the lane.

That evening I mentioned the matter to Mum, and she quite casually said that she would mention it to Dad.

I must say I was pretty on edge for the next day or two, but on the third evening, Mum and Dad suggested I come into their room, and we all three sat on the bed together.

'So Eli Page wants to walk out with you,' said Dad. 'We are both very appreciative and actually quite flattered that you want to talk to us about it first before giving him an answer.'

'Your asking us for our thoughts has made us take the matter very seriously,' said Mum, 'and we've been praying about it together.'

'What do you think about it yourself?' asked Dad.

I told them what Eli had said about wanting a serious girl who he could love, and I said that I was rather attracted to him.

'But we need to get to know each other,' I added.

'There are things about Eli you need to know,' said Dad. 'Firstly his mother died when he was about a year old. That means he has never known a mother to love him. From all we hear, his father is a good Christian man, a good farmer, and an owner of some of the land he farms. Eli's mother was Richard Page's second wife, and he has children from his first wife, but she died a couple of years before he married Elisabeth, who was Eli's mother. This means that Eli has stepbrothers and stepsisters older than him. They all work on the farm, and since we hear that Richard Page hasn't been so well recently, I guess all the sons have learnt to take a lot of responsibility. It's true that Eli is high-spirited and has been thought of as one of the ringleaders for the more rowdy element in the area, but basically he comes from a good family, and your mum and I are not against you getting to know him better.'

'But, Selina,' interrupted Mum, 'there are a couple of other important things we want to say, aren't there, Samuel?'

'Yes,' said Dad. 'Firstly, we have good reason to believe that God's grace has given you new life. You love God and are trusting in Jesus Christ for salvation, aren't you?'

No one had ever challenged me quite as simply as this about my faith in God before and I hesitated.

'Yes, Dad,' I said at last. 'You and Mum have taught me to believe in God and have shown me how real he is to you, and he's become very important to me too. When Mr Mannington has been preaching, I've been aware that apart from Jesus' death for me, I have no hope of pleasing God. I love the Lord Jesus for what he has done for me, and he's my friend whom I talk to every day.'

'That's lovely to hear,' said Mum. 'We've prayed for you every day since before you were born, as we have for all of you, and it has thrilled us to see God touching your life and drawing you to know him personally.'

'But what this means,' added Dad, 'is that God's Spirit within you now makes you think differently from those who are not born again, so it's very important that you don't marry anyone who doesn't have God's Spirit. The Bible warns Christians not to be unequally yoked with unbelievers. Were this to happen, you would find you would seriously regret that you could have no understanding together on the things that really matter to you as a believer in Jesus. So our advice is to get to know Eli but to take it slowly. Pray for him and, if possible, with him. He comes from a believing family, and the fact he is looking for a serious girl is very positive. But don't let the relationship develop if you sense there is no grace of God in his heart.'

'The other thing we decided we should say to you,' said Mum, 'is a bit more delicate, and we thought we would say it by way of an illustration.'

'Do you remember hearing about William Huntington?' asked Dad. 'He had a lot of influence as a preacher here in Sussex although his main church was in London. He was somewhat eccentric, and people either loved him or hated him. He worked very closely with Jenkins in Lewis and, in fact, is buried in the graveyard of Jireh Chapel, Lewis. He only died in 1813, so your Mum and I heard him preach a number of times. Anyway what we want to say is that Mr Huntington had a romance as an unconverted young man which led to a pregnancy. The father of his girlfriend had severe doubts about the young William and refused to allow his daughter to marry him. William then found that he was legally bound to pay maintenance for his illegitimate son which he couldn't in any way afford. This forced him to leave home, and he became a homeless tramp for a number of years. To avoid being found, he changed his name from Hunt to Huntington and for many years lived in fear of being discovered and being sent to prison for the debt he couldn't pay.

'Wonderfully,' continued Dad, 'he eventually found God's forgiveness in Jesus and became a preacher. If you find yourself tempted to have a sexual relationship outside the commitment of a legal marriage, remember the mess that poor young William Hunt got himself and his girlfriend into. God's way is always the best way. He designed both the bodies and the different temperaments of male and female to come together in a life-long commitment to one another. The sexual act is not something to play with but rather the ultimate way in which the wife gives herself to her husband after a commitment has been publicly made in the marriage service. In this way, in the words of scripture, "the two become one flesh".'

We were all silent for a while, and then I murmured in a subdued tone, 'Thanks, Dad, that's given me a lot to think about.'

I found my way upstairs with my candle and lay for a long while in thought and prayer before falling peacefully to sleep.

Chapter 6

Courtship and Death of Eli's Father

The first time I walked out with Eli was a beautiful Sunday evening. Eli had called round to see me again during the week, and I had agreed to spend an hour or so with him after the Sunday evening service. He had come along to our little chapel in Ripe, had sat at the back, and afterwards we met under an agreed oak tree just outside the village. I had suggested this as it would have provoked immediate gossip if we had been seen together at the chapel. As we walked across a freshly mown field, smelling delightfully of drying hay, I remember a blackbird was singing beautifully in the trees and that we had disturbed one or two rabbits enjoying their evening meal of grass and dandelion leaves along the hedgerow. We sat together on a fallen tree trunk and simply talked.

I shyly asked him to tell me a bit about himself. He began by saying no girl had ever asked him that before, all they had seemed to be interested in was a kiss and a cuddle behind a haystack.

This had embarrassed me a bit at first, but I soon realised he had intended it as a compliment. He told me that he had worked for his father on the family farm for as long as he could remember. He enjoyed farming and hoped one day to have a farm of his own. He confessed that he had been a bit wild and was now ashamed of many things he had done and how he had blasphemed God's name without a second thought. This gave me the prompt to ask him straight out whether he knew God's peace through knowing his sins were forgiven. This startled him rather, for his reaction was to say that that wasn't a question he had expected to be asked on his first date with a new girlfriend. But after a minute or two of silence, he said, 'No, Selina, I don't have that peace, but in recent days, it's become the most important thing I need.'

We then chatted a bit more about farming, and I told him the sort of things I did in our market garden. He then walked me back to our cottage, and as we parted, he asked me whether I would agree to walk out with him again, and I assured him I would be happy to. We arranged to meet in a similar way the following Sunday.

My sisters knew I was meeting Eli that evening, and they were very curious to know what had happened. No! I hadn't held his hand, and no, he hadn't kissed me.

'What did you do then?' asked my youngest sister.

'Oh, we just talked,' I answered.

'How boring' was the response.

I said no more but went to sleep with a little smile on my face and lightness in my heart.

The next Sunday, Eli wasn't at the service, and I found it difficult to concentrate on the sermon. However, when it was over, I walked towards the agreed oak tree, and there was Eli waiting for me.

'I'm sorry I didn't make the service, Selina,' he said. 'One of our cows was calving, and Dad needed my help. I only just managed to get away in time to be here now.'

I must say it was a great relief to me that he had such a plausible excuse. I knew enough about farming to realise that although Sunday was our day of rest, the animals didn't understand this, and life went on every day the same for them.

We followed the same procedure as the previous Sunday and chatted generally about all sorts of things. As we parted, Eli's tone changed, and in quite a low voice, he said, 'You know what you asked me last Sunday,

Selina. It shook me a bit, but can you pray for me? I really need God's peace. I'm trying to change some of my behaviour, but it's not easy. When I can get away from the farm, I usually have a couple of evenings out with the lads, and this past week, I didn't enjoy it as much as usual. I kept thinking about you.'

It soon became public knowledge that Eli and I were walking out together, and it was good to be able to be seen together without me feeling embarrassed. Hellingly is just six miles from Ripe, and if Eli couldn't borrow his father's horse, he would walk across to see me. Sometimes he was able to use a pony and trap, and then we would ride out together. Eli, although somewhat reluctantly I think, gradually gave up his evenings out with the lads. We agreed that when he could get away, he would meet me on at least one of these evenings and that helped him a lot. We both enjoyed nature and walking through the countryside, and we really began to value each other's company. I felt my heart going out to him, and I longed to be able to give him female love and the care that he had been deprived of through losing his mother at such a young age. We didn't talk a lot about spiritual things, but I knew that Eli still hadn't found God's peace.

One evening, he shared with me how tortured he was in his mind about this lack of assurance that he was really a child of God. Our preachers often mentioned that God's children were chosen in eternity past before the creation of the world. This is a wonderful thought once you knew that through the death of Jesus Christ you have been accepted by God, but for Eli at that time, it felt to be a doctrine that shut him out of heaven.

Then something happened that really shattered poor Eli; his father died. It was the 7 February 1837 when God called him home, the year after we had begun to walk out together. Eli was nineteen years old, and the fact that he was now an orphan hit him hard. The funeral was held in the Lower Dicker Chapel and Richard Page, aged sixty-three years was buried in the chapel graveyard alongside his wife, Eli's mother, Elizabeth, who had died 4 September 1818 when Eli had been a mere baby of eleven months. Little Naomi, Eli's sister, was also buried in the same grave. She had died three months after her mother, at the age of four years and eleven months.

I went to the funeral and was able to give poor Eli a certain amount of support. Although it was a sad day, there was also a note of victory in the service. Mr John Vinall of Lewis took the service. He gave us some interesting facts about Eli's dad which I wonder whether Eli himself had ever heard before.

Richard Page had been born in 1773 in Wilmington, a neighbouring village to Hellingly. He had lived there with his first wife, Philadelphia, until her death in 1807 and had farmed land left to him by his father. His father, Nicolas Page, had died when Richard was a year old but had owned 'copyhold land' in both Wilmington and Arlington. He had left the Arlington land to his older son, John, and the Wilmington land to his younger son, Richard. The two sons came into the possession of this land on their twenty-first birthdays. The Wilmington land included a pub called the Black Horse.[9]

Richard Page and his wife Philadelphia had been faithful members of the Anglican Church, and Richard had been appointed a church warden in the parish church of Wilmington in the year 1800. Philadelphia was buried in the churchyard at Wilmington in January 1807. However, prior to his second marriage in 1811 to Elizabeth Verrall, Eli's mother, Richard Page had come under the influence of gospel preaching, and although Mr Vinall had not acknowledged it, this was almost certainly from John Vinall himself as he had preached widely around the villages of East Sussex. Richard and his second wife, Elizabeth, both found spiritual freedom through a personal faith in Jesus Christ, and after their marriage, they had made their home in Hellingly and become members of one of the group of independent chapels in the area under the pastoral care of John Vinall.

Mr Lewis pointed out that Richard Page had had a sad life. He had lost both his parents before his eighth birthday, then two wives and two

---

[9] John Richard Thomas, *A Page in Time*. Unpublished family research of the Page family.

daughters. His little daughter Jane had died soon after her birth from Philadelphia in 1806 and little Naomi, from his second wife Elizabeth, soon after the death of her own mother in 1818. His four surviving children, Philadelphia, John, Ruth, and Eli would severely miss the guiding influence of a God-fearing father, and he commended them to the loving care of their heavenly Father, quoting the reassuring words of David in the Psalms: 'When my father and mother forsake me then the Lord will take me up'. [10]He assured the gathered company of relatives and friends that he had no doubt of Richard Page's acceptance into glory through God's grace, which had led him into a personal faith in our Lord and Saviour Jesus Christ. He then exhorted the children to seek that same grace for themselves to ensure they would, when the time came, be reunited with their parents in heaven.

It was a very moving service, and I know it touched Eli greatly. Around the grave after Mr Vinall had laid Richard's outward frame to rest in sure and certain hope of the resurrection, we sang together softly but meaningfully John Newton's wonderful hymn 'How sweet the name of Jesus sounds'. I'm quoting it right through because it meant so much to us then and continues to do so this day.

> How sweet the Name of Jesus sounds
> In a believer's ear!
> It soothes his sorrows, heals his wounds,
> And drives away his fear.
> It makes the wounded spirit whole,
> And calms the troubled breast;
> 'Tis manna to the hungry soul,
> And to the weary, rest.
> Dear Name, the Rock on which I build,
> My Shield and Hiding Place,
> My never failing treasury, filled
> With boundless stores of grace!

---

[10] Psalm 27:10.

By Thee my prayers acceptance gain,
Although with sin defiled;
Satan accuses me in vain,
And I am owned a child.
Jesus! my Shepherd, Husband, Friend,
O Prophet, Priest, and King,
My Lord, my Life, my Way, my End,
Accept the praise I bring.
Weak is the effort of my heart,
And cold my warmest thought;
But when I see Thee as Thou art,
I'll praise Thee as I ought.
Till then I would Thy love proclaim
With every fleeting breath,
And may the music of Thy Name
Refresh my soul in death!

Chapter 7

Eli's Conversion and Our Marriage

After his father's death, you could say Eli's life really took off! He missed his father greatly, but the scripture quoted by John Vinall at the funeral really gave him hope. The Lord would take him up. He brought this promise to God earnestly in his prayers and besought the Lord to reveal himself to him and assure him of his acceptance as his child.

I was with Eli when that assurance came. It was in a service in the new chapel they were in the process of building at Upper Dicker. When finished, it could seat 400 people, but the new regular minister at that time, Mr Cowper, who had provided the initiative for this building, began using it to preach in almost as soon as it had a roof on! Anyway in that particular sermon, he began by describing the human heart in all its selfishness and deceitfulness, and in quoting the scripture, 'For all have sinned and come short of the glory of God', he appeared to be condemning the whole human race to God's judgement and condemnation. But then he talked about grace. He showed God's love in sending his eternal Son Jesus into the world to die for sinners and then began to describe how this grace of God moves within the evil heart of a man or woman. At first the Holy Spirit makes them aware of their sin and causes them to hate it, then it causes them to cry for mercy, before showing them God's wonderful remedy in the cross of Jesus Christ. I knew this was affecting Eli, and by the end of the sermon, he had a wonderful happy look on his face. He had grasped the point that Jesus had done everything necessary for his salvation and that all the despair and wretchedness he had been feeling about himself during the past year or so had been of the Holy Spirit, preparing him for this wonderful moment when he would see the gospel clearly and would welcome Jesus as his Saviour.[11]

As we walked out of the chapel, Eli said to me, 'I can die now.'

'Not just yet, I hope, Eli,' I answered. 'I need you, and perhaps God needs you here too for a bit longer to tell others about his grace.'

Those words came out without my planning them, and I didn't realise at the time how prophetic they were.

The next radical thing in Eli's life related to me. He asked me to marry him!

We had walked out to our favourite log. The place we had sat on our first date. Eli took my hand and said, 'Selina, I love you. I've loved you for a long time, but I'm realising more and more how important you are to me. Do you find it in you to marry me? I promise to look after you to the best of my ability for the rest of my life, and next to God and our Lord Jesus, I want no one else by me for my comfort and happiness.'

My heart was beating wildly as I answered, 'Eli, I promise with God's help to be the helpmeet he intended for you. I've loved you for many months too, and it will be my greatest joy to be your wife.'

Eli then explained that now his father's affairs had been settled, we would have the means to run our own farm. We could have Clifton Farm, Arlington, right next to Bowleys Farm where Eli had been brought up. It sounded wonderful, and we agreed to try and arrange a wedding as soon as possible.

We were married in the parish church in Ripe on the 12 February 1838, almost exactly one year after Eli's father died. We were both still

---

[11] For Eli's own account of his conversion, see appendix 1.

legally minors, Eli being twenty years old and I ten months younger and still nineteen. The witnesses to our marriage were my brother James and Eli's sister Ruth.

St John the Baptist Church, Ripe, Sussex

After the wedding and a celebratory meal with our families and a few close friends, we rode across to Clifton Farm, Arlington, now part of Upper Dicker, and Eli carried me over the threshold into our first home.

Our marriage night was wonderful. I think physically Eli enjoyed it more than me, but I was so happy to be able to give myself fully to the man I loved with a clear conscience. Ringing in my thoughts were his words, 'I take this woman to be my lawful wedded wife to love and to cherish and to have and to hold till death does us part.' I relaxed in Eli's arms, feeling myself loved as never before.

This was the beginning of the rest of my life.

Part 2

Clifton Farm, Arlington
1838–1842

Chapter 1

Our Early Home and Daily Routine

The first home I shared with my new husband, Eli, in the farmhouse at Clifton Farm was a mansion compared with my own family home. Farmhouses tend to be larger than the average village cottage, partly because of a farmer's status and partly because it was common for unmarried farm labourers and female servants to live-in with their boss and his family. We had two large rooms downstairs in addition to the kitchen and six bedrooms upstairs. For water, we still depended on a well in our courtyard, but the luxury for me was that we had a hand pump over the large, fairly shallow sink in the kitchen which pumped water out of the well straight to the point I needed to use it. There were two privies in the yard, one for the family and another for the servants. Our family privy had two wooden seats, a normal size one for the grown-ups and a lower one with a smaller hole especially for children's bottoms! The buckets had to be emptied regularly.

Our house was situated up our own farm track off the Camberlot Lane which runs northwards from the Dicker. The lane continues past Bowleys Farm, where Eli was brought up, and then past Camberlot Hall and across Dicker Common towards Lower Dicker. There's an interesting but disturbing incident that happened to Eli's father on Dicker Common which I'll tell you about soon.

It thrilled me to be able to make a home for Eli and myself, and for the first few months, it was just the two of us living in the house. Eli had inherited some furniture from his father's home, and one of his pride and joys was a big four-poster bed which had belonged to his parents. Eli once made the comment, 'Just think, I was conceived in this bed, and now our children will be too!'

Eli loved being married; he said it gave him a real sense of pride and responsibility to have a wife, and he was certainly a changed person from the young man who had behaved so irresponsibly. We both knew, however, that this was not just his new status as husband and farmer but his newfound faith and his confidence that he was God's child. He used to say to me, 'Selina, my darling, we must never forget that we were chosen by a gracious and loving god in eternity past to know and serve him.'

One of his favourite scriptures in those early days was in Paul's epistle to the Ephesians: 'For we are his workmanship, created in Christ Jesus unto good works, which God hath before ordained that we should walk in them.'[12]

We had quickly to get into a pattern of daily life as the work of building up the farm was very demanding, but an important part of our daily routine was our times of family prayer. Of course in the early months, it was just Eli and me. We were up early and, after a couple of hours work, would sit down about 8 a.m. to a breakfast of chunky home-baked bread and fried eggs and, when possible, sausages or bacon. Following breakfast, Eli would read a short passage of the Bible and commit the work of the day into God's hands. Later our children and as many of our farm labourers and house servants as could be spared from their duties would join us for this time of Bible reading and prayer. Then, after the evening meal, Eli would have a further Bible reading which all those living in the house were expected to attend unless it was

---

[12] Ephesians 2:10.

their evening off. It's now Eli's habit to make a few expository thoughts on the scripture passage we read, and I remember well the first occasion this happened, and I'll be telling you about this. When Eli is away, it becomes my duty to lead these family devotional times, and I must say they then tend to be rather shorter!

It was a great excitement and challenge to begin to run our own farm. Our acreage wasn't large; in fact, after a couple of years, Eli was able to rent a few more fields, which once his father had rented before him, and together this gave us enough acreage to get ourselves going. Eli's father had been very proud of a small herd of Sussex cattle, and after his death, as with much of the other livestock and equipment, Eli and his brother agreed to split the herd between them. This gave us three milking cows, a heifer due soon to calf, two castrated oxen as working animals, and two further bullocks that were being fattened for beef. It was agreed that the two brothers would share the Sussex bull for his fatherly use as required.

Sussex cattle are an ancient breed in the county, smallish as cattle go with a dark red-brown coat. They have some excellent qualities. The females are mild animals and good mothers, and although the bull can be more temperamental, the breed produce very good quality beef, and they are excellent draught animals for pulling ploughs and wagons, etc. Through the influence of his father, Eli had a very high regard for the Sussex breed and would not willingly choose another. His aim was to build up the herd to at least six milking cows and to fatten their offspring for beef, perhaps also buying in a few additional calves for fattening too.

The heifer produced a fine female calf which pleased Eli a lot, and soon he was able to buy two more young bullock calves for fattening, and at this point, we were able to rent the additional acreage of grazing land to free up two of our fields for wheat. The farm had a small pigsty, and we bought in a sow already in pig, and she gave us ten little piglets for fattening too.

It was hard work. Eli needed to be up early to milk the cows, and we both worked as many hours as God gave us daylight.

The daily yield of milk had to be dealt with. In those early days of our farming, it was not so usual for people to drink milk, but they did like butter, so we turned most of our milk into this beautiful yellow spread which made bread so tasty. The skimmed milk left after we had taken off the cream for butter was, of course, still very drinkable, but we had far more than we needed for ourselves or to sell, so most of it was given to the pigs or the calves. It fattened them up well.

When we were first married, it was my job to make the butter. We had a cool room for this, and Eli would bring the milk and pour it into largish, shallow earthenware dishes, which were made for the purpose and called setting dishes or pancheons. The cream in the milk would then fairly quickly rise to the top and could be scooped off, and this process was called skimming. We had a routine for this as the cows were milked twice a day. I would skim the cream from the morning milking during the late afternoon after it had had time to rise and then the cream from the evening milking first thing the next morning. The skimmed cream was stored in a special urn, and then at least twice a week, I would make butter.

Butter making is a laborious job! The cream has to be kept moving until it thickens and turns into butter, and this can take several hours. In earlier years, the farmer's wife used what they called a dasher. This was a wooden stick constructed with cross-sticks on the end which was then lifted up and down, up and down in an urn of cream until the butter appeared. I was very proud to have a butter churn to do the job which was somewhat easier and quicker. This was a wooden barrel which is laid on its side with a handle sticking into one end which turns paddles inside the barrel. On the side of the barrel which acts as the top, there is an opening with a lid, so you could pour in the cream and take out the butter. Later I had girls to help me with this job, but in the early days of our marriage, I had to do it myself.

To keep up our spirits when churning the butter, we would often sing, and I remember one of the girls who came to work for us introduced an old traditional butter-churning song. It went like this:

> Come butter come, come butter come. Peter stands
> at the gate, waiting for a buttered cake.

I found this quite harmless, but Eli wasn't very happy about our dairy maid singing it. He explained that it was originally sang to call in good fairy spirits to help make the butter (it always was a bit of a mystery how milk can be turned into delicious butter), and then by referring to Peter waiting at the gate, the intention was to warn away evil spirits, who might stop the process but who would be fearful of the apostle Peter!

We made different types of butter, partly as people wanted it and partly for our own convenience. Butter that had to be kept any length of time needed to be salted, and this is sometimes referred to as Irish butter or *gruiten*, which I think comes from the Irish language. Some people, ourselves included, much prefer fresh butter, that is without the salt, but this has a shorter life and needs to be kept as cool as possible and be eaten fairly quickly. It's also possible to make a sweet-cream butter, but this needs to be made immediately from the cream before it has time to sour. We do this on demand for special customers and charge them a bit more for it, but our normal procedure was to let the cream accumulate over a few days and then make the butter twice a week, and by this time the earliest cream has soured somewhat.

I also cared for the chickens. The farm had an old chicken house when we took it over, and Eli was soon able to do it up and make it fox-proof. The chickens roamed around the yard during the day and as it got dark made their own way into their house. We just had to remember to shut it up once they were in. The chicken house provided them with straw-lined egg boxes in which to lay their eggs, and it was only rarely that some silly hen would insist on laying hers somewhere in the yard. The breed of chicken we chose was the light Sussex. They had a white body with a black tail and black wing tips, and their necks were white with black stripes. Their eggs are large and a creamy to light-brown colour, and we were told we could expect them to lay around 250 eggs a year. We have always found them a very satisfactory breed, and our rough calculations indicate that they have come up to expectations in the number of eggs they gave us.

I enjoyed my chickens in those early days of our marriage. They were my own special bit of the farm. In those days, we had about eighteen hens and a rooster. I remember that I had a special name for our first rooster. I called him William. I think because when he sat on top of the hen house and crowed, I could imagine that it was William Huntington preaching. I know that's a bit mean and irreverent, and I never told anyone the reason for William's name, but I think Eli guessed. He would sometimes refer to William by name, and it usually gave him a smile. It's amazing how animals have their different personalities, and it was definitely so with my hens. Some were much more forward than others and tended to be more bossy although they all submitted without question to William. Occasionally there were one or two who we couldn't get to leave the egg boxes, and when this happened, we generally gave in to their mother instincts and gave them some eggs to sit on in a special box in another shed. In this way, we got little chicks and kept up the number of our little flock even when the fox got one or two as occasionally happened even in broad daylight.

Our pigs are another story, but I'll save that till later.

Our days and weeks had a definite pattern. We worked hard, but it was one of the periods of my life that I look back to with greatest pleasure. Eli and I were getting to know each other. It was just the two of us in the house, and we planned and worked together. I mostly agreed with his suggestions because he had already had many years of farming experience with his father and brother, and he was the one who had the final responsibility, but it always thrilled me that he would discuss things with me, and I would like to think I sometimes had an insight into things in a way that he didn't.

Chapter 2
Sundays at Lower Dicker

Sunday was a special day for us. We did as little work as possible and ensured that the cows were milked and the animals fed and watered in time to wash and change for chapel. We had special clothes for chapel, and in those days, I remember Eli had a very smart greenish-brown linen smock-frock with a large collar, bright green button, and some rather fine light-green stitching. These clothes are out of fashion now, but most of the men wore them to church in the early days of our marriage. They were fairly loose with tubes, as we called them, that is, un-ironed pleats running lengthwise down the full length arms. Eli's was thigh length and was something like a long loose shirt made of thick linen. I wore a full-length dress with a large shawl around my shoulders, pinned at the front with a rather nice brooch which had belonged to Eli's mother.

We worshipped regularly at the independent chapel at Lower Dicker where Eli's parents were buried. The chapel had no regular pastor and was considered a daughter church of the bigger chapel in Lewis where Mr John Vinall was pastor. He was able to arrange ministers for us most Sundays, and every now and then, he preached to us himself, but because of his other commitments, this was mostly on a weekday evening.

The building was very simply built, and the front door opened directly into the chapel itself which was lined with plain wooden benches, with a desk at the front and a raised pulpit behind the desk. A door beside the pulpit led into a room behind the hall which we called the minister's vestry. On both sides of the front desk were two short benches set at right angles to the rest of the seats, and these were for those leading the singing. In our chapel, we had two or three men with good voices who were able to pitch the right note and lead the rest of us through the hymns. Things have changed more now, but at that time, we didn't have hymnbooks and some of our number couldn't read anyway, so the leader for that day would read the verses one by one, and we would sing them from memory. We soon learnt the most popular ones, and then it wasn't necessary for each verse to be read out. Our favourite hymns were those by Isaac Watts, John Newton, and Charles Wesley.

I must tell you about one particular Sunday because it proved to be a very significant day which influenced the rest of our lives. It was a beautiful summer's day. Eli was in the middle of haymaking, and although part of him found it difficult to stop work for the Sunday, on that morning he had really sensed the Lord's presence and blessing. He had found himself singing in worship as he had milked the cows and completed the necessary chores before leaving with me for the morning service at the chapel. He told me how he was finding great pleasure in the fact that this was God's day and that although the warm sunshine, the melodious song of the birds, and the beauty of all the tints of nature's growth around us reflected the glory of God, he had a far greater reason to worship the great god of heaven and earth. The Son of God had died for him. He had been redeemed by the precious blood of Jesus, and he was a child of God. As we talked together along the lane to chapel, his enthusiasm inspired me too, and we both felt our hearts overwhelmed with God's love to us.

That morning Mr Vinall hadn't been able to find us a preacher, and Mr Richard Guy, who was appointed to lead the service, called on various men to lead the congregation in prayer before he read a passage of scripture and some meditative thoughts that Mr Vinall had sent him.

For the first time ever in public worship, Mr Eli Page was requested to pray. Although he started in a hesitant way, the Holy Spirit seemed to take Eli over, and his prayer was soon one of eloquent worship and praise in line with all he had felt in his heart and spirit that morning. It was obvious to me that the great blessing Eli had felt whilst milking the cows had been God's preparation for the part he had planned for him to play in that Sunday morning worship service. The scripture passages which Mr Guy read to us and the meditative thoughts were also a blessing, and we returned home with a sense of having really met with the Lord.

Chapter 3

Our Household Increases

Early on in our marriage, I discovered I was pregnant. Although this didn't surprise me, I decided to say nothing about it to anyone until I was absolutely certain. Pregnancy and all it involved wasn't talked about much at that time, and Eli really had no idea what to expect and how he should behave towards me. He couldn't understand my morning sickness, and eventually, I told him that I thought it was because I was going to have a baby. Although this thrilled him, it also frightened him because he knew there was a risk he might lose me. He very wisely suggested that I went and chatted to my mum about it, which I did.

Mum gave me a lot of useful tips and assured me that she would be available to come and help me when the baby showed signs of coming into the world. Basically, I carried on with my life as much as usual, but there was a heavy workload with a big house, the dairy, the chickens, and not the least, looking after Eli! One evening Eli mentioned that he ought to have someone to help him on the farm, and I took the opportunity to point out my own predicament and that if he wanted me and the baby to keep safe, I ought to be able to rest a bit more. He saw the point at once and, very graciously for Eli, apologised that he hadn't thought of this himself but rather only about his own growing workload. Anyway we agreed there and then to pray about finding the right people to come and help us in the house and on the farm.

Eli got his helper first. His nephew, Trayton Parris, the son of his half-sister Philadelphia, who was about the same age as Eli, was already employed elsewhere as a farm labourer. They had always got on well together, and when Eli suggested to him that they could work together, he jumped at the opportunity. We came to an agreement with Trayton, and within a couple of weeks, he moved in with us at Clifton Farm and was employed on the farm in an official capacity.

I very soon got my assistant too. We had a family by the name of Wenham with us in the fellowship at Dicker Chapel; they had a number of children and were eager for the eldest daughter to go into service. When they knew I was looking for a girl to help me in the house and dairy, they suggested that Eliza should come to live with us and undertake these duties. Eliza was just thirteen when she came to us; she was a good little worker, eager to learn, and appreciated the freedom of being away from home.[13]

Our first child arrived in the autumn of 1838. My mum was with me. Eli had rushed down to Ripe with the pony and trap to pick her up when I had begun to feel pains. She had insisted Eli went to pick up a close friend of hers too, who had helped her with her babies so I was well looked after. I'm deeply thankful to God for his help at that time as everyone knew of mothers who had died in childbirth and in thoughtless ways kept telling me about them as I had got bigger and bigger with baby Richard. Giving birth is far from a pleasant experience, but the joy of cuddling my own baby, of knowing he was a part of me and Eli and so totally dependent on us, and of bringing him to my breast to feed on my own milk somehow made all the pain worthwhile. I realise that it's not always so with the birth of babies, but Eli and I really praised God that he had been so gracious to us.

Eli stayed out of the way during the birth, but as soon as he heard our baby's cry, he came rushing to see me. He had been praying hard

---

[13] 1841 Census, Eli Page, Clifton House, Arlington.

and was so relieved to see me alive, albeit weak and weepy. We had already agreed that if it were a boy, he should be called Richard. Our firstborn son was to be named after Eli's father whom he had so much respected.

Chapter 4
The Gruesome Side of Farming

Our first year of farming was a moderate success. Eli had been able to sow a few acres of wheat in the spring, and this had grown well. Thankfully, Trayton was with us just before harvest, so he was able to help Eli scythe the corn and tie it into sheaves. The sheaves were then stored in one of our barns to be threshed as required or, as time allowed, during the winter months. We had also been able to cut a reasonable amount of hay in early summer, I had helped with this, and we now had a good-sized haystack to draw on for the cattle during the winter. I was very impressed with Eli's attempt at thatching the haystack, and he had told me that this was one of the skills his father had taught him.

Our regular income came from the sale of butter and eggs, and Eli had been able to sell two bullocks which had fattened up enough to give a good price, and he had also sold on six of our fattened pigs. We kept back one female pig for breeding and one to kill for our own use. We also hoped there would be sufficient wheat to sell a few sacks through the winter, but we needed a good proportion of it for our own use. The chickens needed it for food, and then as we required flour for bread and cakes, we would take a sack of grain to the mill, where our miller Tom Sawyer would grind it for us.

The day for slaughtering our pig had been planned well ahead, subject to dry weather. It was a major event, and I still remember my first experience of this gruesome task. As Eli reminded me, a farmer is a farmer and we breed animals for food and you can't eat live animals. He also pointed out that God has sanctioned this when he said to Noah, 'Every moving thing that lives shall be food for you. I have given you all things, even as the green herb.'[14]

We waited for the onset of winter for the slaughter, as the meat keeps longer when the temperature is lower, and then planned a convenient day subject to dry weather. Preparations began the day before. Eli set up a pulley and rope system strong enough the bear the weight of our pig, and we made sure we had a large trough, big enough to lay the dead pig in, and enough suitable containers for the meat. Knives were sharpened in readiness for action.

Early the next morning, I got the fire going and began heating up a large cauldron of water. Once the cows were milked and chickens fed and other urgent chores completed, Eli got a rope around the pig's back legs and hauled him up on the pulley. Trayton was there to help, and I had recruited one of my sisters to help with the cutting up of the meat, although she refused to come until the gruesome first stage of the process was over. Amidst much squealing, from the pig of course, Eli cut its throat. It was very quickly dead, and we allowed the carcass to bleed as much as possible before lowering it down into the trough we had prepared for it. We then poured on water, as near to boiling as was possible, to remove the hair. Under these conditions, most of the hair comes off quite easily. Eli and Trayton then lifted the carcass on to wooden boards, and together they scraped off as much as possible the remaining hair with a sharp knife and a shaving razor. While this was happening, I had been heating up another cauldron of water, and when it was boiling, I got the men to carry it out to the pig which they had put back into the cleaned out trough, and it was my job to splash it over the carcass and give it a thorough wash. Next came the rather

---

[14] Genesis 9:3.

unpleasant business of cutting the pig open and removing its intestines and inner organs. Much of this was kept for our use. The liver and kidneys were good food, and the intestines were washed out and used as sausage skins.

Next using very sharp knives and a cleaver, the carcass was cut into various joints of meat, and over the next few days, we treated it in different ways. The buttocks were salted and pressed in order to produce ham. The ribcage meat was salted and smoked in order to get bacon. Then salt was rubbed thoroughly into each piece of meat and all surfaces are covered. Much of the meat was then cut and ground and turned into sausages, which meant mixing it with a special recipe of herbs and stuffing it into the washed-out intestines. The lengths were then twisted at suitable intervals so individual sausages could be easily cut off for cooking. None of this meat could be kept for very long, although the smoked joints would keep longer, and this meant we would often share it out among our family and church friends, and by making the slaughter day as near to Christmas as possible, it made very acceptable Christmas gifts.

Chapter 5

An Additional Challenge

One evening Richard Guy from the chapel called in to see us. We were just about to have our evening meal. Both Trayton and Eliza, who were then living with us, were sitting with us around the table when we heard the knock on the door. It was unusual for us to have callers at that time of evening, but when we saw who it was, we invited Mr Guy to sit round the table with us and share our supper. I had baby Richard in his cot beside me, having just given him his milk. All was peaceful, and I was pleased that I'd made more than enough substantial vegetable soup that evening to eat with some of my home-baked bread. Mr Guy apologised for calling in this unexpected way but said he had something he'd like to discuss with us after supper. Eli opened one of the bottles of elderberry wine made by my mother, and we feasted together. It was good to get to know Mr Guy somewhat. He had been a blacksmith by trade but, although now officially retired, still worked some hours a week with his son in the family business.

When Trayton and Eliza had left us after supper, Mr Guy explained that many of the congregation at the chapel had been blessed by Eli's prayers. That Sunday when Eli had for the first time been asked to pray remained in everyone's mind, and following that, he had often been asked to lead the congregation in prayer. Mr Guy continued to say that several of the chapel friends had felt that Eli had a God-given gift and that he should be encouraged to preach. Having spoken to Mr Vinall about it, on behalf of the chapel, he would like to invite Eli to preach the sermon on one of the Sundays that Mr Vinall was unable to find them a preacher. What did Eli think about this?

I was flabbergasted. My Eli, a preacher! To me at that time preachers were very holy people. I saw them as men called by God to the solemn responsibility of bringing God's Word to us ordinary people. I knew Eli inside out. I slept with him every night; he came in sweaty every evening from the farm. I'd seen him cut the throat of pigs, ring the necks of chickens, castrate bullocks, lose his temper with our workers, there was nothing especially holy about Eli!

Eli said very little by way of an answer to this invitation.

'Mr Guy,' he said, 'I appreciate greatly the honour you've offered me, but I need to think and pray about it. I can only do this if I'm certain it's God's calling.'

'Thank you, Eli,' answered Richard Guy. 'That's the sort of answer I hoped you would give. But bear in mind that part of God's calling is the recognition of a person's gifts by other Christians.'

As we went to bed that night, I was longing to hear what Eli thought about the whole thing. He said very little, but before we went to sleep, he took my hand and prayed that we might be ready for whatever God wanted from us.

The next few days went by much as usual. Eli was up early to milk the cows and feed the pigs, etc. Trayton was there to help, but up to now, Eli very rarely left him to do these morning chores alone. Eliza was proving a great help to me, and while she was raking out the ashes in the kitchen grate, laying it with small twigs which would light afresh with a spark from the tinder box in order to get water heated up, I could quietly feed Richard. He always sensed when I was impatient to get on, so it was wonderful to be able to let him take his time and to hear the work being done in the kitchen below. I used this time for my own prayers and found myself now talking to God about our future, for I knew that if Eli became a preacher our lives were going to change.

The men always came in hungry and thirsty for their breakfast at about 8 a.m., and I aimed to have something sizzling in the frying pan over the fire by then. Our pig kept us in bacon for a few weeks. I mostly kept the sausages for our evening meal, but there were always chicken eggs. The pig had given us a good supply of fat, much of which I had melted down into lard so frying chunks of bread in lard and then adding a couple of fried eggs gave them good sustenance for the day. We always had a Bible reading and prayer around the breakfast table, but with our workers with us, Eli couldn't pray in detail about personal things, but I was able to sense what lay behind some of the desires he was expressing. In fact, I was sure Eli's prayers were becoming more real and earnest and less formal.

After a few days, I dared to ask him how he was thinking about the chapel's invitation to preach.

'Selina,' he said, 'I've wanted to talk to you about it, but somehow I've been having such a battle in my mind that I haven't known how to start. My first reaction was simply, how can I preach? I'm just a like a child. I've had no training as a preacher. I'm a Sussex country farmer. But did you notice that reading we had the other morning from Jeremiah? It almost brought me to tears. I had to stop for a minute or so to blow my nose.'

I had noticed those verses and Eli's reaction to them, and it was partly this that had given me the courage to talk to him about the subject.

Eli got out the Bible that was beside his bed, turned to the Old Testament book of Jeremiah, and read from chapter 1:

> Then the word of the Lord came unto me, saying, 'Before I formed thee in the belly I knew thee; and before thou camest forth out of the womb I sanctified thee, and I ordained thee a prophet unto the nations.' Then said I, 'Ah, Lord God! Behold, I cannot speak: for I am a child.' But the Lord said unto me, 'Say not, I am a child: for thou shalt go to all that I shall send thee, and whatsoever I command thee

thou shalt speak. Be not afraid of their faces: for I am with thee to deliver thee, saith the Lord.'

Then the Lord put forth his hand, and touched my mouth. And the Lord said unto me, 'Behold, I have put my words in thy mouth.' [15]

As Eli read these words again to me in the solitude of our own bedroom, he broke down and sobbed. It wasn't until then that I realised how much pressure my husband had been under as he had battled with the question as to whether this was God's calling or not. If it wasn't, then how dare he stand up in God's name before a congregation? And if it was, could he really trust God to help him, to give him words to say and the unction of the Holy Spirit to say them effectively? He might disgrace himself and, what was even worse, the honour of God.

Eventually, Eli turned to me and in a broken voice said, 'Seli, I'm going to have to say yes. Will you stand behind me, to pray for me and support me? I've no idea how I'm going to do it!'

I hugged and kissed him, and we snuggled down together.

The next morning, Eli was up again at the crack of dawn, and another day got under way in the normal pattern. As I sat in the old rocking chair beside our four-poster bed with little Richard at my breast, I mused on the night before. Part of me was thrilled at what was happening. God was calling my husband to be a preacher! But another part of me recognised that the way ahead could be hard, and I had no idea what to expect. I prayed silently, committing our future days fully into God's hand, and as I prayed, I felt an amazing sense of peace. I looked down at little Richard sucking contentedly at my breast and thanked God for him, and then it struck me that I too was just like a baby before God and in a way through my prayer I was sucking at God's breast. At first I felt it was blasphemy to have such a thought, but then I believe God gave me his peace about it, and I found it such a wonderful idea and it helped me tremendously. I needed God, just like

---

[15] Jeremiah 1:4–9.

Richard needed me, and he would sustain and strengthen me just like my milk was nourishing Richard.

At the end of breakfast, Eli reached across for the family Bible and continued the reading in the book of Jeremiah. For the first time that morning, Eli made a short, very short, explanatory comment about the verses he was reading.

> 'Turn, O backsliding children,' saith the Lord, for I am married unto you: and I will take you one of a city, and two of a family, and I will bring you to Zion: And I will give you pastors according to mine heart, which shall feed you with knowledge and understanding.[16]

'I believe,' said Eli, 'that what God promised here to Israel of old, he is still doing today for us Gentiles. He is calling one of a city and two of a family and bringing them through faith in Jesus Christ into his invisible church. And he is giving them pastors and teachers to feed them from his Word.'

When Eli came in at the end of the day, he looked exhausted.

'What a day!' he said. 'It's been a different sort of battle. I'm much more peaceful in my mind, but it's as if all the forces of nature have been opposing us today.'

---

[16] Jeremiah 3:14–15.

Chapter 6

Eli's First Sermon

I shall never forget the first time Eli preached. We'd both prayed a great deal about it. Eli had shared with me his thoughts about the preparation of his sermon.

'Basically, Seli,' he said, 'I'm not a scholar, and I've not got the time to sit for hours writing out a sermon. In fact, I think it would be a disaster if I did it that way. As I thought about it, I remembered David going to fight the giant Goliath. King Saul wanted to give him a coat of armour and a heavy sword, but David refused saying, "I've not tried them, I'll go as I am with what I know, my sling!" You remember the story. When I pray publicly, I just pray and wonderfully God directs my thoughts, and I believe I should do something similar when I preach. I shall pray beforehand for a text and then meditate and pray about it, try to understand it in its context and to have some main points in my mind and believe that if God wants me as his mouthpiece, he'll help me. As I see it now, every sermon will be a miracle.'

Something in me told me that Eli was being a bit simplistic, but on the other hand, I realised that if he was going to preach, this would have to be his way. I knew I would probably be more fearful than Eli the first time he stood in the pulpit, and I would certainly be praying for him. I also knew that the people at chapel liked Eli and would hear him with sympathy and prayer and not in a critical way.

It was a Sunday morning in late February when Eli preached his first sermon. There was a lot of interest when it had been announced that Eli Page would be preaching that Sunday, and the chapel was almost full. This didn't seem to deter Eli at all, and I noted a sense of confidence and, dare I say it, almost pride as he stood in the pulpit. It struck me that it was comparable to a soldier in uniform, proud to represent his king and country. He announced his text from the New Testament in 2 Corinthians chapter 10:

> For though we walk in the flesh, we do not war after the flesh: (For the weapons of our warfare are not carnal, but mighty through God to the pulling down of strong holds;) Casting down imaginations, and every high thing that exalteth itself against the knowledge of God, and bringing into captivity every thought to the obedience of Christ.

I had been praying with some trepidation for my husband prior to the announcement of his text and the beginning of his sermon, but as soon as he began to preach, I felt a complete calm and sat back with little Richard, as good as gold, on my lap and listened to God speaking, at least that's how I felt. As his wife, I felt a responsibility for Eli, but as God's servant he was no longer my responsibility, he was God's, and I knew God could look after him far better than I could!

Eli explained that the apostle Paul in his ministry had seen his service for God as a spiritual battle for the minds and hearts of his fellow men. He had realised that it was hopeless to try and win those hearts for God with human resources but that God had provided the spiritual weapons of prayer and the preaching of the gospel which were supernatural. Nothing and no one was too strong to withstand these weapons when God was at work by his Holy Spirit, and in this way, the sovereign God was building his kingdom. Eli spoke of his own conversion as a miracle and evidence of the power of these spiritual weapons. He said his confidence in God's power and sovereignty and his purpose to save men and women from their own foolish, sinful thoughts and ways through the preaching of the gospel of the love of Jesus was the only reason he was standing in the pulpit that Sunday. He referred to the story of David and Goliath, to the dry bones that Ezekiel saw, and he closed by stating the words of Jesus: 'I will build my church; and the gates of hell shall not prevail against it.' [17]

I knew, as we left the chapel, that this would not be the last sermon Eli preached, and I couldn't help wondering what lay ahead of us.

---

[17] Matthew 16:18.

Chapter 7

Springtime in Sussex

Spring brought a very busy time on the farm as Eli was determined to use the land to full advantage. He had managed to plough the land in the autumn that he intended to sow, and the winter cold with the occasional frost had helped to break up the clods. We had two oxen that he had used to pull the plough, and they were now brought back into use to pull the harrow in order to break up the soil further and to give as fine a tilth as possible before sowing the grain. Thankfully, our soil wasn't too heavy, although still rather clayey, and it was possible to start harrowing earlier than in some areas where the ground has more clay and is heavier and wetter. Our Weald, which is the name given to the land lying between the chalk North Downs, north of us, which run from Surrey down to the White Cliffs of Dover, and the South Downs which lie south of us and run from Hampshire in the west through to the coast at Beachy Head near Eastbourne, is a mixture of clay and sand, some areas being more clay and others more sand.

Eli always maintained that oxen are far better than horses for farmwork, and our Sussex breed are his favourites. After being broken-in when about two years old, these castrated male cattle will then give a good six years work before being fattened for the butcher. Through his training and experience on his father's farm, Eli knew what he was doing with oxen, and I loved to watch him at work. He always had his ox-goad handy, which was a thin hazel stick about eight or nine feet long with a piece of iron wire filed to a point in one end. However, once trained the oxen respond well to voice commands. The guttural grunts Eli used were common Sussex farm language but sounded to me as though the oxen had taught Eli their language rather than the other way round. A sound something like 'Mothawoot' meant come hither, and 'Yahawoot', go thither.

Oxen are far harder to shoe than horses as they don't readily allow their feet to be picked up as horses do. However, if they are used primarily for field work and not on hard surfaces, it's not necessary to shoe them, and none of our oxen were ever shod.

Eli was determined to grow both wheat and oats. He explained to me that oats do better than wheat if it's a wetter and cooler summer, so he wanted to 'hedge his bets' as the phrase goes. Oat straw is also softer and makes better bedding for the animals than the coarser wheat straw, and oats make a good animal feed for our horses. At that time, we had two ponies which we used for riding and pulling our two-wheeled trap.

It was hard work, and Eli decided we should employ a further worker. Although he had done his sums and calculated that we could afford to do this, there was a good degree of faith in it too, as anything can happen in farming. We prayed about getting the right person, and soon another young man, David Burton, joined our household.[18]

Although there was always too much to do, I was determined to enjoy the springtime. Whenever possible in an afternoon, I took Richard out in a little wooden cart that Eli had found and repaired for me, and we walked around the country lanes enjoying the fresh air, the sunshine, and the new growth around us. I loved the countryside. It was so alive, and I watched with interest all that was developing around me. Two of our main trees are the oak and the ash. They are quite different. The oak usually grows into a sturdier tree than the ash, and one of its characteristics is the frequent ninety-degree bends in its branches. I always watch to see which comes into leaf the soonest in

---

[18] 1841 Census, Eli Page Clifton House, Arlington.

spring, as there is a saying that 'if the oak comes out before the ash, we will only get a splash, but if the ash comes out before the oak we shall surely get a soak.' That year the ash came into leaf first, and I remember telling Eli that it would be a wet summer. He laughed and jokingly commented that according to God's Word if, as a prophetess, my prophecy proved to be false, I should be stoned as a false prophet! When during the summer it never seemed to stop raining, I reminded Eli of my prophecy, and we both wondered whether there really is any truth in the ash and oak saying.

We had swallows nesting in our barn, and I was very excited to see the first one safely back from Africa. I noted that it was the 15 April and since then have often found that it's exactly that day that I see the first swallow swooping around the farm. House martins return much the same time. They nest under the eaves of our farmhouse, and although they can make quite a mess on the ground below, I love having them there. On a summer evening, I could watch them for hours as they swoop around. Although they do this to catch the flies and insects they feed on, I'm convinced that at the end of day, they are doing it just for fun. I've often wished I had wings and could join them!

Because Richard and I mostly walked the same lanes—at least it was I that did the walking, Richard lay in his little cart and gurgled—I got to recognise new things that were happening. There was one spot where we regularly saw a robin. He was often sitting on a particular tree stump or in hawthorn hedge next to it. One day as we came by, I said to Richard, 'I want to show you a lovely little bird with a red breast.' Richard smiled up at me, and I took him out of his cart and sat him on my knee where he too could look across at the robin still sitting on his favourite perch. We sat quietly. First the robin sang us a little song, and then he flitted off looking for grubs. We sat still, the sun warming our backs pleasantly. Before too long, back he came into view and darted down into the bottom of the hedge. Yes, as we listened carefully, we could hear a soft chorus of chirping. 'Richard, my little man,' I said, 'I think we have discovered a robin's nest.' I laid Richard back in his cart and, once the robin had flitted off, carefully separated the grass and cow parsley and peered at a low bank behind a narrow ditch. I had to look very carefully, but at last I saw it. Tucked into the bank above an exposed tree root in a lovely little cavity was the nest with tiny, almost featherless little birds crouching low in their comfortable looking home.

'Richard,' I said, 'God has given me you, and we have a nice farmhouse where we live with Daddy, Uncle Trayton, David, and Eliza, and God has given our robin friend four little babies, and they have their little house under the hedge. God looks after us, and he looks after them. He's a wonderful god.'

We found other birds' nests on our afternoon walks. I didn't always actually search for them, but I had a good idea where they were. There was often a skylark soaring in the sky above a particular field. It was delightful to hear its song as it rose higher and higher in the blue sky. I decided that it must have its nest somewhere in this field, and one day, we watched it dive down into the grass. I didn't go looking for its nest as I remembered that my dad had once told us that larks are very clever; they never drop down exactly to the spot in the grass where they have their nest, but once having got out of sight in the vegetation, they flit silently through the grass to their nest, and it can be some yards in any direction from where they have landed. I knew that that field was due to be cut for hay shortly and hoped very much that the fledgling skylarks would be old enough to leave their nest before this happened.

I didn't manage to get out for a walk every day; often it took a lot of determination to leave things in the house for an hour or two, but I know it was good for Richard and it also helped to bond us together and I quite think also gave him, right from an early age, a love for the countryside.

Chapter 8

A Distressing Family Incident

One Sunday midday as Eli, I, and little Richard were returning home from chapel in the pony and trap down Camberlot Lane past Dicker Common, Eli remarked that the common land had originally been very much larger before much of it had been fenced off. Its purpose had been to provide free grazing for the poorer people to use for any animals they might have. He then asked me if I'd ever heard what happened to his father one winter's night when he was walking home across the common.

'No, I don't think so, Eli,' I said. 'What, did he fall into the ditch in the dark?'

Eli laughed. 'No, something far more serious than that. It was reported in the papers and was the talk of the neighbourhood for a long time. It made Dad quite famous.' [19]

'Now you've got me curious,' I said. 'Tell me.'

'It was shortly before Christmas in 1823,' began Eli, 'so I was only just six at the time and didn't understand all that was happening or realise how serious it was. I remember one breakfast seeing Dad hobbling around and all bandaged up round his head. As you know

---

[19] *Sussex Advertiser* (15, 22, and 29 December 1823). Quoted fully in appendix 2.

my stepsister Philadelphia, who was seventeen years older than me, mothered me and brought me up after my mother died, and she told me all about it later.

'Dad was walking home across the common from a tithe feast in the inn at Horsebridge, and he said he half-sensed someone was following him. In fact, Dad had got quite deaf as he became older, so he really wouldn't have heard things that you and I would hear clearly. Anyway when he was well away from the village, and remember it was a dark evening in December, the fellow attacked him. He clubbed Dad almost unconscious and raided his pockets. He must have seen Dad doing some transaction with another farmer at the feast because Dad was in the unusual position of having a cheque for £36 in his pocket, as well as a sovereign and some silver.'

'Wow!' I exclaimed. 'That's a fortune! What's a farm labourer's wage now? Nine shillings a week?'

'Yes, I reckon Dad had just been paid for his whole harvest,' Eli retorted.

'Did he get the money back?' I asked.

'Thankfully, it was a cheque from the bank at Hailsham, so there was no way the robber could have cashed it. He must have realised this as it was found later in the ditch.'

'How about your dad, was he badly hurt?'

'Oh, Dad had a good hard head, and he soon recovered and was able to crawl home. But he could have been killed of course,' said Eli. 'Even at that age, I remember well how Dad would regularly thank the Lord in our family prayers for delivering him from death!'

'Did they ever find out who did it?' I asked.

'Oh yes,' said Eli, 'quite easily. It was a fellow named James Bennett, my stepbrother John knew him. He was a carpenter in the village and a similar age to John. He had a reputation as a good worker, but somehow the devil must have got control of him, and he had turned really vicious. It was said in court that even his father was terrified of him and refused to live with him. It's frightening to think what people can become left to themselves. I sometimes wonder what would have become of me if God's grace hadn't changed my heart and I hadn't got you!'

'Oh, Eli, you would never have done a thing like that.'

'I hope not, Seli, but I've realised that you can't trust the human heart an inch if Jesus hasn't changed you. Anyway, James Bennett hadn't been very careful, and footprints from the place on the common where it happened led straight across a ploughed field to the house where he was living.

'James got the death penalty for it. Dad pressed for clemency, and we heard later his sentence was reduced to life and he was deported to Australia. I know Dad used to pray for James Bennett, and after Dad's death, I found a newspaper cutting amongst his papers which stated James was transported to New South Wales, Australia, in July 1824 on the ship *Mangles*.[20] I hate to think what life must be like out there with all our criminals. It must be a foretaste of hell! Although I understand it's a big place.'

I was quiet the rest of the way home, thinking about what Eli had said. Not so much about Australia but just how much a blessing it is to know Jesus and to have been set free from the power of evil and sin through his life in us. I realised that Eli didn't think badly of James Bennett even though he nearly killed his father. I have heard him apply the quote by John Bradford a number of times to this situation and others with the words, 'There but for the grace of God goes Eli Page.'

---

[20] www.convictrecords.com.au/ships/mangles/1824.

Chapter 9

Another Baby and the Birth of a Plan

As the summer advanced, I realised that I was pregnant again. I was a bit frightened at first but was able to talk to God about my fears, and gradually I found a peace and calm at the thought of another birth, which I'm sure came from him.

'Seli, my darling, I think you should have more help in the house.' This was Eli's response to my announcement to him one evening in bed that there was another baby on the way.

'God has given us a large enough house to have another young girl with us. It gives them better training than is often possible with their own families, a sense of independence, and in many cases parents are pleased to have one of their children out of the home to give more room for the younger ones growing up.' Such was Eli's reasoning, and there was a fair amount of truth in it.

I think Eliza must have been giving a good report about life at Clifton Farm with the Pages because several parents had asked us whether we were needing another housemaid. The girl who actually came to us was my niece Sarah. She was just eleven at the time, and I wondered how she would cope away from home. She shared a room with Eliza who proved also to be a good little teacher, showing Sarah how things were done in our household and being a good friend to her.

I'm convinced that Eli's prayer time each day, with our entire household together around the meal table, bound us together and helped to form us into a loving family, better able to bear with one another's idiosyncrasies. I'm sorry to say that Eli was the most impatient of us and was liable to react harshly when things weren't quite right. This sometimes brought the girls to tears, but I was usually able to smooth things out, and they knew they could always talk to me about things that troubled them.

Eli was now preaching every now and then at chapel, and I knew the people appreciated his sermons. He was also getting invitations to preach in other villages. Small independent chapels had sprung up all around Sussex and only a few of them had pastors or regular ministers, so there was a demand for preachers whom these congregations could respect and who could bring them God's Word in a way that fed their souls. Because of his farming responsibilities, it was clear to Eli that he couldn't accept all the invitations he received, and I know this worried him as he wanted to put God first in his life. I know he prayed about it, and one evening he shared with me how he was thinking.

'Seli,' he said, 'I believe we have two alternatives. Preach I must, God has clearly called me to this and he is opening many doors of opportunity. I could give up farming and concentrate on preaching, trusting God to supply our needs. I have been challenged by this, but I'm not convinced it's right for us, at least not at this time. The alternative is to work and expand the farming so that we have the potential for more income and can employ more workers which should, if all goes well, and it can with God's approval and blessing, free me up to spend more time preaching.'

I listened quietly to his thoughts. I must say they sounded very optimistic, but I didn't voice this to Eli. I knew he would need my encouragement and support and not my criticism if we were to go down this road.

'Eli,' I responded, 'we need to keep praying. If God provides us with the opportunity for more land here or a bigger farm somewhere else, then I guess we should see this as a sign that he wants us to expand.'

'Thanks, Seli, you're a wife in a million,' answered Eli.

It's amazing how flattering men can be when they are getting their own way, I thought. But I really did respect and love Eli, and if this was the road down which God was leading him, then I was proud to be his wife and to stand by him.

Little John arrived on the 12 February 1840.

Chapter 10

Man Sows, God Gives the Increase

We had another two farming years at Clifton Farm, Arlington. We all worked hard. My two girls were a great help in the house and dairy, and with three men now working the farm and with the extra acreage we were now renting, Eli could increase the small herd of bullocks for fattening, and we were also able to add two more sows to our resident pig herd. Each sow produced two litters of piglets a year which we fattened. A good proportion of their diet was the skimmed milk from our milking cows which was left after we had taken off the cream for butter. Each time the sows were ready for the boar, Eli was able to fetch a sturdy 'gentleman' called Boris from a neighbouring farm, and in return, we gave back two of the piglets. The arrangement suited us well. We also ensured our small herd of milking cows kept producing calves, and Eli had a part share with his half-brother in the Sussex bull they had inherited from their father.

When John was ten months, I discovered I was again pregnant. Eli was very nonchalant about this, in my mind far too much so. On the one hand, with each of my pregnancies he had a degree of fear for my health and survival, but after two successful births with no real complications, he showed less anxiety.

One evening, when we had had time to get used to my new pregnancy, Eli quoted to me the verses from the Psalms: 'Lo, children are an heritage of the Lord: and the fruit of the womb is his reward. As arrows are in the hand of a mighty man; so are children of the youth. Happy is the man that hath his quiver full of them: they shall not be ashamed, but they shall speak with the enemies in the gate.'[21]

Although my natural reaction was to say 'It's all right for you as a man. You enjoy your part in producing children, and we women have the suffering', I didn't actually voice this thought as I guessed he would then quote Genesis and point out that the hardship of farming, contending with weeds and thistles and diseases in the livestock is what he must suffer as the result of sin's curse and the pain of childbirth was my part. The fact that I knew he did work hard and that he accepted fully and prayerfully the responsibility of caring for me and our children helped me to feel calm about the whole situation.

The year of 1840 was a very dry year in contrast to the year before. The spring was particularly dry. It enabled Eli to get the soil prepared and the spring corn sown in record time, but he did begin to get anxious when the April showers failed to materialise. Thankfully there were signs of growth which helped him to appreciate the fact that there is a fair amount of clay in our soil which retains the moisture better than more sandy soils of some other parts of the Sussex and Kent Weald. He brought all these concerns to God in our daily prayers with our staff, and when May and June provided a fair amount of rain, we all joined in praising our heavenly Father and in fact the crops did very well, and when August was again a rainless sunny month, they were able to harvest a good crop.

I tried to get out as much as possible on sunny afternoons, and now with John in the little cart and Richard tottering along holding my hand, our progress was slow but what did that matter? We sometimes used our walks as an opportunity to deliver butter and eggs to our

---

[21] Psalm 127:3–5.

customers in the village, and they would often invite us in for a cool drink of some cordial they had made.

The Harmans were members of the congregation at the chapel, and it was always a delight to spend half an hour or so with old Mrs Harman in her little house. She made the most delicious drink from balm leaves which she grew in her cottage garden, and she usually had a jug of it keeping cool in the little pit her husband had dug for this purpose in a shady spot in the garden. One such visit remains particularly in my memory.

It was a warm afternoon in August. Eli and the men were busy with harvest, and leaving the girls making butter, I set out with both John and Richard in the cart. Although Richard rebelled at this initially as he now loved walking, I was firm with him as we go along faster this way and I knew I needed to be back to make supper. The sun was hot, but a number of sturdy oak trees thick with foliage gave us good shade at regular intervals along the lane. Everything was peaceful, and even the birds must have been having an afternoon snooze. John was soon asleep, and Richard was enjoying the jog along the rutted road. The Harmans lived in a small thatched cottage on the edge of the village which stood a little back from the lane. It was some little while since I had called on Mrs Harman as I normally send one or other of the girls to deliver the butter and eggs we sell, and as we approached the cottage, it struck me just how pretty it looked. We stopped at the gate, and I lifted Richard down so he could walk up the garden path. As I lifted the latch and ushered Richard in before me, the beauty of the garden must have struck him almost as much as it did me. Out on our walks, we regularly picked flowers to take home to display in a vase in the kitchen, and this must have been Richard's immediate thought. He dropped on his knees before the bright orange marigolds, which formed the border of the four-foot-wide flower bed running down to the cottage, and before I could stop him had picked one of the blooms.

'No, Richard,' I exclaimed, 'no more. These belong to Mrs Harman.'

I took him by the hand, and together we admired that lovely garden. Behind the marigolds were snapdragons and wallflowers interspersed amongst clumps of dahlias in a range of magnificent colours. Then at the back, as if standing guard over the less tall members of that family garden, were a double row of fully blooming hollyhocks in a range of colours from deep purple to light yellow and white. It was a cottage garden at its best, and the buzzing of bees gave sound to the beautiful picture, and the flitting of butterflies from bloom to bloom gave movement. I could recognise small tortoiseshells, red admirals, peacocks, painted ladies, and was that a clouded yellow?

'Look, Richard,' I said. 'Look at those lovely little blue butterflies.'

I knew Mrs Harman must have worked hard on this garden and was probably bringing water from a nearby stream to water these delightful plants every evening, but essentially, these were God's colours and designs. They were living and vibrant, and my mind went to the cry of the angel seen by Isaiah in his vision: 'The whole earth is full of His glory'.

Mrs Harman had seen us coming, and as we walked up the garden path, she was waiting for us in the open doorway. She was framed by light mauve clematis flowers, which were climbing around her cottage door, an older lady with whitish hair tied tightly back into a bun and wearing a full-length dark blue pleated dress with a bonnet of a similar colour adorning her head. But what was most obvious about her was her beaming face. It was obvious that she was pleased to see us.

'It's lovely to see you, Selina,' she said. 'I was hoping you would bring the butter and eggs this week as I've got something exciting to tell you. Do come in with those precious children and have some of my cool balm tea. I'll just fetch the jug from my cold store.'

Like most country people, Mrs Harman had a little pit dug in the ground in a shaded part of the garden which was covered with a slab of stone. This helped to keep the milk and other drinks cool in hot weather.

We left John under the shade of an apple tree and sat around her kitchen table. Mrs Harman gave Richard some wooden blocks to play with on the floor, and she and I sat sipping our lemony flavoured cold tea.

'Selina,' she said, 'something wonderful has happened, and humanly speaking, it's because of your Eli.'

I listened with interest.

'You may not have known that my Harold has been suffering recently,' she continued.

'I'm so sorry. I didn't know,' I said.

'I suppose you would call it soul trouble,' she explained. 'But it was very real and has been affecting every part of his life. He's talked to Mr Vinall about it, and he has sat and prayed with Harold but nothing seemed to shift it. It really all started with me. For years I was a good church person, but when I've analysed my form of Christianity, I think I went to church more to earn God's favour and to ensure the smoke went up the chimney than for any other reason. Then nearly two years ago, I heard Mr Vinall preach and realised for the first time that God was a loving and merciful god and that it was in love that he had sent his Son Jesus into the world to atone for his people's sins. Mr Vinall said he is calling us to trust him and enjoy daily fellowship with him as our heavenly Father. This gave me tremendous joy and changed my whole attitude to life. Harold didn't understand but was happy to let me go along to chapel each Sunday. Then a few months ago, he began to come with me. "Doris," he said to me, "something has made you a different person. You are far happier and more content than you used to be. I've heard you singing to yourself as you do the housework and tend to your plants, and even they seem to respond to your new, loving attitude." So Harold began coming with me on Sundays. However, instead of making him happy, it made him miserable. The more he heard, the worse it was. The preaching we hear tells us we can do nothing to gain a place in heaven, and this is what Harold seemed to hear so loud and clear that the message of the mercy that there is in Jesus never touched him. He would tell me over and over again that he felt hopeless and helpless. It was so bad that it affected his work and his sleep.'

'So what has happened?' I asked excitedly. 'You've said there's good news.'

'Last Sunday, your Eli was preaching,' continued Doris Harman, 'and although he said some very simple and obvious things which must have been said many times, the Holy Spirit used his sermon in a powerful way to set Harold free. You were at home with the children, but Eli's text was "the Lord gives grace and glory". In the course of his sermon, Eli made the point that God will often make us feel helpless and hopeless before we can receive his grace. It was those two words which aroused Harold's interest and focused his attention. They are just the very words he had been using about himself. Then your Eli went on to say that Jesus came into the world not for the self-righteous but for the hopeless, and he quoted the words of Jesus, "Come unto me, all ye who are weary and heavy laden and I will give you rest." I was watching Harold's face and praying hard. I knew what his question would be and somehow your Eli did too. "Perhaps you are asking," he continued, "what does it mean to come to Jesus? Basically, it just means trusting him, taking Jesus at his word, accepting all that he offers, loving him, and obeying him." Then Eli quoted Jesus again and it was Jesus' words that set my Harold free from all his misery. "Whoever comes to me I will in no wise cast out." Harold looked at me with tears running down his face. "He won't cast me out," he murmured. "He won't cast me out!" I think if we'd been at home, Harold would have sobbed in relief, but being in chapel, he braced himself and simply wiped his eyes and squeezed my hand.

'Your Eli must go on preaching, Selina,' Mrs Harman continued. 'He's young, and I'm sure he has a lot to learn, but God is with him. Don't let him get proud, I'm sure you'll find ways of deflating him if he begins to think he's indispensable to God, but do tell him what I've told you. It will encourage him.'

I walked home with a wonderfully happy feeling in my heart. God was building his kingdom and using my Eli. I couldn't help wondering though where it was all leading.

Chapter 11

Harvest and Winter

The end of summer and beginning of autumn is one of the busiest times for a farmer's wife. Harvest provides all sorts of produce which needs to be preserved to provide nourishment for the winter. We had apple and plum trees which had been fairly heavy with fruit, and I'd also been able to pick a good supply of wild blackberries with the intention of bottling apples and blackberries together. The girls could help me with the bottling of fruit, and I also made a good supply of jam. We had several varieties of apples and some were good keepers. Eli had allocated me some shelving in one of barns for storing the apples, and I had to ensure that only good apples, which we had picked with our own hands from the trees, were put into store. Any bruise, however slight, would cause the apple to decay, and the decay in one apple would affect all apples it was touching. I stored Bramleys, which were large green cooking apples and delicious when baked. We also had several trees of Cox's orange pippin. These stored well and were lovely sweet eating apples. Having carefully placed good undamaged apples on the shelves, I covered them with straw to protect against frost and felt a similar satisfaction to that which a squirrel must feel when hiding nuts for a rainy day.

We had two pigs to kill that year for our growing household, and we planned this to give us meat for the longest possible time. Eli decided if we killed one shortly before Christmas, we could feed the other a little longer and have him in about February. These occasions always give us plenty of work cutting, salting, and smoking the meat and making sausages.

It's unusual for us to have really cold winters in Sussex in southern England, but that winter of 1840 to 1841 was hard. Serious frosts started coming by middle December, and apart from a few weeks of slightly less cold weather, the temperatures stayed much lower than average for many weeks. We keep the cattle and ponies inside during the colder weather, but this makes much more work. Eli had devised a system of channels to bring water to them, but under freezing conditions, this can freeze up and then water has to be carried by hand. Thankfully, however cold it gets, the water deep in our well never freezes, and with the hand pump in the kitchen and not in the yard, this doesn't freeze either.

But cold weather adds many complications to everyday living. The only fire in the house is in the kitchen, so we all tend to congregate there in the warmth until sleep calls us to brave the cold and dash upstairs with our candles and get under our blankets and eiderdowns as quickly as possible. During the dark evenings, we have supper earlier than in the summer and are usually in bed by nine o'clock, if not sooner, and in very cold weather, I have the children in bed with me to ensure they keep warm.

Mornings are even more of a challenge in real frosty weather, and as we went into 1841, we had several weeks of low temperatures. It was then no use taking water upstairs the night before to wash in before dressing, as it froze overnight. I had trained the girls to get up before me to light the kitchen fire and put a cauldron of water on it to heat up, but in such weather, I had to pull some clothes on first and come down and fetch water to take back upstairs to give myself and the children a quick wash. Eli and the men would have got up sooner and, being a bit hardier, given their faces a quick wash in the kitchen sink before going out to milk the cows. They get out there as quickly as possible because, as Eli has often said, on frosty mornings, the cow stall is warmer than the house. I know some farms where in winter the farmworkers prefer to sleep in straw in the cow shed because it's warmer than their bedrooms! I wonder whether the farmer's wife is then willing to have them back in the kitchen for breakfast! Although I must say, even our men don't smell the most fresh when they come for their meals. Thankfully, in a remarkable way, God has so designed us that our senses get used to familiar smells, and it's only guests who notice.

Once the animals have been dealt with, there's not so much the men can do on the land in the depths of winter, so one job reserved for these weeks is threshing the corn. At harvest time, the corn is tied into sheaves and taken into the barn for storage. Then what is not required immediately is left like this until the winter. Beating the corn by hand using a flail keeps the men warm and provides work for those difficult winter days. The grain is then separated from the straw and sacked up and the straw stored for animal bedding. Another winter's job was felling a tree or two, sawing them up, and slitting the logs into a suitable size for our kitchen fire. We aimed to have a supply of suitably prepared firewood so that the logs had at least two years, preferably three, to dry out. Dried wood provides more heat. Felling trees in winter helps quicken the process of drying as there is less sap in the wood when the tree is not feeding leaves, blossom, or fruit. As we cut down trees, Eli always tried to ensure, as much as possible, that new ones were taking their place.

I remember the evening that winter when Eli came in and said he was sure there was snow on the way. The wind had been in the east for some days, the temperature had not risen above freezing all that week, so when the wind veered towards the south-east and brought snow across from Poland and Germany, there was little chance of it melting quickly. It came overnight, and as I lay in bed, I knew something was different. I had a disturbed night; the children too seemed to sense something and were unsettled. A good six inches of snow had fallen by morning, and it was still coming down being blown around the house in a steady wind. William, our proud rooster, generally arouses me before dawn, but that morning he seemed so muffled I wondered whether he had a sore throat. I tried to look out of the window but, as had been often the case that winter, Jack Frost had painted some lovely fern-like designs on the inside of the glass, and I could see nothing. I was determined to know what had happened outside and remembered a trick my father had taught us children. I warmed a copper penny in my hand for a minute or two and then placed it on the iced window pane. Almost immediately I had a spyhole through the frost, and although it was still dark outside, by putting my eye to it, I could see white everywhere, and yes, those were swirling snowflakes blowing against my window. I suppose in those days, I was still young at heart. Snow like this didn't come to us very often in Sussex, and I must say I was really excited about it. Still, work had to be done! The men would soon come in cold and hungry, demanding thick chunks of bread, fried in plenty of pig lard, and big fried chicken eggs. I trusted the girls had got the fire going. But first I had to feed John. That morning, I snuggled back into bed and nursed him under the blankets. We both appreciated this method on a cold morning. Richard was still sleeping beside me, so once John was satisfied and I was sure he didn't need winding, I lay him back alongside Richard and, being Eli's son and knowing what was good for him, he was soon back in the land of nod.

It snowed off and on for several days. The men cleared a good path between our back door and the animals, and thankfully, we had all that we needed to feed ourselves and our livestock. Water had to be carried to them, and we were thankful for a steady supply of unfrozen water from our well.

I ought to, perhaps at this point, tell you how difficult it could be to light the fire in the morning before lucifers were commonly available. We tried as much as possible to keep the kitchen fire in, that is to keep it alight all night. Usually if we heaped wood ash over a burning log before we went to bed, the log would continue to burn very slowly under the ash, and there would be enough life in it in the morning to get flames going again with dry twigs. However, sometimes the fire went out, then we had to start it again from scratch. What we used was flint and steel and tinder. The tinder consisted of a linen rag which had been set alight and allowed to burn till it was of a dark-brown colour. The flame was then put out, and the resulting brown rag, which will relight easier than unburnt rag, is stuffed in a round tinderbox. The ones we used were about five inches in diameter and about one and a half inches deep. The tinder rag was compressed down in the box by a piece of lead about one-fourth inch deep with a little knob on top for lifting it out. We then used an ordinary piece of flint broken so as to give one or two sharp edges and a piece of steel shaped something like a capital *U* and about three inches long, to get a spark. The rag was arranged so as to give as many free edges as possible, and holding the steel by one of the arms, the sharp end of the flint was then brought down sharply in a downward direction against the other arm of the steel and directed at a free end of the rag. After a few attempts, and if all went well, a spark would set the rag alight, and it would smoulder along one edge. Then we used a match to get a flame. Matches were made by gypsies who sold them to us at the door. They consisted of a very thin piece of wood, preferably softwood from a conifer tree, about half an inch wide and six inches long, cut into a diamond-shaped point at each end and coated with brimstone. The gypsies would make these by melting brimstone in an iron spoon and dipping the end of the match into it.[22]

It took considerable practice and skill to make the spark fall on the tinder and cause it to begin burning, and sometimes if the girls hadn't managed to get the fire going by the time I came down, I had to take over. As you can imagine, there was always great relief if the log in the fire was still glowing enough in the morning to get fresh twigs alight.

We had to wait several years before self-lighting matches became available for us. We called them lucifers, and you can imagine what a difference they made to everyday life. They were something of a

---

[22] Nathaniel P. Blaker, 'Flint and Steel', *Sussex in Bygone Days* (first published in 1906, for private circulation only, under the title of 'Reminiscences of Nathaniel Paine Blaker', new edition, revised, extended, and largely rewritten, December 1919). See www.freepages.genealogy.rootsweb.ancestry.com/~blaker/reminiscences/flint.html.

novelty at first, but then quickly replaced tinderboxes even in the most conservative households.

Still, I must get back to my story. Before the snow had gone that winter, the two boys developed whooping cough. This worried me considerably, but thankfully, the lanes were clear enough by then for me to make a hurried visit to my mother for her advice.

'First and foremost, keep them warm,' she said. 'They need an even temperature, so you'd better keep the kitchen fire going all night and sleep with them down there. No carrying them upstairs to the cold air in the bedroom.'

'I'm already doing that,' I said. 'I remember how you used to look after us when we had coughs and colds in the winter months. But have you got any of that medicine you used to give us for our cough? I remember it was essentially honey, but you had some herbal root in it as well.'

'Thankfully, I have,' said Mum. 'I make some every autumn for just such needs as this. I'll give you some for the boys, and I'll also tell you how to make it because you need to be making it too as your family and household increase.' She looked at me meaningfully.

I said nothing in response to her look but agreed that her suggestion was a good idea, and although I was eager to get back to my little patients as quickly as possible, I listened carefully to Mum's recipe.

'The herb I use is elecampane,' said Mum. 'Sometimes it's referred to as horse-heal because we use it on horses too, but don't let that worry you. I grow it in the garden and each autumn dig up some of the roots and cut them up into little pieces. Then I bottle them in honey. Just simply put the small bits of root in honey in a little pot. You can shake the pot about a bit for a day or two to make sure it's mixing well, and after about a week or so, it's ready for use.'

'I remember now,' I said. 'You used to give us a spoonful or so, and we sucked the honey and then chewed the bits of herb before spitting them out.'

'Exactly,' replied Mum. 'It doesn't hurt to swallow the bits of root, but it's good to chew them well to get the benefit out of them. Most children love it because the main taste is the honey.'

'How about John?' I asked. 'Isn't he a bit young for this? He's not one till the twelfth of next month.'

'There is another way of taking it if you find he's not happy sucking on the honey and bits of root,' Mum said. 'I'll give you some dried elecampane root, and you'll need to cut it up and boil a couple of egg cups full of it in a quart of water. Let it boil for about twenty minutes, then add enough honey to make it pleasant to drink. You can add a little lemon juice too if you've got any. Then drain it to get rid of the bits of root and give John spoonfuls of it. You can't give him too much unless the honey makes him sick.'

I gave Mum a kiss and walked home as fast as I could with my medicine, praying that God would bless it to the boys and heal them quickly.

It took a few weeks before they were free from their coughs, but thankfully, by keeping them warm, they didn't get seriously ill.

That winter was full of many challenges, but what I hadn't realised at the time was that by the next winter, our minds would be already concentrating on preparing for the move to a new farm.

Chapter 12

A Bigger Farm

Eli had for some months been looking out for a larger farm to rent. He had become convinced that this was God's way for him to have more time for preaching. It seemed a back to front way of thinking to me—to give yourself more work so you can have more free time! Eli had explained it to me more than once.

'With more potential for income, we can employ more men and that should free me up from the routine, everyday chores,' he had said. Then added with a smile, 'A bigger farm should give us a bigger farmhouse and plenty of room for more children, who of course can all help on the farm!'

I throw a cushion at his smiling face. 'I'll fulfil my wifely duties,' I said, 'but you had better make sure I get all the help I need in the house!' What gave me comfort in all these grand plans was the fact that I knew Eli wasn't lazy. He didn't just have big ideas in his head; he was prepared to roll up his sleeves and work all the hours God gave him. The men admired this, and it inspired them to work hard too.

Since becoming aware of his true identity as a child of God, Eli had given up his pub evenings, but occasionally he would call in at our local, the Plough Inn, to chat to other farmers. It was either there or at a farmer's market that he heard that a farm in Ticehurst was becoming available. When he mentioned this to me, I can't say I was enthusiastic. Ticehurst is a good twenty miles north of the Dicker, and living there would mean I wouldn't be able to call in and see my mother so frequently, and I wondered whether our girls' parents would want them to move so far away from them. We agreed that we would pray about it, and Eli would make further enquiries.

When Eli saw the farm, he was delighted with it. It consisted of ninety-five acres of land some of which was already used for hop-growing. Although hops were a new crop for Eli, he knew there was profit to be had from it if managed properly, and it was a challenge that excited him.

One afternoon in March, we took the pony and trap and Eli drove me and the boys over towards Ticehurst to show me Limden Farm. It was a day of bright periods when the sun showed itself for brief intervals before thicker cloud driven by a steady south-west wind obscured it again. The air was beautiful. We could sense that the warmer weather was on the way, and I really enjoyed the ride. I love our Sussex countryside. Primroses were showing in sheltered spots and hazel catkins were dancing in the breeze in the hedgerows. We drove straight to Limden Farm which is just north of Stonegate. Eli had already looked over the farm, so we spent our time looking at the farmhouse and outbuildings. I was pleased to see that there was a smokehouse close to the house in the yard. This would make it easier for us to smoke out pig meat. There were several things that we agreed needing improving, but Eli assured me this wouldn't be difficult, and in general the farmhouse provided everything we were already enjoying at Clifton Farm, and I told Eli that I was happy to leave the final decision with him.

I was now getting heavier with our third child, and on the 2 July 1841, our first daughter, Ruth, was born.

Eli was delighted to have a little girl, and Richard and John were intrigued to have a baby sister. My two girl assistants, Eliza and Sarah, had become so much part of the household that I sensed they saw the advent of Ruth almost as a gift of a sister to them too. We soon got into a new routine which included meeting the needs of Ruth as well as that of everyone else. Without discussing the matter with Eli, I took the step of breastfeeding Ruth downstairs in a kitchen chair and was relieved to find that everyone, including our farm employees, accepted this without showing signs of embarrassment. I think Eli would have been against it if I had asked him first, but when he saw how naturally I was able to do it without drawing attention to what I was doing and how the rest of the household accepted it as a natural thing to do, he was happy about it.

I'm convinced that the Bible reading and prayer time which Eli led each day helped to mould us together as a household, and apart from minor, and occasionally not so minor, upsets, which mostly I could defuse fairly quickly, we were a very peaceful home.

Eli decided it was the right thing for us to move farms, and although this was unsettling at the time, we both very quickly learned to thank God for guiding us on in his sovereign purpose. Limden Farm was to bring new experiences, new challenges, a considerable growth in our family, and above all, a home in which we experienced God's Spirit with us.

Part 3

Limden Farm
1842–1856

Chapter 1

The Move

Eli made the necessary arrangements for us to finish the year at Clifton Farm and to move to Limden Farm in time to prepare the ground and sow crops for the next season.

Moving was a major event. We reduced the livestock as much as possible, selling off the bullocks we were fattening, but it was important to take our milking cows with us and also the oxen we used for farmwork. We also had two ponies for riding and drawing the trap and a larger carthorse for farmwork. When the time came, these larger animals had to walk the distance to Limden Farm, and driving the cows up the country lanes took a full day. After thinking it over, Eli decided to sell off the pigs and get in fresh sows on the new farm. He also decided to buy a larger cart as this would help with the move and also would be useful for the larger acreage we were moving to. We were able to mount the henhouse on the cart so my hens could be transported without difficulty. We were pleased that all our staff wanted to stay with us, and once we got to Limden Farm, Eli engaged two further farmworkers, one of whom had had experience in hop farming which pleased Eli tremendously.

One of the biggest wrenches for us was leaving out chapel friends. They were very sorry to lose us, but Eli assured them he would be happy to come and preach for them occasionally. Many of the folk spoke of the blessing they had received through Eli, and I think the fact he was such a young man and spoke with such certainty of his faith in Christ and belief in the scriptures enabled them to overlook deficiencies in his preaching which they would have been less able to do with someone more mature.

Our plan was to take the cows first and then to move our farm implements and things from outside of the house on one day and then our household goods and furniture from inside the house on another day. On the day we had scheduled for moving the farm stuff, our chapel friends arrived in force. We were overwhelmed by their kindness. They brought two largish wagons, and with our own as a third, they manhandled everything on board and drove with Eli and the men to Limden Farm, unloaded, and returned for another three wagon's full. They kindly arranged for another contingent of men to repeat this the following day when we moved the furniture and household goods. I was so thankful to them as otherwise the move would probably have had to have been drawn out over several days. My mother was able to look after Richard and John for a couple of days, and I and Ruth and the girls stayed on at Clifton Farm after the last loads were gone to clean the house. Eli returned on the wagon of one of our chapel friends and then drove us over in the pony and trap. The second stage of our married life had begun.

Chapter 2

A New Location with New Experiences

The little town of Ticehurst lies in the northern part of East Sussex nearer the Kent border. As Eli explained to me, the soil in this area is essentially clay lying on a base of sandstone. The countryside is more wooded and more rolling; by this he meant there are dips up and down, whereas our previous farm was more level. The very name of the early settlements here, Ticehurst and Wadhurst, describe the location well. The word 'hurst' or in Old Saxon 'hyrst' means a 'wooded hill'. This type of farmland lends itself more to pasture land than cereal growing, but it has been found that hops do very well here also.

Limden Farm had a total area of ninety-five acres of which about 10 per cent was woodland. Eli was excited about the challenge of a different type of farming. We would maintain a small number of milking cows, increase our herd of bullocks for fattening, have up to four sows producing piglets for fattening, and we would grow sufficient corn for our own use with some small amount to sell, but apart from hay for cattle fodder in the winter months, our main growing crop would be hops. Eli explained to me that some of the woodland was coppiced, that means the trees had not been allowed to grow tall but had been cut down to mere stumps out of which many small branches grew. A few years growth then provided sticks which could be cut and used in the hop fields for the hops to grow up, and there was a good market for them. If he saw there was sufficient demand for hop sticks, he would think about increasing the area of coppiced woodland.

The farmhouse was about two miles from Ticehurst which was our nearest bigger village, and if I needed to go shopping there, I would have to take the pony and trap; however, we are pretty self-sufficient, so there is not a lot we need to buy regularly. Our address was Limden Lane, and this runs from Stonegate, south of us, up to the Ticehurst to Wadhurst road. From Stonehurst, our lane runs north, drops down Mabbs Hill, and then dips a bit further down to the river Limden, and our farmhouse lies in the dip there, just by the river which runs through the middle of our farm. Stonegate is our closest village, and although there are not many shops there, I was pleased to discover that it had a smithy, a post office, and a grocery and draper's store.

One of my main concerns which I talked to Eli about was the availability of Christian fellowship. Our chapel friends in Arlington and the Dicker had meant a lot to me, and I know to Eli too, so I hoped very much we would be able to find local people who loved Jesus and the Bible like we did. Eli's answer was that we would have to find out. He knew there was a Calvinistic chapel in Flimwell, just north of Ticehurst, and another in Burwash and also at Shover's Green which were all well within travelling distance.

It took us several weeks to get ourselves sorted out and into a manageable routine. We had brought William, our Sussex rooster, with us, and he soon took up his duty of waking us all up at the crack of dawn. The hens went off their regular laying for a week or so, but they very soon adjusted to their new surrounding, and I would chat to them when I fed them each morning and collected the eggs. This was one job I didn't want to give to the girls to do. Much of a housewife's work can become just drudgery, and my contact with my hens took me out of the house and away from the children and just the twenty minutes or so that it took helped my day. I would often talk to God at the same time. Thank and praise him for the fresh air, which was somehow still fresh even when pig smells wafted by! I would also thank him for the hens, cows, horses, and the pigs. They were our livelihood and although we were eventually going to kill them and eat them, my understanding of God's Word was that he has given them to us for this purpose. We treated our animals well. We aimed that they should have a good life and then be killed as humanely as possible.

One thing I was determined to do on our new farm was to have a kitchen garden. We had grown some vegetables at Clifton Farm, but I had always felt there could be more. I also wanted a flower garden. The lane ran close by the house, and I was determined to find time to make a good impression to those passing by. I had in mind Doris Harman's flower garden and decided it would be a good reason to go back and call on her for some tips.

The children took a lot of my time. Ruth was just seven months when we moved and Richard was about three and John coming up to two years old. I was very thankful to have the two girls still with me. They had grown into our household and were willing and capable helpers and loved the children. Ruth particularly was a little favourite. She was the most docile and happy of our babies so far. The girls had been intrigued to watch her eyes change from blue to brown, just like her father's, and she was happy to lie for hours watching the boys playing. People told me that it was my own relaxed manner which helped the children to be gentle and easy to control, and if this is so, I just thank God for it. I would have been even more thankful about this if I'd known at that stage how big our family was to become!

Eli was able to buy two sows already in-pig, so we soon got our new pig herd going. They were due to farrow in about six weeks which suited us fine. One of the cows we had brought with us was due to calf in April, so we really began to think that things were moving on our new farm. Eli got one of our fields ploughed and harrowed, ready for wheat, and we were just able to get the seed in before it got too late in the season. He had a good-sized plough, and because of the heavier clay soil, he needed our two oxen to pull it. God blessed us with some soft drying winds in early March which prepared the soil well for harrowing, and Eli was pleased to be able to get a reasonable tilth for sowing.

Chapter 3

A New Crop

The hops were more of a challenge to Eli because this was a new crop to him, but thankfully, our farm had a hop field already established. Eli had already reaped quite a lot of information about hop-growing, and one evening he explained it to me and it thrilled me a lot that he wanted to do this.

Apparently our variety of hops was called white bines. Like all hops, they are perennials, that is, the same plants last several years, in fact, up to twenty years. They produce a massive root system, but the outward growth dies off in the autumn and needs cutting back to its base. It will then grow afresh the next year. Our hops were planted in flat-topped mounds with three plants to a mound. The mounds were then nine to ten feet apart, which means there are approximately 900 mounds to an acre. When planting the hops, a hole is dug in the centre of the mound about a foot square and a foot deep and two of three hop plants planted in each hole. The distance of nine feet between the holes allows for plenty of light for the growing plants. Sticks are very important for the hops to climb up, and ideal sticks are about nine to ten inches round and not more than fifteen to sixteen feet in length. Each mound needs three or four sticks, and they need pushing about eighteen inches into the soil to keep them stable and should slope slightly outward to give light down the middle. The best wood for this job is chestnut or alder and part of our woodland was coppiced chestnut trees, so this enabled us to produce our own hop-sticks and also, as Eli hoped, have sufficient to sell. A few needed replacing, but Eli reckoned most of the existing sticks could be reused for at least one more year.

During the growing season, the hops fields need quite a lot of attention. The plants will climb the sticks, always winding around them in clockwise direction and attaching themselves with tiny little hairs from the stem and back of the leaves, but this needs to be controlled and some of the stems tied into place with lengths of reed to ensure they grow in a way that makes best use of the sunlight. Then they needed to be kept relatively free from weeds. But as Eli said, this work would come in due course; in the immediate, he needed to ensure the plants were well manured. He had heard that the best fertiliser was dung, soap ash (sodium carbonate), and bracken, all of which is rich in potash. This year he would use whatever he could easily get hold of and then aim to be better prepared for the following year.

There was another interesting thing that Eli explained to me. There are male hop plants and female ones. Essentially, it's the female plants we need to produce the hops, and the flowers don't actually need to be fertilised to produce the little leafy cone-like structures which we harvest. It has been fairly normal practise to have one male plant to every hundred female ones.

There was going to be a lot more interesting things to discover about hops as the season progressed, and while the hop field was quite close to the house, I was determined to keep an eye on how things developed. I couldn't help asking Eli one more question though, 'How were hops used?' I knew they were used in beer-making, and I gathered from Eli's cautious answer that he didn't know much more than I did about this. What he did say was that perhaps I should find the recipe, and we could make our own beer. He thought it was quite easy to get a licence to do this. I almost wished I hadn't asked the question!

Chapter 4

New Neighbours

As the weeks went by, I began to enjoy our new house. It was lovely to be so close to the river. It wasn't a big river, and it flowed fairly slowly, but it seemed to me to be alive. It was ever-moving, ever-changing, and it attracted birds and other wildlife which we hadn't seen at Clifton Farm. I hoped very much there would be otters on our river, as this was an animal that I'd only heard about, maybe also a kingfisher or two! There were certainly fish in the river, and already I could imagine Richard and John wanting to catch them when they were a bit older. In the immediate, I realised that there were dangers as well as excitements in having a river nearby. What if it flooded? Did we need to fence it off to protect the children from falling in? I would have to talk to Eli about these things.

Spring weather soon began to arrive, and I disciplined myself to find time to walk the children at least two or three times a week. Now it was Ruth in the little cart and sometimes John alongside her. Our lane was pretty rough, which made it hard going with the cart. Also being in a dip meant whichever direction I went, it was uphill. However, that had its compensation as I knew coming home would be easier! On one of these spring afternoons, a horse approached us as I was pulling the cart up an incline with all three children enjoying the ride. It just happened that at that moment, we were all laughing together, and as the horse approached, its rider, an oldish man with a short greyish beard and sideburns, obviously couldn't help being amused by us.

'You must be Mrs Page,' he said. 'I'm James Ford, from Stores Farm, just down the lane. I'm pleased to meet my new neighbour.'[23]

Eli had mentioned the various farmers that lived around us and had already met some of them, but I had been more confined to the house.

'It's good to meet you too,' I answered. 'Everything is still new to me here, and we've been very busy settling in.'

'You look to be a very happy little family,' he added. 'I know my wife would like to meet you. Perhaps one afternoon you would like to call by? I'm sure the children would like to see our rabbits, and I know Mary would love a chat.'

I thanked him very much and said I would love to come.

'Would Thursday be a good day?'

Mr Ford assured me that his wife was always at home and, although usually busy, would love to have an excuse to sit down and enjoy a bit of company.

We continued our walk, and I was thrilled to find celandines and primroses in the hedgerows, and we caught sight of a red squirrel clambering up an old oak tree. We stopped for a few minutes, and I whispered to Richard that if we stood very still, Squidge the Squirrel might peep out at us from behind the tree trunk. After a little while, our patience was rewarded, and there he was peering at us timidly. I'm not so sure that Richard saw him, but I certainly enjoyed this encounter with another of our neighbours! We returned home with a lovely bunch of primroses for the kitchen, and I felt it had been a very worthwhile afternoon.

That evening after our regular evening prayers, I mentioned to Eli that I had met Mr Ford and that he had invited me to visit his wife.

'Yes, do that,' he said. 'I've spoken to Mr Ford myself, and he seems a very pleasant sort of man.'

---

[23] 1841 Census, James Ford, Stores Farm, Ticehurst.

The following day was Wednesday and proved to be one of those days when nothing goes to plan, and I began to wonder if I would manage to free myself that Thursday to make a visit to Mrs Ford at Stores Farm. Thankfully, things came together much better the next morning, and at about two o'clock, I set out with the children to make my first official visit as the farmer's wife of Limden Farm. I had in fact suddenly realised that I had quite a status. Our farm was by no means small, and this gave Eli and his family a distinct respectability in the neighbourhood.

I found Mrs Ford an older lady than I had expected, considerably older than my own mother, but she was very welcoming. She had a very black kettle simmering over the fire, and the kitchen gave the impression of being well cared for. There was fresh sand on the floor, and the large oak table was spotlessly scrubbed. She invited me to sit down at the table and produced blue willow pattern cups, saucers, and plates from the dresser, set a plate of home-made rock cakes in front of me and proceeded to make a pot of tea. Richard and John looked eagerly at the cakes, and this soon took away any shyness they might have had. Our hostess lifted them up one at a time on to a wooden bench which ran the length of the table against the far wall and placed a small rock cake in front of each of them. Just at that moment, a little head appeared round the door.

'Come in, John,' said the old lady. 'There's a cake for you too.'

'John is my daughter's child,' explained Mrs Ford. 'He's living with us at the moment.'

John was considerably bigger than Richard but was happy to ease himself on to the bench next to my two boys and to be given a cake.

'How old is John?' I asked.

'He's just had his ninth birthday,' said Mrs Ford. She said no more, and I sensed there was some embarrassment about John. He seemed a happy little boy, and despite their age differences, he looked pleased to have children in the house. After they had devoured their rock cakes, John asked his grandma whether he could take Richard and John to see the rabbits. I was a bit concerned about my John going without me, but Mrs Ford assured me it was quite safe, and she asked her grandson to take special care of the little boys. He went off proudly with my two in tow.

I had Ruth on my lap and rocked her gently as she opened her eyes.

'So how are you settling in?' asked Mrs Ford.

I explained that it had been quite a wrench for me to leave the Dicker, where we had made some good friends and where I knew I could call on my mother easily.

'Do you have help in the house?' enquired Mrs Ford. 'It's a largish place, and with the three children, your hands must be full.'

'Yes,' I said. 'I've got two very helpful girls. They are young, but we get on very well. Sarah is my niece, and Eliza was with us first and was proud to take Sarah under her wing and teach her all she herself had learnt. They look on me almost as their mother and love the children, especially Ruth here.'

'It makes so much difference if there's harmony in a household,' commented Mr Ford. 'Ours hasn't always been so harmonious, but things are somewhat better at the moment. Our children weren't really interested in the farm, and that has been a cause of irritation to my husband. Our two youngest are still living at home, John is now twenty-six—I guess that is older than you, my dear—and Hannah is just twenty-one. John works for Samuel Read, the blacksmith in Stonegate, and Hannah helps out in the grocery store there. Thankfully Stonegate is within walking distance for them.'

'Oh, I often see a young lady walking past the farm,' I said. 'That must be Hannah!'

'It will be,' answered Mrs Ford. 'There's nobody else comes down the lane regularly. I'm not so sure how long she will be at home. She's walking out with a lad from Ticehurst. He seems nice enough. We'll just have to see. John is the son of my other daughter, but sadly she died soon after he was born. The poor father was distraught, and I agreed to have John with me. He's finding his feet again now at last, and from comments he's made to us when he comes to see John, there's likely to be another wife soon. I hope very much this will eventually mean a home for John. I'm not as young as I was and haven't always been so well in recent weeks.'

At that moment, Richard came running through the door followed closely by my John. The older John came along behind, looking pleased with himself.

'I said they could have one of my baby rabbits each,' he said to his grandma. 'Is that all right?'

'Well, if their mummy and daddy say so, certainly,' answered Mrs Ford with a smile.

I thanked John very much and said that we would need to ask Richard and John's daddy to make a hutch and that it might be best if they were two little girl rabbits.

'No, Richard,' I said. 'We can't take them today. Daddy will need to make a home for them first.'

I was pulled out of the house by two little boys to admire their new pets. Richard had chosen a black one, and John wanted one with white on his tummy. I assured them that once Daddy had made a hutch, we would come again to fetch them.

'It's all very kind of you, Mrs Ford,' I said as we took our leave. 'I'm so glad we're neighbours, and you must bring John to see us very soon too.'

Chapter 5

Finding a New Church

It was important for us to find a fellowship of believing Christians as soon as possible, which could be a spiritual home for us. Our persuasion was Calvinistic, that is we embraced the reformed doctrines clarified in the writings of the Geneva reformer, John Calvin. However, there were two streams of Calvinistic belief and practise amongst the many chapels of Sussex. Some were Baptist, practising baptism by full immersion on confession of a personal faith in Jesus Christ. Other congregations had members like ourselves, who could trace their Christian roots back to either the influence of Selina, the countess of Huntingdon, or that of William Huntington and didn't practise adult baptism. We generally called ourselves Independents.

Selina, countess of Huntingdon, had been Anglican. She saw the doctrines she believed and which she encouraged her preachers to preach as those clearly expressed in the Church of England prayerbook. For years she had avoided supporting preachers who were not ordained clergymen of the Anglican Church. The eighteenth-century evangelical awakening in Britain came initially through the preaching of men like the Wesley brothers, George Whitefield, and William Romaine in England, and Daniel Rowlands in Wales, all of whom were men ordained by Anglican bishops. However, pragmatism had gradually eroded this deep-seated adherence to Anglican practise. The Anglican

Church had for the most part rejected these faithful preachers who had seen their first allegiance to the Word of God, and the spiritual hunger of the people called for more faithful preachers of the gospel than the established church could supply. Hence, Selina had arranged for the training of her own ministers, and of course these did not qualify for ordination by bishops. However, she encouraged her ministers to remain as faithful as possible to the doctrine of the Anglican prayerbook, and this meant they were essentially paedobaptists, baptising the children of believers into the fold of the church. I myself was baptised as an infant in the Heathfield Independent Chapel. The Methodist Church had the same practise, but following the teaching of John Wesley and these chapels, unless they specified otherwise, were not Calvinistic in doctrine.

Also those chapels established by William Huntington and his followers were not Baptist in any form. Mr Huntington's experience of the Church of England had been very negative. He had looked for spiritual help there and found none. The Methodists had helped him to faith in Jesus Christ, but he had very soon rejected their Arminian teaching and embraced the Calvinistic doctrines. Church ordinances, however, had never been an important consideration to him and in swinging away from the idea that they can impart grace he virtually ignored them completely. I guess that Eli's position at this stage of his life was more Huntingtonian than anything else, although he wouldn't have given himself this name. Until very much later when he embraced a Baptist position, Eli was not baptised, and none of our children were baptised as infants. To Eli the work of God's grace in a person's life, leading him or her to embrace Jesus Christ in faith and trust as their only hope for eternal salvation, was the vital issue. Church order was to him at that stage in his Christian life a secondary matter. However, not everyone thought like this, and so the attitude of our local chapels to the ordinances of baptism and the Lord's Supper did have some influence as to where we were to finally settle for regular Christian fellowship.

As a result of the movement of God's Spirit in the eighteenth century, it's a wonderful fact that the majority of the larger villages of

Sussex in our nineteenth century have nonconformist chapels where devout believers gathered regularly and the Word of God and the gospel of his grace is clearly preached. We are in fact spoiled for choice, but we still had to find out who was who and what was what.

Within about two miles from Limden Farm, we have Calvinistic chapels at Shover's Green to the north of us and Burwash to the south. If we extend the radius to five miles, we could add at least Flimwell, Wadhurst, and Pell Green to causes of truth as we called them, where we would be comfortable to worship. Eli was soon to travel further afield to preach, but we decided that we would try to get to know the Christians in both of the nearer chapels and then decide which of these to attend regularly.

Having made some preliminary enquiries, we decided to try Burwash first, so on the earliest Sunday possible, Eli drove me and the children and the two girls south down Limden Lane through the toll gate at Stonegate and on to Burwash. Sussex seems to be full of toll gates, and there are a whole range of charges depending how you are travelling, but on a Sunday, if you say you are going to church and are in respectable clothes, they let you through free!

The Burwash Chapel was an independent fellowship and at that time had a pastor Mr James Weller. At the end of that year, Mr Weller moved on to open a new chapel at Robertsbridge, but both Eli and I appreciated his preaching in the spring of 1842.[24]

We were given a warm welcome and quickly decided this was the right chapel for us. Our pastor was a youngish man in his mid-thirties, and he and his wife, Martha, had three children, Mary, Mercy, and Joseph. Joseph was about the same age as John, and the two girls were a few years older. It made a lot of difference to have other young families attending chapel, and Martha Weller brought her children regularly to the Sunday morning service which encouraged me to persevere with our three!

---

[24] Ralph Chambers, 'Burwash', op. cit., vol. 2, 123.

Chapter 6

New Challenges

Late that April, I had the suspicion I was pregnant again. Ruth was a quiet and passive baby but still less than ten months old, and I must say it was a challenge to my faith to have to think about coping with yet another birth and another baby. Still, this must be some months off yet, and I found that the only way I could cope was to live one day at a time and trust God for the future.

Our hops crop helped to take my mind off worrying about giving birth again. Eli was very excited about this new venture, and I had been extremely interested in watching the crop grow and then hearing his plans for harvesting it.

I was amazed at how fast the hops plants grew. Once they got going, they seemed to race up the poles, and then only when they reached the top and the shoot was waving about trying hopelessly to find some new thing to grip on to did side shorts start to develop. It's the hops' flower clusters from the female plants which we eventually harvest. We call them seed cones, and they look like miniature fir cones but are soft and leafy rather than hard and brittle. They are used as a flavouring and a stability agent in beer and give it its bitter, tangy flavour.

The time to harvest is late September. The moisture content when they are harvested is about 80 per cent, and the hops need to be dried straight away to about 6 per cent. During storage, the moisture content will then increase slightly to the required level of approximately 10 per cent. We had our own specialised barn for drying the hops. In the south of England, this is called an oast, but I believe further north in the Midlands, where hops are also grown, it would be called a kell.

Our oast is about eighteen feet long and eight feet wide and is divided inside into three rooms. The middle room is the drying area. Here there is a brick canopied furnace, just over a foot wide, about six feet in length and two feet six inches high. Above the furnace in this inner room is the drying floor. It's constructed of lengths of one inch square timber lying one-fourth inch apart, just too narrow for the hops to drop through, and is about five feet above the floor of the oast. The harvested green hops are delivered into the room at one end of the building and then carefully spread out on the drying floor to a depth of about eighteen inches. Drying can take between six and twenty hours but on average about eleven hours. There is no easy way of measuring the moisture content, but an experienced eye can get it about right. Eli later explained to me that as a good guide, if the central stem of the hops breaks instead of simply bending when you bend hops, then it's dry enough. When dry, the hops are raked off the drying floor into the third room where they are left to cool for about ten days.

Charcoal is used as the fuel for the furnace, and as you can imagine, to dry several acres of hops requires a great amount. As he thought ahead for our first hops harvest, Eli was determined to make his own charcoal, or at least some of it.

Eli often commented that it was a great blessing to have the river Limden running through our land. There is obviously a fire risk when drying hops, and the positioning of the oast has allowed for this. It was far enough from the house to avoid setting fire to our home if it were to go up in flames, and it was close enough to the river for a ready supply of water if needed. Also as he thought about a location for the clamp for producing charcoal, the nearness of the river was again important as water was needed to keep the outer soil and turf covering of the clamp moist. I'll be telling you more about our efforts at charcoal burning later.

I got into the habit of calling in on Mrs Ford fairly regularly. Stores Farm was only about a quarter of a mile up the lane, and when I managed to get out for a walk with the children, Richard would always hope to call in to see John. We wouldn't stay long, but the children would play together, mostly happily, and Mrs Ford and I would chat. She was very interested to hear how Eli and I had met, and I told her about the transformation of Eli after his father's death when he had become troubled about his soul and the judgement of God. Mrs Ford was particularly concerned when I mentioned that Eli had not been baptised as a baby. I explained our understanding of the Bible's teaching, that being made right with God was entirely through faith in Jesus Christ and what he had done for us in dying on the cross. The assurance of salvation, which Eli and I had, really impressed her, and she confessed that sometimes she would lie awake at night worrying about death. I quoted to her one or two Bible passages and prayed with her, and it was wonderful to hear later that she had found peace in committing herself to the mercy of Jesus, the Saviour of all those who trust him.

My two boys now had their rabbits. Eli had made them a suitable hutch and had gone with Richard and John to choose their new pets and ensure that both had female bunnies. Maybe later they might be persuaded to breed rabbits for meat, but we decided at this age it was better for the boys to have their first bunnies simply as pets. Richard was able to have the black one he had first chosen, and he decided to call it Blackie. John's was black and white and the name he chose had nothing to do with its appearance. John simply said, 'It's Becca.'

'That's a silly name,' said Richard.

'Not a silly name,' retorted John. 'My bunny is Becca.'

I assured Richard that it wasn't a silly name, and anyway it was John's rabbit and he could call it what he wanted.

I realised later the origin of John's bunny's name. I had been telling him and Richard some of the stories in Genesis the evening before, and John in particular had reacted with surprising interest to the account of Abraham's servant riding off on a camel to find a wife for Isaac. He had listened attentively when I told them how God had led him to find Rebecca who had been a farmer's daughter looking after her father's sheep!

Something else helpful came out of Eli's visit with the two boys to Stores Farm. James Ford had been pleased to chat with a fellow farmer and confided that he didn't have the same strength and go in him that he used to have, and although his farm was small and with one labourer and the occasional help of his son he was able to keep up with regular things pretty well, it was the extra jobs he never managed to get to that often worried him when he couldn't sleep at night. For instance there were a couple of old elm trees close to the house which really needed to come down. He was afraid every time there was a strong wind that if one or other blew down, it could do a lot of damage to the farmhouse. He tentatively suggested to Eli that if he and his men had time to fell these trees, he could have the timber. This was just the time when Eli had been toying with the hope of being able to produce his own charcoal, and one of the problems he had foreseen was that although we had woodland, if he started felling trees for charcoal we would soon use mature trees far quicker than new ones could grow. He therefore recognised James Ford's offer as being God's provision and so timely and had shaken hands on the deal immediately.

Eli told me later that the wood from these substantial trees had considerably more value than the time it would take to fell them, and he had in mind to make it up to the Fords in other ways. Perhaps they would appreciate some bacon when we next slaughter one or two pigs!

Eli was somewhat worried about cutting down James Ford's elm trees. He had had some experience of tree felling with his father, but these were hefty trees, and it was very important that they dropped in the right place so as not to damage any of the buildings. He talked to Trayton and David and the other men about it, and they decided they would saw off some of the larger boughs before cutting the trees down fully. He then went across and talked to Mr Ford about their plans and found his agreement.

I knew Eli had the job much on his mind, and on the morning chosen to start the work, he brought the matter up in our morning prayers, asking God for his wisdom and help in the task and praying for protection from accidents and that the trees might fall correctly to avoid damage to the buildings. Before they set off, I heard Eli impressing on the men that their safety was of primary importance, and they were not to take unnecessary risks.

'Take your time,' he said. 'Ensure ladders are firmly placed before you climb up them, and when you are sawing off branches, anchor yourself to the trunk of the tree with one of the ropes. You may need to use two hands on the saw, and the rope will steady you and hold you if you were to slip. It's not bravery to take risks, it's foolishness.'

In the event, I think it was Eli who went up the trees and cut off most of the branches. He used a handsaw to bring the branches down and then got the men cutting them into manageable lengths using a two-man saw. By the end of the first day, they had the timber from the branches they had cut off safely back at Limden Farm and then concentrated on felling the remaining, rather bare-looking trees on the second day. Richard heard that Daddy was cutting down trees at John's house, and we walked up there in the afternoon just in time to see the second tree fall. I was very impressed that it landed exactly where planned. Mr Ford came up to us, and we watched the final moment together with bated breath.

'Your husband knows what he's doing,' he said. 'By cutting first well into the tree on the side he wanted it to fall, taking out a good-sized angled chip slanting downwards into the tree, and then making a straight cut into the back slightly higher up with his axe, he was able to control the direction and angle the tree would fall. I know it in theory but am a bit too much of a coward in my old age to put it into practise. It's great to watch it happen and to see the theory actually works.'

I asked Mr Ford about his wife as I had begun to sense she was struggling with life somewhat. He thanked me for my friendship with her and said he knew she was very appreciative of my visits.

'She doesn't complain,' said Mr Ford, 'but I'm beginning to think there's something seriously wrong. The trouble is neither of us has much confidence in doctors. There are certain plants that she boils up and drinks. I just hope they help!'

Eli left the job of sawing and splitting the trees to two of the men, and he was very satisfied with the amount of timber the two trees provided.

Chapter 7

Charcoal Burning

In one of the chapels where he preached, there was a retired old man who had spent his life burning charcoal, and one morning after Eli had chatted over the day's work with the men, he saddled Jehu and set off to find him. Jehu was a recent acquisition. He was a rather beautiful grey stallion, and Eli was enjoying him tremendously.

I didn't see Eli immediately when he got back, but that evening, he looked very satisfied with himself but was eager to give all the credit to God.

'It's a wonderful privilege to be in the Christian family,' he said. 'We have brothers and sisters everywhere. Old Jack Sawyer was delighted to see me, and it was humbling to hear how he appreciated my preaching. When he heard my ideas, he offered to come and oversee the work of producing our charcoal. He has lived alone since his wife died a few years ago and is very happy to come and live with us for a few weeks.'

I stifled my immediate reaction to this news and expressed delight that we would have an expert on the job. I was aware that producing charcoal wasn't as easy as it sounded and had secretly been afraid that Eli was attempting more than he could reasonably manage. I admired Eli very much but had always been a bit concerned about his attitude that what anyone else could do, he could as well, if not better.

Jack Sawyer was to arrive the following Monday, and Eli asked me if I could go and fetch him in the pony and trap. I left the children with Eliza and Sarah and set off across country in the direction of Mayfield where Jack lived in a little cottage.

I really enjoyed the ride. It was good to get out of the house without the children and to jog gently along lanes lined with hawthorn hedges full of many blossoms and with the warmth of the sun on my head and the song of birds in my ears. Some of the fields were being cut for hay and the scent of cut grass drying in the sun was almost intoxicating. My natural reaction was to talk to God. To praise him for the wonder of his created world, to acknowledge my own littleness, and to commit myself and my family happily into his sovereign care.

I thought about the new baby I was now certain was developing inside me, and somehow being outside in the world of nature, vibrant with life, I was able to thank God for it. Life was God's gift. I was seeing it and experiencing it in so many forms. The whole of nature seemed to be rejoicing in the sunshine. The birds were singing—yes, that was a skylark above the field, soaring high and singing its little heart out. Along the grass verges there seemed to be an unending choir of crickets, all chirping in chorus and competing in volume. And there in the background a louder and deeper croak which I could now identify as a corn crake in the hayfield. I reined in Charlotte, my pony, and stopped a moment to listen and watch. Because I was seated on the trap, I could see over the top of the hedge and so had a good view of the field. I now heard a new sound, a higher-pitched *cheep cheep* and then a long *oo-oo-oo*. A hen corn crake must be calling her chicks. I waited and watched, and then to my delight, I could see them—a brownish, moorhen-shaped bird feeding amongst the freshly cut grass stalks followed by a number of little black chicks. I was able to count ten babies! I was thrilled by the experience. This was God's world, and Eli and I were part of it. The life growing in me was also his gift, and it was more precious than all I could see and sense around me because it was being endowed with the very image of God himself and would be capable to having a relationship with its Creator in a way that no animal or bird could ever have. I set Charlotte into a trot again with a singing heart. I, Selina Page, was part of God's marvellous creation, and a new human person was coming into being within me. At that moment, I could see everything in a really positive light. God was at work. He called us simply to trust him, to be faithful to him, to accept his providence with joy, and work with him and for him. Trust and acceptance were the keys to peace and relaxation, and at that moment, I felt this peace in a remarkable way.

I found Jack Sawyer's cottage without difficulty and sat in the sun outside his back door as he made his final preparations to come back to Limden Farm with me. He was a clean-shaven, small man with a somewhat wizened but kindly face, tanned dark brown by years of outside work. The darkness of his skin accentuated the whiteness of his hair, and I found his whole appearance and demeanour very attractive. Although he must have been in his seventies, he appeared fit and active. He flattered me by saying what a privilege it was to be picked up by such a beautiful young lady! The ride back was fairly uneventful, but as we jogged back along the country lanes through Witherenden Hill and Stonegate, Jack expressed his pleasure in having the opportunity to use his life's experience in helping Eli, who obviously he respected greatly on account of his preaching.

The next days were hectic. The farm was haymaking, but Eli spared one man to work with Jack on the charcoal project and called by to keep an eye on things as often as he could. They chose a site to build the clamp which was both near the river and as near the source of timber as possible. There were a few fallen trees and branches in our woodland and also two further trees which Eli decided to fell to provide sufficient wood to make a satisfactory burn, and he used the oxen to drag the trees and branches across to the spot chosen for the clamp.

The principle of producing charcoal is to burn timber in a controlled way very slowly. The fire needs oxygen to burn, but the amount of oxygen entering the fire must be minimal. This is achieved by piling lengths of timber around a central chimney made from four posts and then building outwards and upwards with more and more timber, as compact as possible, until the finished construction is a circular igloo-shaped object. The outside is then covered in straw, mud, and turf so that the timber is completely closed in. Once constructed, fire is introduced in the bottom of the clamp as far in as possible and, once the wood is alight, the entrance closed up. The aim is to allow the wood to burn very slowly, taking about five days. During this time, the burning clamp needs to be watched day and night, and at any sign of fire breaking through the outer coating, it must be damped down and new damp soil added.

Picture used under licence from 'Museum of Rural Life', Reading University, England.

Jack explained this to us carefully the first evening he was with us.

'We shall need a little hut or tent at the site of the clamp,' he added. 'I and my helper will need to take turns sleeping during the night. It's important that one of us is on duty at all times watching the clamp and can wake the other if there is an emergency.'

Jack would have preferred the timber to have seasoned for a year or two before being burnt for charcoal, but Eli had been able to find some old seasoned logs and branches that had been lying about for some time, and when they mixed this with the newly cut wood, Jack was fairly confident that they would be able to get a reasonable result.

We enjoyed having Jack Sawyer with us. He liked talking about his life as a collier in Ashdown Forest and told us about different experiences in which he had proved God's care of him. He also told us about the independent fellowship he was a member of in Mayfield. Although at that time we had no idea what an important role this chapel was to play in our lives in the future, we were very interested to hear about it as Eli had already preached there once or twice. Jack spoke very warmly of Mr William Burch who, as an itinerant preacher, had been the means of bringing together this small fellowship of believers in Mayfield.[25]

He would visit them regularly to preach and encourage them from the scriptures, and up until recently, they had met for this in the cottage of one of their members. However, Mr Burch had contacts in different parts of Sussex and Kent, and one of his supporters had generously financed the building of a chapel for them in Mayfield. The most recent news was that Mr Burch had been called to be the resident minister of a similar independent fellowship in the village of Staplehurst over the county border in Kent. This had been a great disappointment to Jack and the Mayfield friends, but they had been cheered to hear from William Burch himself that a condition of his acceptance for the call to Staplehurst had been that he would be free to continue regular visits to Mayfield and one or two other villages where he was seeking to establish young Christian believers in the faith.[26]

During his time at Limden Farm, Jack was pleased to come along to Burwash with us for the Sunday services and to meet our pastor Mr James Weller. He also joined in our family devotions with enthusiasm,

---

[25] Ralph Chambers, 'Mayfield', op. cit., vol. 2, 63.
[26] Ralph Chambers, 'Staplehurst', op. cit., vol. 2, 13f.

when the charcoal burning didn't keep him away, and on a few occasions, Eli asked him to lead our Bible readings and prayer.

The charcoal earth-burn, as Jack called it, was a reasonable success. I took the children out to see it when the clamp had been constructed. It was circular and about nine feet across and seven feet high at its highest point. It apparently couldn't be much bigger than this as the men needed to be able to reach to every point of the surface to moisten down and repair the earth and turf surface if the fire broke through. The wood needed to burn with as little oxygen as possible, and if the fire were allowed to break through the surface, it would tend to suck in air and burn too fast to provide the charcoal. There was more than enough wood for a second clamp so, whilst keeping guard over the first, Jack and his helper also constructed a second one nearby. Each clamp took about five days to burn after which it was allowed to cool and then dismantled. Jack himself was pleased with the result, and he was the expert!

Eli decided that he would need at least double this amount of charcoal, and Jack expressed interest in returning again the following month once he had fulfilled one or two commitments at home.

That summer, my father died. He was seventy-eight. You may remember me saying that my mum was dad's second wife, so he was actually seventeen years older than her. Dad had been getting weaker for some months, but it was still a shock when he died. It was good to have a caring pastor when these things happen. Mr Weller came up to see me soon after the funeral, and it was good to be reminded that although we had lost Dad from our lives here on earth, he was now with Jesus. Despite my natural sadness at Dad's passing, my faith in the reality of glory as the true home for believers brought me real comfort. I was able to talk to Mr Weller about my memories of Dad, and he then prayed for me and my mum and the rest of the family, and I found his whole visit extremely helpful.

Eli suggested we call our next baby boy Samuel, after my father, which pleased me greatly. My response was to wonder if it was little Samuel then making his presence felt within me as we spoke together!

'Eli,' I said, 'isn't there a scripture which talks about generations, one after the other, praising God's name? It would be so lovely if we could produce another Samuel to continue praising God as my father did.'

Eli found the verse I meant, and the next day in our family devotions, he read Psalm 145, which is one of David's psalms of praise and includes his confident statement of faith: 'One generation shall praise thy works to another and shall declare thy mighty acts.'

Samuel was born on the 18 December that year.

Chapter 8

Grain Harvest

However, first came harvest, a very important time on any farm. Our acreage of corn was relatively small, and our men were basically able to cope with this themselves. I remember, however, that in our first year at Limden Farm, we'd had a longish spell of wet and windy weather, and when the sun finally came out, Eli was very keen to get the harvest in as quickly as possible before the rainy weather could return, so he really needed extra help. During the summer, people, both men and women, come into the country areas from the towns looking for casual work over the harvest period. Eli always preferred to engage local people he knew, particularly those from the chapels where he preached, but with the sudden improvement in the weather, everyone was busy with harvest at the same time, and the people he knew had already found work on other farms, so he took on two men who came by the farm asking for work.

The most colourful of these was Gunter. His father was Irish, but his mother had her roots in Prussia. He was a charismatic figure but with an eye for detail and a persistence which kept him at a job until it was done. Eli liked him, and he in return had a great respect for Eli. The corn was cut and bundled into sheaves in record time, and as was the custom, we all celebrated full-heartedly the bringing in of the last wagon load. Big-Foot, our carthorse, was decorated colourfully with whatever flowers could be found in the hedgerows together with roses from the farmhouse garden, and we also found some bells to tie into his harness. Thankfully, Big-Foot was a very patient horse. Our workers and their girlfriends, wives, and children all accompanied the wagon on its journey down the lane, singing merrily, and that evening, we put on a harvest supper for them all. The weather was good enough to be outside, which was ideal, and we set up trestle tables in the field behind the house on which we laid out the food and everyone helped themselves and found somewhere suitable to sit.

There is traditional food for these occasions, and a harvest supper is not complete without large helpings of caraway seed cake, pumpkin pie, and 'Brown Georges', which are large apple turnovers. I had also baked several large loaves of bread, and we had our own home-made butter and cheese. Of course we had to provide drink too, and Eli had bought in a barrel of beer for the occasion. When everyone had well eaten and he considered it the right moment, Eli stood up on the tree stump on which he had been sitting and thanked everyone for their help and then, being Eli, read a selection of verses from Psalm 104, acknowledging that all that we receive comes to us from God. He also took the opportunity to remind us all that God's provision goes far further than food for our bodies and that Jesus Christ spoke of himself as the bread of life who gives eternal life to all who repent of their selfish lives and trust themselves to the Saviour. One of our number could play the fiddle, and he struck up a harvest hymn or two which we all sang with gusto. Gunter then raised his glass and called for three cheers for Eli and myself and then he added, 'And most of all, three cheers for Eli's Master, from whom all these blessing come!'

Eli was initially somewhat taken aback at this, but he appreciated that Gunter's motives were good, and although not a traditional way of thanking God, he trusted that it came from Gunter's heart. The loud cheers echoed around the house!

Once the corn had been cut and the sheaves safely gathered in, the local women were allowed to glean the cornfields, searching for ears of corn which our men had missed. Taking an example from Boaz in the

Old Testament, Eli would tell our harvesters to ensure they weren't too thorough when cutting the edges of the fields. He knew that the ears of corn which got left wouldn't be wasted and that housewives with large families really valued the free grain they could gather. Interestingly, after a few years, Limden Farm had quite a reputation as a very fruitful farm for gleaners. Eli wasn't afraid of being thought a careless farmer for leaving an above average number of ears of corn in the fields as he knew his men were with him in this and would proudly mention in their local pub that their boss left their wives enough grain to make gleaning worthwhile.

However, even gleaning had to be organised, and it was traditional for a farm or a number of farms to appoint a Harvest Queen. One of our newly appointed labourers was a local man with a wife and family, and Eli suggested to him that his wife be appointed the Harvest Queen for Limden Farm. Both Bob and his wife appreciated this privilege, and Ann Bearman proved to be a very capable queen. Her job was to ensure that each of the gleaners had an equal opportunity to gather the left grain. They would need to apply to her for permission to join the band of women, but Eli had instructed her not to discriminate and any who wanted should be allowed to glean his fields. Our acreage of grain wasn't large, so there wasn't a lot left to find after one day's gleaning, but normally the women continued to search for about three days. Ann stipulated the hours when gleaning was allowed and would ring a bell at the start and finish of the day and for the midday break when I provided some bread and cheese and a couple of jugs of balm tea. Not all the farmers' wives did this, but I must say the appreciation and loyalty it provoked made this little effort worthwhile.

Chapter 9

Harvesting Our Hops

After the grain harvest came the harvesting of the hops, and we most certainly needed outside help for the finicky job of hand-picking these. All types of people come into Sussex and Kent for the hops harvest, and for many, it's the only holiday they can afford. It means hours of work, but there's also the enjoyment of the open air life and of being part of a small community in a completely different environment.

A team of hop pickers needs a leader, and it was normal for this to be one of themselves rather than one of the regular farm labourers. Eli had formed a high opinion of Gunter as a conscientious worker and someone whom he could trust, and he offered him the opportunity of finding six or seven pickers and organising them into a team. Gunter was sleeping in one of our barns and cooking for himself on a campfire, and Eli allocated one of our men to help him prepare the barn as a temporary home for a group of pickers. It was cleaned out thoroughly, and we provided palliasses for them to stuff with straw to sleep on and built a brick fireplace with a metal grid for them to cook on. Eli's attitude was that to get and keep good pickers, who might also return in future years, he needed to provide facilities which were better than average.

Harvesting our crop of hops took the best part of three weeks. It was a busy but merry time. Gunter had selected his team well. Our first hops harvest at Limden Farm was a special time for us all as it was a new experience, so I remember that year well. Our adult pickers consisted of four women and two men and Gunter. Three of the women had husbands and families who they had been able to leave in the care of their mother or mother-in-law. If circumstances allowed, most working-class husbands were happy about their wives and older children coming into the countryside for a few weeks at harvest time, as it gave a good opportunity to earn some very useful additional cash in a healthy environment. Two of the mums had children with them, so in addition to the adults, we also had five children aged seven to twelve working alongside their mums. The children added their pickings to those of their mother's and so increased the family earnings.

Payment was made according to the number of bushels picked, a bushel being a dry measure of a capacity of eight gallons of water, and there was a strict procedure to ensure fairness and accuracy. Eli had entrusted Gunter to be the hops measurer and tally man. Each day before picking started, Gunter took six longish sticks, allocated one to each picker, broke off about one third of the stick which he gave to the picker and kept the longer part himself. These were the tally sticks. Eli explained to me that the word 'tally' comes from a French word meaning to cut. During the day, at fairly regular intervals, Gunter would go around the pickers to collect the hops they had picked. Each worker picked into a basket, and Gunter would tip these hops into an accurate bushel basket to measure the quantity before adding them to his larger collecting container. Having agreed the quantity with the picker, he would take his part of that picker's tally stick, ensure it was the right stick by matching the break with the picker's own part of the stick, place both sticks alongside each other, and with a knife make one or more cuts across both of them—one cut for every five bushels. He would then also record the quantity in a record book against that picker's name. At the end of the day, each picker were given hop tokens according to the number of bushels he or she had picked, and because the two parts of the tally sticks could be matched up, there could be no ground for disagreements. We had five-bushel tokens, ten-bushel tokens, and twenty-bushel tokens all engraved with the initial EP, for Eli Page. On average a conscientious worker could expect to pick about twenty-five bushels a day, and at that time, a five-bushel token was worth 10d. (10 old pence).[27] The picker was able to use these tokens instead of money at our local shops and inns, and at the end of season, Eli would redeem them with normal money either from the workers themselves or from the local shopkeepers.

Once off the plants, the hops needed to be dried straight away, and Eli and two of our own farm labourers looked after this process. Until later when we had a good farm manager, Eli liked to oversee most things himself, and although drying hops was a new process for him, he had asked advice and had already got hold of the essential principles. He was also pleased to have one man who had had a fair amount of experience with hops. Our own charcoal, produced under the guidance of Jack, provided the majority of the fuel needed to keep the oast fire burning, but Eli did have to buy in a bit of extra that first year.

The drying process sets the speed of harvesting the hops as it's important not to get a build-up of picked hops waiting to be dried. Gunter was happy to cooperate with Eli on this, and after a sufficient number of bushels had been picked on any one day, he would call a halt to the picking. In general there was a happy spirit amongst our picking team, and they had a repertoire of traditional songs which echoed around the field as they picked.

It was an understood thing that Sunday was a rest day, and since most of the pickers came from too far away to go home for their day off, Eli decided we would provide a Sunday high tea for them and for any of our own farmworkers and their families who wanted to join us. This was to be somewhat similar to the celebration meal we would lay on for all the workers at the end of the hops harvest but not quite as elaborate. We had talked about it together. Eli had wondered how we could get

---

[27] Until 1971 in Britain, one pound was made up of 240 pence, and twelve pence then made a shilling, hence twenty shillings made a pound.

a little closer to our workers and how to share with them God's Word, and this seemed a good way of doing it.

We talked to Gunter about it, as he was their leader, and he was enthusiastic. It proved to be a great success. The meal and a small barrel of beer were obviously appreciated, and all were content to sit with their stomachs full to listen to Eli as he warned them of God's judgement on sin and the good news that Jesus had come into the world to save sinners. He also told them of his own conversion and of what this had meant in his life. Some of our pickers came back to us year after year, and we have a real hope, in the case of at least two of them, that God has touched their hearts and drawn them to him. I know that what impressed them and prompted them to take Eli's words seriously was the fact that he wasn't a professional clergyman but a working farmer whom they had come to respect.

Chapter 10

Years Roll By

That first year at Limden Farm set the pattern for the years that followed. As far as the business side of our farming was concerned, Eli concentrated mainly on hops and cattle fattening with a small acreage of corn, but also in a small way and mainly for our own household use, we had my hens, a few pigs, a few ducks on the river, and a kitchen garden where we grew vegetables and soft fruit. We also had a small orchard of fruit trees. These were mostly apple, but there were also a couple of pear trees and a few plums. Later we had a few beehives which helped to ensure the fruit blossom pollinated well and also provided us with delicious honey. I'll tell you a bit about that later as our experience of beekeeping was quite exciting at times.

Our years in the Ticehurst area were also very productive as far as our own personal family was concerned. Samuel, our fourth child and named after my father, was born on 18 December 1842, then during the next fourteen years, God gave us six daughters. Orpha was born on 10 September 1844, Naomi on 16 July 1846, Mercy on 18 February 1850, Mary on 1 December 1851, Elizabeth on 7 October 1853, and Dorcas on 17 February 1856.

Between the births of Naomi and Mercy, in 1848, we had a little boy, Ebenezer, but God only entrusted him to us for just over a year and then took him to himself in June 1849. This was a difficult experience for all of us. Ruth was just about eight years old then, and she had loved her little brother fondly. It gave us the opportunity to talk to the older children about death, to tell them about Adam's sin of disobedience to God, and that death was the consequence of this but also how Jesus had come to bring a resurrection to a new life. We told them that we had committed little Ebenezer to Jesus and that we could look forward to seeing him again one day in heaven. I know that Ruth never forgot her little brother, and both Eli and I were very moved when much later she called one of her sons by the same name.

We had a service in the chapel at Burwash for Ebenezer, and then together with a few family members and friends, all the children gathered with us round the grave in the parish cemetery in Stonegate as Eli committed that little body into the ground, looking in faith to Jesus on behalf of our precious thirteen-month-old son whom God had seen fit to take from us.

Although he never said so, I think the death of little Ebenezer jolted Eli into a greater awareness of the brevity of life as it seemed to arouse him to take every opportunity to preach the Word of God and to seek to awaken as many as would hear to think seriously about eternity and to seek to know their part in the redemption provided in Christ Jesus. Eli had for some years been accepting invitations to preach at Sunday services at independent chapels in Sussex and Kent on an occasional basis, on average probably twice a month. He had seen it necessary to concentrate on establishing the routine of farming Limden Farm, but now after the death of Ebenezer, he began to take on more engagements which meant he was away most Sundays and also occasionally on a weekday evening. Our farmworkers soon realised that if they wanted to stay with us, they had to learn to think for themselves and make their own decisions on everyday issues. Although Eli was a considerate boss, I know very well that he didn't suffer fools gladly and had little patience when the men made avoidable mistakes. He often used to tell me that farming and preaching actually fitted well together and most of his sermon preparation was done on the hoof. In his case, the hoof being either his own two feet whilst at work on the land or on horseback as he rode the lanes either on farming business or to his preaching engagements.

As you can imagine, my own life during these years revolved around the children and running the household. My two girls, Eliza and Sarah, who were helping me in house, moved on. Eliza married a shoemaker and moved to Herstmonceux, and Sarah, my niece, moved to Brighton as a maid in the household of a Yorkshire wine merchant. Each of the children were given daily jobs to do as soon they were old enough, and in 1846 Eli's niece, Ruth Parris, the daughter of his stepsister, Philadelphia, joined our household. Philadelphia had lost her husband in 1843, leaving her with twelve children, and then tragically, she herself died three years later. Different members of the family gave homes to the younger children, and the older ones were able to find positions as farmworkers and housemaids.

Ruth came to us. She was just seven years at the time, a few months younger than Richard. Limden Farm was conveniently placed for the national school in Stonegate, which was just a mile or so down the lane, so she was able to go to school with Richard and John, and our Ruth started very soon afterwards.

Each generation sees changes and developments, and we were thankful that our children had the advantage of some formal education. National schools were springing up all around Sussex by this time. They were linked to the state Anglican Church and either used a church hall or a building near the church. The Stonegate school had its own building, and the teacher at that time was Mary Read, whose brother, William Read, farmed Stonegate Farm and was a friend of Eli's.[28]

The National Society for Promoting the Education of the Poor in the Principles of the Established Church in England and Wales had been founded in 1811 and was the brainchild of Joshua Watson. Eli used to sometimes talk about Joshua Watson and had a great respect for him. Mr Watson certainly didn't share our nonconformist views, but he was a devout Christian within the Anglican Church who was

---

[28] 1851 Census, William Read, Stonegate Farm.

prepared to devote himself sacrificially to promoting Christian teaching and ethics within British society. The stated aim of the National Society was that 'the National Religion should be made the foundation of National Education, and should be the first and chief thing taught to the poor, according to the excellent Liturgy and Catechism provided by our Church.' Having accumulated a considerable wealth as a London merchantman, Joshua Watson retired early from business to use his money for practical Christian purposes. He has sometimes been referred to as the best layman in Britain. Our children certainly benefited from his national school in Stonegate. In some areas, there were also non-denominational schools known as British schools, and these were founded by the British and Foreign School Society. Schooling didn't become compulsory until my grandchildren's time, from 1870 onwards, when all children between five and ten were legally required to go to school.

All our children were expected to work as soon as they were able, and Eli was very strict with them about this. He believed that it was a scriptural principle that, unless there were obvious reasons otherwise, those who didn't work shouldn't have the right to eat.[29] Even while they were pupils at school, each had specific jobs allocated them, and once they left school, when they were ten or eleven, they were expected to pull their weight in helping to run the house and the farm.

After our niece Ruth Parris's twelfth birthday, we employed her officially as a housemaid. This didn't mean she was our servant; we all served each other. Her formal employment was Eli's suggestion as he thought it would help her to get another job later if she had a recognised position in our household.

---

[29] 2 Thessalonians 3:10.

Chapter 11

New Friendships

Around the time Naomi was born, I got a new friend. I had been visiting Mrs Mary Ford when I could, but she was really my mother's generation, and sadly her health steadily degenerated and she died, much to the distress of her husband and family. It comforted me greatly that my friendship with her had helped her to find peace in trusting Jesus for her eternal salvation, but I missed having her as a neighbour whom I could call on with the children and chat to. But then a new family moved into South Limden Farm, the neighbouring farm in the Stonegate direction down Limden Lane. I called to welcome them to the area with a jar of honey from our bees and found a very friendly housewife about my own age named Ann. She had three children of her own, her oldest, Sophia, being a little older than our Ruth, and then in addition, there were various other relatives, including an elderly uncle, living-in who were helping her husband Henry to run the farm.[30]

I realised quickly that Ann had her work cut out to care for this largish household and, like myself, wouldn't have much time for social activities. However, I liked her, and knowing how helpful it is to have

---

[30] 1851 Census, Henry Harmer, South Limden Farm.

friendships outside the family circle, I was determined to find time to visit as regularly as I could and to try to nurture a friendly relationship.

My friendship with Ann took time to develop. I would call on her when I could, but this wasn't so frequently, and I sensed some reticence on her part to talk about herself or her own real feelings. I wondered at first whether this was because of our Christian position but later came to the conclusion that no one had really ever been interested in her as a person before. She had always had simply to conform to the view of firstly her father and then her husband, and they weren't in the habit of asking her opinion about anything. The fact that her husband, Henry, was twelve years older than her and had been married before hadn't helped this situation.

One afternoon when I had managed to escape from the household chores, I arrived at Ann's kitchen door with my youngest three, Samuel, Orpha, and Naomi, and found Ann near to tears. I sat down with my arm around her and let her sob for a while and eventually she was able to talk.

'Selina,' she stammered, 'please forgive me for being so silly. I've been fighting tears all day and just seeing your friendly face at the door was more than I could bear.'

'Is it something you can tell me about?' I asked.

'I've feared for some time that I was pregnant again, and today I'm sure,' Ann answered. 'I'm scared stiff.'

Having already by that time given birth to six children myself with varying degrees of anxiety, discomfort, and severe pain, I could well sympathise with Ann's fear.

'I hate being a woman!' said Ann. 'When I was younger, I couldn't wait to be married. I imagined it must be wonderful to have a man of my own who loved me. Don't get me wrong, Selina, Henry and I get on fine most of the time. I love my children and would do almost anything for them, but when little Henry was born three years ago, I had such a bad time of it that I've done my level best not to become pregnant again. It's taken any pleasure there might have been from being in bed with my husband, and now it's all going to happen again!'

I did my best to comfort Ann, but we both knew the pain and danger of giving birth to children.

'Ann,' I said, 'I can only tell you the way I've coped with pregnancies. I believe it's the woman's calling in life to produce children, to mother them and love them, and to bring them up to be the next generation. You'll remember that the first woman God made was called Eve, which means the mother of all living. She was made to be a helper for the man and the mother of children. Men can't produce children, and although it's painful, only we can do it. I've tried to be proud of the privilege of being able to do this, and each time I feel a baby inside me, I think of the miracle of another little human being which will have its own personality and its own soul. I pray constantly for my children and start praying well before they are born. Somehow this helps me to look forward to their birth rather than to fear it.'

'Oh, Selina,' cried Ann, 'that's wonderful, but I'm not sure I could think like that. Last time was so awful I was sure I was going to die.'

'Look, Ann,' I answered, 'I'll do all I can to help you and if possible I'll be with you during the birth. I'll pray for you, but please try and talk to God yourself about your fears. It's wonderful to know that he loves us and cares for us personally. When Naomi was being born, I consciously stretched out my hand and imagined I was holding God's hand, and it gave me so much strength.'

I continued to visit Ann as often as possible, and after that afternoon, our friendship really took off. She used to say how wonderful it was to have a close woman friend with whom she could share womanly things. I don't think she had really had a proper friend before. I encouraged her to come with us to chapel, but it's so difficult for a wife and mother to get away on a Sunday when the husband isn't supportive in this.

Ann's fourth child was born safely, a delightful little girl who they named Ellender. I didn't manage to be there at the birth, but I visited Ann the next day as soon as I heard the baby had come.

'Selina,' said Ann, 'thanks so much for coming. It wasn't as bad as with little Henry. I stretched out my hand to God as you said, and I really believe he was there. I felt new strength and courage and suddenly baby Ellender came, and she's so lovely.'

Another neighbour whom I got to know well was a very different person. Sarah Fuller was also about my own age and lived on another neighbouring farm where her husband was employed as a farm labourer.[31]

Both George and Sarah were Christian believers and were part of the fellowship at Burwash, but somehow I could never get alongside Sarah as an equal. When I visited her, she received me she as if I were Lady Page making a charitable call. It was true that my status in life had risen. That I was now the wife of a farmer employing five men and with servant girls working with me in the house (I prefer to say 'with me' rather than 'for me') and also being the wife of a respected preacher of the gospel raised my status amongst the Christian community. However, I had no wish to be seen on a higher plane as I recognised that all was of God's grace, that Sarah was my sister in Christ, and that we are all equal at the foot of the cross. Eventually, I managed to get somewhat closer to Sarah, but it took a long time.

As I got to know Sarah and her background, I began to understand the reason for her feelings of inferiority. Her mother had been born deaf. What this meant in the 1780s when she was growing up in a poor village family was that she had had no chance at all to progress in life. Unable to hear, she was unable to learn to speak and so was classified as deaf and dumb. Such people became little more than animals and were totally dependent on charity. Some village lad had taken advantage of Keziah's innocence and helplessness, and she became pregnant and Sarah was the resulting child. Relatives who had been converted through the evangelical preaching that was wonderfully sweeping through Sussex at that time had taken both mother and daughter into their home and cared for them. However the stigma of being an illegitimate child of a deaf and dumb mother is a burden that is not easily lost. The gospel had been Sarah's salvation in every sense. The Burwash fellowship had taken both Sarah and her mother under their wing, and Sarah had blossomed

---

[31] 1851 Census, George Fuller, West Limden Farm.

as a Christian young lady and won the heart of George Fuller, a local farm labourer. Through God's grace, she now had a home of her own, and George had been willing for them to take Sarah's mother, Keziah, into their household too. The more I got to know Sarah and George, the greater respect I had for them.

One day Sarah opened her heart to me about her longing to have children. I felt this so ironic as it came not so long after Ann's expressed terror of being pregnant again! Sarah and George had been married a year after Eli and I, but in their case, no children had been forthcoming. We talked about it, and I made the suggestion that perhaps they should consider fostering children. I pointed out that this doesn't rule out having one's own children and experience has sometimes shown that having other children to look after takes the pressure off longing for your own and foster mums have then fallen pregnant themselves.

Sarah and George took up this suggestion, and soon little Emily joined their household for a while and then after a year or so Sarah took in a little baby named Naomi.

As far as I know, Sarah never had children of her own, but I'm sure the Lord blessed that little household for the love they showed to others.

We kept in touch with Sarah and George after we left Limden Farm, at least it was Eli more than I. He would occasionally return to preach at Burwash where they were in fellowship, and one evening when he came home after such a visit, he told me about a conversation he'd had with George. George was beginning to get unhappy at work and had asked Eli if he knew of another job going. Since Eli had good contacts around through both his farming and his preaching, he was able to recommend George for a position of farm manager, or farm bailiff as this was often called, in the Mayfield area.[32]

This worked out very successfully, and Eli would bring greetings home to me from Sarah when he preached at Mayfield.

I often saw the case of Sarah as an example of how God can bring those who trust him out of a desperate situation and establish them in

---

[32] 1861 Census, George Fuller.

life. I thought of Sarah when, one evening for our Bible reading, Eli read Hannah's worshipful prayer from the book of Samuel:

> The Lord maketh poor, and maketh rich: he bringeth low, and lifteth up. He raiseth up the poor out of the dust, and lifteth up the beggar from the dunghill, to set them among princes, and to make them inherit the throne of glory: for the pillars of the earth are the Lord's, and he hath set the world upon them. He will keep the feet of his saints, and the wicked shall be silent in darkness; for by strength shall no man prevail.[33]

---

[33] 1 Samuel 2:8–9.

Chapter 12

Bringing Up the Children at Limden Farm

We were at Limden Farm, Ticehurst, for fourteen years, between 1842 and 1856. Our oldest three children, Richard, John, and Ruth, were born during our time at Clifton Farm, so they, and also Samuel, Orpha, and Naomi, who were born during our earlier years at Limden, each had all their formal schooling at the Stonegate National School down Limden Lane. School was not compulsory, and some parents had little time for it and preferred their children to help in the house or to earn them pennies in any way they could find. We insisted that our children went regularly to school and did their household jobs both before and after school hours. They started school when they were four or five and attended until they were ten or eleven years old.

Miss Mary Read was the teacher, and as with all the national schools, the school day was very Christian-orientated with prayers to begin and end the day and the liturgy and catechism of the Anglican Church playing an important role in the syllabus. Our thought on our children's schooling was that it supplemented what we taught them at home. Eli was very strict with them. At mealtimes and when in the company of adults, they were only expected to speak if spoken to, and

171

obedience was expected without question. Eli had a cane which he used quite freely, and any form of disobedience was taken very seriously indeed.

I talked to Eli about his rather harsh discipline, and he explained to me that his father had, in his mind with the afterthought of maturity, been too lax in disciplining him when he was a child. I guess the main reason for this was that Eli had lost his mother at a very young age, and his father had tended to spoil him. Eli had become quite wild as a teenager, and more discipline from his father would perhaps have prevented this. Eli also wanted his thinking and behaviour to be directed by the Bible, and he often quoted the verse in the book of Proverbs: 'He that spareth his rod hateth his son: but he that loveth him chasteneth him betimes.'[34] I know too that he took very much to heart the sin of his Old Testament namesake who, although a godly priest, had been judged by God because he had not restrained his sons who were abusing their privilege as priests.[35]

In bringing up the children, Eli also believed that experience was one of the best teachers, and to his mind, it was asking for trouble in the future to shield our children too much from danger. One example of this was the river. It ran very close to our house and across one of our fields. When the children were very young, it was a constant source of worry to me that they might fall in it and drown. Eli was adamant that we shouldn't fence it off. Let them learn about the river, he said. Take them to it. Sit with them beside it. Let them feel the current and warn them that if they fall in, they might die. Make it clear too that if we ever saw or heard that they had pushed one another in, they would be thrashed. In this way, our children learned to both love and respect the river. It was their friend, they took a real interest in the wildlife that lived there, and I'm thankful to say we never had a serious incident in relation to it.

---

[34] Proverbs 13:24.
[35] 1 Samuel 3:13.

Our children knew that we loved them, and we encouraged sensible conversations and tried to answer their questions to the best of our ability. Nearly all of them took a lively interest in the countryside around us. They learned to identify the birds, butterflies, and many of the flowers on our farmland, and when they returned from school after walking up Limden Lane, the subject of conversation was often something they had seen on the way. The boys loved to collect birds' eggs. I must say at first I wasn't too happy about this, but Eli encouraged it.

The beginning of their interest in birds' nests began, as far as I can remember, the day we watched a pair of moorhens building a nest in the reeds beside our river. I explained to Richard and John that birds built their nests in many different places, and each species of bird has its own habitat and has eggs of a particular shape, size, and colour. The mother bird, having laid her eggs, she, and sometimes the male bird as well, will sit on them to keep them warm for two to three weeks until the baby birds hatch. The boys were used to the idea of this, having seen the way our hens produced their young, but they were intrigued at the idea of the wild birds' eggs being different colours. After a day or two, when we went to look at our moorhen's nest, we discovered one single egg in it but no sign of the birds. The boys were delighted to see the egg. It was brownish with darker spots and squiggles, and I explained to them that the colour and marks helped to make it more difficult to be seen by predators. That evening they talked to their dad about the nest and egg, and I'm afraid it was Eli's suggestion that they might like to collect eggs.

I was somewhat perturbed.

'Eli,' I said, 'you'll have to show them how to do this without disturbing the birds more than necessary. I'm looking forward to seeing the baby moorhen chicks on the river with their parents, so I would hate them to forsake their nest.'

Eli saw the point and explained to the boys that they should only take one single egg from a bird's nest and that it was important not to disturb the nest by battering down the vegetation around it as this exposes the nest for other birds and small animals to find, many of whom would love to have an egg or a young bird for dinner.

The next day Eli went along the river with the boys, and to Richard and John's delight, there were now two eggs in the nest.

'We'll just take one,' Eli said, 'and possibly the mother won't even notice.'

As a mother myself, I thought this hope rather optimistic, but I guess Mrs Moorhen hadn't had time to establish any form of relationship with her potential offspring, so maybe Eli was right.

When they got home, Eli showed them how to blow the egg. He broke a thorn off a rose bush and carefully pushed it into each end of the egg, making one hole a bit bigger than the other. He then put the smaller hole to his mouth and carefully blew out the contents of the egg through the slightly larger hole at the other end.

'You need to be very careful not to squeeze the egg as you blow it,' Eli explained. 'The smaller the egg, the more fragile it is, so learn to hold it very gently and don't blow too hard.'

I'm thankful to say that stealing one of our moorhen's eggs didn't seem to upset her, and she went on to lay another six. When she had finished laying her brood, both she and Mr Moorhen shared the responsibility of keeping them warm, and after three weeks, out hatched seven little chicks. The first I knew of the hatching was when the boys came running into the kitchen to say the nest was empty. Did I think a fox had got them all? I had warned them of this possibility if we were to expose the nest by walking through the reeds to it too often. Happily the next day, the news was far better. The report from my two young ornithologists was that the two parent moorhens had been spotted proudly swimming though the reeds surrounded by at least six little black chicks.

The second egg in the boys' collection was a very different colour and size. One day whilst feeding my hens, I had seen a shy little brown hedge sparrow collecting what looked to be nesting material, and I suggested to the boys that if they watched very carefully, they might discover where the bird was building its nest. I wasn't surprised when a day or two later they rushed in to show me a beautiful little bright-blue egg, which they had even managed to blow themselves.

The children continued to collect birds' eggs for a number of years, and the interest gave them a very good understanding of our Sussex birdlife, and it was a good topic of conversation with their father who himself had a deep interest in all aspects of God's creation around us.

I recollect some years after this when a minister friend from Brighton remarked to Eli that he was surprised he allowed his children to collect birds' eggs that Eli maintained there was biblical permission to take the eggs or young from a bird's nest. This was a bit tongue in cheek as the reference in Deuteronomy 22:6 is no doubt giving the Israelites under the old Mosaic law permission to take eggs or young birds from a nest for their food rather than merely for their interest. What is very revealing here is that the Creator God is concerned that the mothering instinct he has given his creatures should not be taken advantage of to their detriment. The Israelites were not permitted to take the parent bird which was guarding her young. She must be allowed to go free. [36]

---

[36] Since 1954 it has been illegal in UK to take birds' eggs from the wild.

Chapter 13

Beekeeping

Whilst at Limden Farm, we had our first bee skeps. Richard was about twelve, and as a personal project for his interest, Eli gave him the task of making the skeps. They were made of straw, and their construction required a fair amount of patience and skill. I remember Eli sitting down with Richard after supper one winter's evening and explaining the principle to him, and at the next opportunity, they got the necessary materials together and Eli got Richard started.

They used straw before the grains had been threshed out, and although the ears of corn were then cut off, this did mean that the stalks were not broken or bruised. Eli had fashioned a sort of funnel out of a piece of old cow's horn with an opening hole about one inch in diameter at the narrower end. First the straw was moistened to make it more pliable, and then a fairly tight bundle of stalks was forced into the wider end of the bone funnel and pulled out of the narrower end as a compressed sausage of straw. Then a longish iron nail was used as a bradawl to make holes at regular intervals in the compressed straw, and lengths of reed were threaded through the holes and wound around the straw sausage to bind it together. The reed also needed to be wet so it would bend without snapping. The aim is to make a continuous length of straw 'sausage', so it's important that there's a continuous feed of new stalks alongside those already going into the funnel to avoid a sudden break or end. The resulting bound straw sausage is then coiled around and around to make a large straw cone. Beginning at the top, the coils increase in diameter as they proceed downwards, and each coil is knitted to the coil above it by the reed thread. The finished skep has a diameter at the bottom of about two feet and narrows down to a point at the top where a circular coil of bound straw makes a handle for carrying.

The bees must be allowed entry into their home, and the simplest way to give them access is by standing the skep on a couple of lengths of wood just deep enough for them to be able to get under the straw.

Richard made four skeps to get us started with our beekeeping, and he did this over some weeks. His skill improved, and the last two skeps looked rather more professional than the first two.

Having made the skeps, Richard came up with an important question.

'Father,' he asked Eli one evening, 'where do we get the bees for our skeps?'

Eli's practice was to help the children to think for themselves, so he put the question back to Richard and asked him what he would do to get some bees.

Richard thought for a moment and then suggested that perhaps by simply putting the skeps out in the open somewhere bees might find it and come and use it for a nest.

'Much like the blue tits came and nested in that box with a hole that you hung on the apple tree,' he added.

'That's not impossible,' answered Eli, 'but with bees, this is unlikely, we will have to help the situation ourselves. In the spring and early summer, a bee colony will produce a second or even a third queen bee, and since a colony can only have one queen, the additional queens are forced to leave the hive and find another home. A good number of worker bees will go with her, and we call this a swarm. We need somehow to encourage a swarm with a queen to take up residence in one of our skeps. What I had already thought of doing is talking to William Read at Stonegate Farm, I know he has a number of skeps of bees, and he may be persuaded to let us leave one of our skeps with him, and when he gets a swarm to capture it under our little bee house!'

'Great, Dad!' said Richard. 'Can I come with you when you deliver the skep?'

'Certainly,' answered Eli, 'it will give you the chance to see his hives and perhaps learn a bit about beekeeping.'

This all went to plan, and soon we had our own family of bees producing honey in one of our skeps.

We put our straw beehive in the orchard, and thankfully, we were in time for our bees to catch the spring fruit blossom.

I had been fascinated by bees ever since I had watched them in the garden as a girl and Dad had told us a bit about them and how these marvellous insects have little pockets in their back legs where they store the pollen they collect from the flowers. I explained this to our children, and together we watched the bees flying from flower to flower, noticing how their back legs became fatter and fatter with stored pollen and then how eventually they would fly back to Richard's straw skep with their 'shopping'.

'They collect both pollen and nectar,' I explained, 'and use essentially the pollen to feed their baby grubs and somehow convert the nectar into honey. This is stored in purpose-made wax containers to feed the colony over the winter.'

We had a lot more to learn about bees, but it was two years before we got any honey for ourselves.

There have been advances in beekeeping since we had our first colony, but in those early days with the type of skep Richard had made, the only way of acquiring their honey for our use was to gas the bees at the end of the summer and then pull the skep apart to get to the honey combs which were attached to the straw walls inside. This meant we always had to allow at least one colony of bees to keep their honey so they could survive the winter and get us started again the next spring with a new swarm or two.

Although at first I had a tinge of guilt when I ate our own honey, knowing that the wonderful little insects that had produced it had been killed so that we could enjoy their winter store, I soon convinced myself that this was in fact what farming was all about. We make God's creatures work for us. The hens produce the eggs we enjoy at breakfast, the cows the milk that we turn into delicious butter, and at the end of the day we slaughter our servant animals and eat them. We fry pieces of our pigs to enjoy with the eggs our chickens lay, boil our cows with vegetables to make a tasty stew, and roast our chickens after having stuffed them with bread and herbs! If God hadn't clearly shown in the Bible that he allowed us to do this, [37]I think I could easily have become a vegetarian.

I didn't share any of these misgivings with the children, but I must say I was delighted when one evening Eli said that he had been speaking at the market with another farmer who also kept bees, and he had heard of a way of getting the honey out of the skep without killing the bees.

Richard reacted with enthusiasm and wanted to know more, so I said nothing but listened with great interest.

'The idea,' said Eli, 'is to make an additional smaller straw skep which sits on top of the larger one. The lower skep would need to be adapted so it has an open flat top the same size as the base of the smaller upper skep. The two skeps must sit nicely together with no access to the upper one from outside. We would then need to place a piece of wood between the two skeps with a number of holes in. What is crucial is that these holes need to be big enough to allow worker and drone bees to crawl through from below but too small to allow the larger queen to enter the upper region. The bee's main living area will continue to be the lower skep where the queen is, but I'm told that the worker bees will use the upper skep as their larder where they make and store their honey.'

'If this really works,' continued Eli, 'at the end of the summer, we can simply remove the upper skep with the honey and don't have to destroy the colony of bees living below.'

'That sounds really clever,' said Ruth, who had also been listening intently. 'I bet it was a woman who thought of that idea!'

---

[37] Genesis 9:3.

Oh, Ruth, Ruth! I thought to myself. *You're a female version of your outspoken father. It's a good thing you've got four sisters growing up behind you to support you in this male dominated household!*

It was then the spring of 1852, and unknown to us, Ruth was to have a total of eight sisters before my childbearing days were over! Boys, you are going to have to look out for yourselves!

Eli made no direct response to his daughter's remark but merely said, 'The proof of the pudding is in the eating, we'll see whether our bees like to store their honey in their living room or in a detached larder. And in any case, if we steal their winter store and want them to survive, we'll have to give them some form of replacement sustenance.'

Chapter 14

Eli Unsettled

Eli worked hard. He loved farming and was always finding new things to do and new ways of doing them. However, there was constantly a tension within him. He had no doubt that God had called him to preach. He loved the Bible. He loved the gospel of God's sovereign grace, and it gave him great pleasure to preach it. The chapels around in Sussex and Kent appreciated his ministry, and he found it increasingly difficult to refuse their invitations to preach for them. Eli had to find the way of combining his responsibilities to the farm, the family, and God's call to preach. Looking back, I sense that God gave him much wisdom and grace in handling these different responsibilities in a way that gave justice to each and honoured his Master.

In the early 1850s we had five farm labourers working for us, and Eli was now able to leave much of the routine farmwork in their hands. But our two oldest boys, Richard and John were also now working full-time on the farm having left school on their eleventh birthdays, and Eli was concerned that the boys should learn their farming skills from him.

The farm served the family. We tried to be self-supporting, which meant we needed to be diverse in our farming to provide ourselves, our children, and to some degree also our employees and various others whom Eli made himself responsible for, with milk, butter, cheese, honey, vegetables, fruit, eggs, flour, bacon, poultry, and beef. I also learned to make a low-alcohol beer using barley and our hops.

Eli used to say to me that farming was the type of work closest to the God-ordained work ordinance given to us in the opening chapters of the Bible. Producing food from the soil was his delight.

We had a certain amount of woodland on the farm at Limden. Many of our trees were sweet chestnut, and by coppicing them, we had a harvest of poles every few years suitable for use in the hop fields. The trees were fairly close together and had been planted with coppicing in mind. Coppicing meant cutting the first single stem of the tree back to within a foot or so of the ground which forced it to sprout a number of new shoots. These, because of the closeness of the other trees, grew straight upwards towards the light providing us with good straight poles. To get the size of poles needed for the hop fields, the new stems needed up to ten years growth. By pruning some of the stems away, we were able to encourage the growth of substantial poles in a shorter time. Unsuitable branches were used for burning charcoal. Managing woodland in this way was new to Eli when we first came to Limden, but it gave variety and interest to the farm which he enjoyed.

At certain times of the year, we let our pigs roam through the woodland. This is really the pigs' natural habitat. They seemed to find all manner of things to eat, and it was really amusing to see them discover a sweet chestnut. Watching them, you could almost imagine their piggy faces lighting up with delight as they crunched away at these delicacies. Another culinary delight for them is the plant pignut, *Conopodium majus.* Above the ground, this plant has heavily divided leaves and produces heads of little white flowers which appear in early summer. But it's what's underground that interests the pigs. The plant produces delicious nuts which grow on the root of the plant in the same way as potatoes do. When they can find them, the pigs love them. But as well as giving the pigs an adventurous time, it's actually good for the woodland to have the pigs there. Their foraging helps to aerate the ground and of course they fertilise it too.

But although things seemed to be going well, I sensed that Eli was becoming unsettled. One evening, he talked to me about it.

'Seli,' he said, 'I don't think it's a good thing for the boys to grow up with hop farming. It gives us a reasonable income, and it's been a very interesting and challenging crop to grow, but I've become convicted recently that it's not really honouring to the god we serve for us to support beer-making. Not that I condemn drinking a pint of beer, but seen in its very best light, beer-making is not helping society, and many would say that as a strong drink, it's destroying it. What am I, as a preacher of the gospel of Jesus Christ, doing farming hops? I'm convinced that food production for man's bodily needs compliments my spiritual ministry, and I can do that with pride but not growing hops.'

'When did you begin to think like this, Eli?' I asked.

'I think I've known it for a long time inside,' Eli answered. 'But I wouldn't acknowledge it even to myself. Then I found when I'm visiting different chapels and get into conversation with Christian people, I talk happily about our small beef herd, about our pigs and our cereal crops and fruit orchard and our bees, but I say nothing about the hops. This made me realise although I could justify this side of our farm to myself as a means of providing for my family, actually when in the presence of other Christians, I am ashamed of it.'

'So what are we going to do?' I asked.

'I guess we will need to move again, Seli,' Eli answered. 'We've got a growing family, and without the hops, this farm won't really support us. It's for God's honour that we want to change direction, and I believe he will provide for us.'

So it became a matter of earnest prayer that God would show us what to do and, if he wanted Eli to stay in farming, that he would lead us to a place where we could serve him with a clear conscience and teach our children a form of farming of which we could all be proud.

God kept us waiting another year, but one day Eli came home looking more cheerful than he sometimes did, and I sensed he had something to tell me. Once we could get up to bed and be by ourselves, he shared his news with me excitedly.

'Selina,' he said as he took off his jacket and unbuttoned his shirt, 'I think there is light at the end of the tunnel. How would you like to be a sheep farmer?'

'Well, I guess we can't get more biblical than that,' I answered. 'Jacob and his family were shepherds. David was a shepherd, and Jesus is our Good Shepherd. But practically, we shall need a far bigger acreage than we have here at Limden if we are going to keep sheep.'

'That's the miracle,' responded Eli. 'At least it will be if it comes off. Today, quite by accident, although in God's eyes I'm sure it was no accident, I met Elizabeth Fuller. Her father farmed Mays Farm, Selmeston, when we were children, do you remember?'

'The Fullers at Mays Farm,' I answered. 'Yes, I remember them. They always seemed pretty well to do. I think Elizabeth was the only child in the family, wasn't she? She would have been a good bit older than me though.'

'That's the family,' said Eli. 'Old Joseph Fuller was quite the gentleman farmer and was related to the Fullers of Waldron who owned the iron foundry at Heathfield which used to make cannons for the Royal Navy. Anyway Joseph died recently, so Elizabeth has inherited, and she and her husband have decided to give up farming.'

'Is that Mays Farm?' I asked.

'No, no!' said Eli. 'Elizabeth married Nathaniel Blaker, and they've been farming crown property just north of the Devil's Dyke behind Brighton. Anyway, the point is that they want to get out of their contract with the crown, and to do that, they need to find another reliable farmer to take over the farm.'

'Are you interested?' I asked.

'I've told Elizabeth I'll go down to Fulking tomorrow to see the farm and talk to her husband, and if it seems right, she'll put our name forward to take over the contract.'

'How big is the farm?' I asked excitedly.

'Well, the Blakers have been farming 700 acres, but a neighbour has expressed interest in taking over part of this leaving the large farmhouse and about 500 acres.'

'Wow!' I exclaimed.

That night, before we went to sleep, we prayed together. Eli thanked the Lord for bringing this possibility to us and asked him to overrule all the details so as to give us the contract if this was his will.

One Saturday evening a few weeks later, when we were alone as a family, Eli turned to the children with a smile on his face.

'How would you feel if we were to keep sheep and move to a manor house and a 500-acre farm?' he asked.

'You are joking, Dad?' said Richard.

'Would I joke about something as serious as this?' said Eli, smiling broadly.

'Where would this be?' said John. 'There aren't any farms like that around here.'

'It would mean moving to the slopes of the South Downs just north of Brighton,' Eli answered.

'But, Dad!' cried Ruth, 'We would need to take Charlotte and Big-Foot, and what about all the other animals?'

'One thing at a time,' responded Eli. 'There's a lot of details to work out, but God has given us this possibility, and your mother and I have decided this is what we need to do. I signed the contract yesterday, and we are due to take over Perching Manor Farm at Michaelmas.'

Part 4

Perching Manor Farm, Fulking 1856 onwards

Chapter 1

A New Challenge

When we moved farms, for what thankfully proved to be our last time, Eli had just reached his thirty-ninth birthday, and I was thirty-eight. We had ten children! Richard, the eldest, was then eighteen, and Dorcas, the youngest, was seven months.

I must tell you a bit about this new location and our new house and farm.

Perching Manor Farm lies immediately to the west of the hamlet of Fulking, and our farmhouse is only about 300 yards from the centre of this very small village. A further 300 yards beyond us is the site of the ancient manor house of Perching, which dates back at least to the eleventh century and seems to have been more of a fortified castle than a house and was probably built by the Norman invaders after 1066. The site is in one of our fields and has been ploughed over for crops, but an indentation where the old moat was is still discernible, and when we first came, there were still old stones from the original manor lying around. Occasionally visitors come to see the site, which annoys Eli when we have crops growing over it. I remember one gentleman being particularly persistent, and in the end, I invited him into the farmhouse for a cup of tea. He told me that at one time, Perching was just as much a village as Fulking, and apparently it was the Black Death in the fourteenth century when so many died from the plague which ended community life there.

A little further west of us is the village of Edburton, and our little communities all lie in a line at the foot of the South Downs. The land south of us rises sharply, and the range of higher ground in our immediate vision undulates to provide three humps each named after the community below them, Edburton Hill, Perching Hill, and Fulking Hill. A little further east, it rises to its highest point of 700 feet, and here is the more well known Devil's Dyke. On the top, there are still the remains of an Iron Age fort, and the views on a clear day are wonderful. John Constable, the famous painter, who incidentally died the same year as Eli's dad, described the panorama from the Devil's Dyke as the grandest view in the world!

The reason for this strange name is due to the rather unique valley gauged out of the chalk to the east of the hill. It's nearly a mile long, and we've been told it's the longest, widest, and deepest dry valley in the United Kingdom. There are a range of different legends about its origin giving the Devil's Dyke its name, and the one our children loved to repeat to visitors goes something like this:

'The devil had been infuriated by the conversion of Sussex, one of the last strongholds of paganism in England, and more particularly by the way the men of the Weald were building churches in all their villages. So he swore that he would dig right through the Downs in a single night to let in the sea and drown them all. He started just near Poynings and dug and dug most furiously, sending great clods of earth flying left and right—one became Chanctonbury, another Cissbury, another Rackham Hill, and yet another Mount Caburn. Towards midnight, the noise he was making disturbed an old woman, who looked out to see what was going on. As soon as she understood what he was up to, she lit a candle and set it on her windowsill, holding up a sieve in front of it to make a dimly glowing globe. The devil looked round and thought this was the rising sun. At first he could hardly believe his eyes, but then he heard a cock crowing—for the old woman, just to make quite sure, had knocked her cockerel off his perch. So Satan flew away, leaving his work half done. Some say that as he went out over the channel, a great dollop of earth fell from his cloven hoof, and that's how the Isle of Wight was made, others, that he bounded straight over into Surrey, where the impact of his landing formed the hollow known as his Punch Bowl.'[38]

Perching Manor
See page 266; Anthony R. Brooks (2008) *The Changing Times of Fulking & Edburton: 1900 to 2007*. Chichester: RPM Print & Design.

Our new house was larger than at Limden, and we were all delighted with it as soon as we saw it. Eli's comment was 'Now, Seli, we will really have the opportunity to entertain guests and hopefully a few angels unawares!'

---

[38] Simpson, Jacqueline, 'Sussex Local Legends', in *Folklore Journal*, vol. 84, 1973.

Actually one of the first 'angels' to take up residence was my mother, Ann. She had really got beyond looking after herself, and by and large, it was a pleasure to have her. She had always been a very practical person, so as long as she was able, she was pleased to help with things in the kitchen and house.

The house faces east with an L-shaped extension out of the back of it on the south-west corner. The front is imposing with the front door in the centre and two largish windows each side. It is built of red brick with typical Sussex inlaid flints. Flint stones occur naturally in chalk so are readily available. There are five large windows on the first floor at the front and a further three dormer windows on a third floor in the roof itself, which is tiled.[39]

It was good arable farming land, so Eli has been able to grow a good number of acres of wheat, barley, and oats. We also kept a small herd of milking cows providing milk and butter both for our own use and also to some degree for the village too. Pigs were also necessary to give us regular meat, bacon, sausages, and that delicious pork fat which makes fried bread so tasty. But the new aspect of farming was the sheep. Eli agreed to purchase the flock of the South Down breed, which were already grazing on the pasture land. We invited an independent valuer to set the price, and both parties agreed beforehand to accept his valuation of the animals, and Eli was satisfied with the outcome. We also kept on most of the existing farm labourers. Things may be changing a little now, but at that time, it was very common for farmworkers to stay with a particular farm for several generations. Sons would often work alongside their fathers and, in due course, take over from them. The result of this was a real sense of loyalty and devotion, and farm labourers would often act and speak as though the farm and its animals belonged to them personally.

Eli and Richard were content to learn the intricacies of sheep farming from our experienced head shepherd George Payne. He appreciated the

---

[39] The house still stands, and since 1983 has been classified as a grade 2 listed building.

trust that Eli put in him, and a good working relationship was soon established. This of course oiled the smooth running of the farm as George learnt to respect Eli and was more than happy to listen to new ideas and to adopt changes when these were agreed to be helpful.

Of our two oldest boys, Richard loved farming, but John never really had his heart in it.

Chapter 2

Exploring Our South Downs

It was a beautiful autumn Sunday afternoon soon after our arrival in Perching. Eli was away preaching, and because we were now living further away from his usual preaching haunts, I wasn't expecting him home until Monday morning. The boys still had their farming chores to do, but the little ones were restless, and I suggested to Ruth that she should take them for a walk to explore the Downs. Orpha, Naomi, and Mercy were enthusiastic to go, and Ruth also agreed to take Mary who was still not quite five. They were away longer than I expected, but I didn't anticipate they could come to any harm so was not really worried.

They came back very excited, but Sunday tea was already laid on the table and the boys were champing at the bit to get tucked in, so I sent the girls to wash their hands at the kitchen pump and told them to tell me all about it later.

'We took the path straight up the hill in front of us,' explained Ruth once everyone had satisfied their appetites. 'I think it's the one they call Perching Hill. Do you think it was named after our farm, or was our farm named after the hill?'

Before I could answer, Orpha interrupted.

'At the top of the hill, we met a nice man with his sheepdog. He said he worked for our dad, and he was ever so friendly.'

'That must have been Mr Payne,' I answered. 'He lives in the shepherd's cottage up Perching Hill.'

'Anyway, he told us a lot of interesting things,' added Orpha. 'We said we'd come up the steep path, and he said it was called the bostal.'

'Yes, I've heard that word before,' I said. 'I think it's a Sussex name for steep paths up the South Downs.'

'He suggested it was easier to use sheep paths even though they meandered around and made the walk longer,' added Ruth.

'Then he pointed out a sort of bank with a shallow ditch behind it,' added Orpha. 'He asked us what we thought it was.'

'Of course we had no idea,' said Ruth, 'but he explained it was the grave of someone who died several hundreds of years before Jesus was born. Do you think he can be right, Mummy?'

The children looked at me for some reassurance that our shepherd knew what he was talking about.

'We'll have to ask your dad to be sure,' I said, 'but I have heard that there are a number of Bronze Age burial mounds along the tops of the Downs, and I guess that's what he was saying. I don't really know when this so-called Bronze Age was though,' I added.

'Wow!' said Orpha. 'It's fantastic to think that people were living here thousands of years ago. I wonder what they were like and how they lived.'

'They couldn't have been Christians like us,' said Ruth, 'because Jesus hadn't yet been born in Bethlehem nor died for their sins. It's much better for us to live now because we can know Jesus.'

I sensed the conversation could now be getting rather difficult, and the next question might well be whether all these people went to hell and I'd rather leave that sort of question for Eli to answer.

'Did Mr Payne tell you anything else?' I asked.

'He had a lovely dog,' said Naomi. 'His name is Jeremiah, and Mr Payne called him Jerry. We all sat down on the grass together, and Jerry lay down and watched us.'

'There were bits of chalk everywhere, so we asked him about this,' said Orpha. 'He said the whole hill was made of chalk, and it stretches right down to the sea at a place called Beachy Head. Maybe we could walk there one day? It would be lovely to get really close to the sea.'

'He also told us,' added Ruth, 'that they dig out the chalk in some places and make it burn in a hot oven by adding charcoal. This turns the chalk into a powdery lime, which can be spread on the fields to help the crops grow better.'

'He gave a name for these chalk ovens,' interrupted Orpha, 'but I can't remember what it was.'

'I think it was lime kilns,' said Ruth, 'and he said there's one that we can go and see up near the Devil's Dyke.'

'Well, it sounds as if you had a really interesting afternoon's walk,' I said. 'What did you enjoy most about it, Mary?'

'She liked the dog,' said Mercy. 'And so did I. He let us stroke him, and he did just what the man told him.'

'Can we have a dog like Jerry,' asked Mary.

'I think Jerry is a very special dog,' I said. 'He's a sheepdog. I guess both his parents and grandparents were trained sheepdogs, and now Jerry has learnt to do exactly what Mr Payne tells him. He can round up the sheep and make them go where Mr Payne wants.'

Chapter 3

Sheep Farming on the South Downs

The sheep we bought with the farm were the South Down breed. These are smallish animals, docile and suitable for both wool and meat. Most years we have had at least one or two to suckle ourselves with a bottle, and they have proved to be very attractive pets which the children have loved. We tried to stop the children getting too attached to these pet lambs warning them that one day they would have to go off to market. Being farmer's children though, they were fairly realistic about this when it happened, and the tears didn't last too long.

Eli talked to me a lot about the different aspects of sheep farming in those early days after we had moved to Perching. He was pleased to have George Payne as head shepherd, who had had considerable experience with sheep, as Eli was very much aware there was a lot for him to learn. By only allowing the rams to run with the ewes in the autumn, we could control to a large degree when the lambs would be born. The sheep had the freedom to roam the slopes of the Downs after lambing and until harvest was over. Then in late summer and winter, they were brought down to our lower arable fields at night, and during bad weather in winter, when they would remain closer to home all day too. This procedure was called folding. One main purpose for folding was to fertilise the fields. Our chalky soil was not particularly fertile, and allowing it to be naturally dunged by the sheep in autumn and winter helped to ensure better crops the following year.

The sheep had to be closely watched by George Payne and his dog Jerry, particularly when they were grazing on the Downs. George knew all his sheep individually, and he had bells which he would put around the necks of those who were more adventuresome. I loved to hear the music of the bells as the sheep roamed, and even when they were nearer the farmhouse at nights, it was pleasant to hear them.

Being a mother myself, the birth of our livestock was always of interest to me, and I took a particular interest in the birth of our lambs. I remember asking Eli about it during our early days at Perching Manor. He explained that the pregnancy time for sheep was a little less than five months, and if the rams ran with the ewes in early autumn, this ensured the main lambing time was February and March. There were usually some ewes which didn't conceive first time, and when this was suspected, they were given another date with the gentleman.

'Will someone need to be with the mother sheep when she gives birth,' I asked. I was aware that Eli always aimed to oversee the birth of calves to ensure we lost as few as possible.

'We shall have the pregnant ewes near the farm when they are due to lamb,' he said. 'In most cases, they will manage to give birth without help, but we need to watch them carefully to be able to deal with any problems. It's not uncommon for ewes to reject one of their lambs, particularly if they have twins or triplets.'

'Will we have to mother these ourselves then?' I asked him. 'I'm sure the children would love to have pet lambs.'

'It's far better if we can foster forsaken lambs to other sheep,' Eli answered. 'Some lambs will be born dead, and the mothers of these are the best ewes to foster the motherless ones, although sometimes a ewe with just one lamb can be tricked into thinking she has two! A forsaken lamb needs to smell right for another ewe to accept it, and there are one or two subtle ways of achieving this.'

'Tell me,' I said.

'Well,' answered Eli. 'If a ewe has given birth to a dead lamb and we have a forsaken lamb which we want her to foster, we can skin the dead lamb and wrap this skin around the live lamb. The mother then smells her own offspring and usually accepts the live lamb allowing it to suckle. Once she's accepted it, we can soon remove its little coat and all is fine. However, if there is no dead lamb and we want to introduce a foster lamb to a ewe with only one baby, then it's often possible to rub the second lamb thoroughly with the ewe's own afterbirth, and it'll then smell right and she'll accept it.'

'It'll be interesting to see how these ideas work in practise,' I said.

There are other significant times in a sheep farmer's year, and I was soon to hear about these too.

Chapter 4
Family Readjustments

Every location has its advantages and disadvantages, and a big disadvantage of Perching at that time was the lack of a suitable school for the children. The close proximity of the village of Stonegate to Limden Farm, with its Stonegate National School run by Mary Read, had proved a great blessing for our older children. They had been able to run or dawdle, as the mood took them, up and down Limden Lane each day, and school and home had fitted together well providing a happy childhood.

When we moved to Perching Manor, Mercy was six, Mary nearly five, Elizabeth three, and Dorcas eight months. Mercy and Mary should certainly be at school and very soon Elizabeth too. They needed to be learning to read and do sums as well as the practical things they were already doing around the house.

Eli raised the matter one evening with a suggestion which to me, as their mother, was mind-blowing!

'I've been thinking,' said Eli, 'I'm not happy with the village school here and think we might need to find a more suitable school we could send the girls away to.'

'Oh no, Eli!' I responded. 'Surely there has to be another way.'

We were both silent for a few minutes, and then I added, 'Neither you nor I had formal schooling, and we haven't done so badly.'

'Yes, I know, Seli,' answered Eli, 'but this is another age. More and more children are now going to school, our position in society has risen, and surely you agree we want the best for our girls.'

We were interrupted by Richard rushing in with some demand requiring Eli's attention on the farm, and Eli's parting words as he went out of the door were gentle and loving, and I knew then that he hated the idea as much as I did.

'We'll think and pray about it, Seli,' he said, 'and we'll talk about it another time.'

I must confess I didn't sleep a lot that night. I loved all our children dearly, and the thought of sending our little girls away to school was more than I could bear. I thought back to my own childhood with affection. It's amazing how one tends to remember only the good bits. How I had loved our simple cottage home and being part of Mum and Dad's life. They had taught us children themselves, giving us enough background learning to build on it in our own way. But I knew Eli wouldn't be happy with me teaching the children, and he had no time to do it.

Yes! I thought. *Our position in society has risen. We are now living in a manor house, running a five-hundred-acre farm with nearly ten employees. But what's the good of that if it destroys family life for our children?*

Then I thought of Ruth. Maybe she could teach the girls, giving them some formal lessons in English and arithmetic. She's been to school and must know how it's done! At the back of my mind, I knew this wasn't a long-term answer, but maybe it would take the pressure away for the moment. With this thought, I eventually managed to go to sleep.

Eli agreed that we could involve Ruth in the girls' education in the immediate and then suggested we should look for a governess who could live-in and teach the girls further. This was a great relief for me, but unfortunately, it didn't work out as I hoped.

Moving across the county of Sussex to our new location brought us in touch with some of Eli's family with whom, up to then, we'd had very little contact. One such person was his Aunt Charlotte. We met her at a chapel service in Brighton, and Eli invited her and her daughter, Eliza, to come and stay with us for a weekend. Eli had never known his mother, who had died before his first birthday, and after this, his father had really lost touch with his mother's side of the family. We now learnt that Eli's mother's brother had married this lady, Charlotte from Henfield. This unknown uncle had since died, and Aunt Charlotte herself wasn't in the best of health and had become quite deaf. However, she had a daughter, Eliza, who of course was Eli's cousin. She lived with her mother and gave her what care was needed but was also a school mistress! Sadly, she also was becoming increasingly deaf which excluded her from being employed in any of the national schools, but she was able to run a small school in the home they lived in, 28 London Road, Brighton. We talked to Eliza about the education of our children, and she suggested that when we felt the time was right, she would be prepared to take the girls as boarders into her little school.

This happened in due course, and by then, I had got used to the idea and knowing my little children were going to a family member helped a lot. We arranged it so that they came and went, not spending too long at a time away from the family nest, but it seemed very strange to me that when we had to fill in the national census in 1861, all five of our younger girls were away from home as boarders with Eliza Verrall.[40] The oldest was Mary who was then aged eleven and the youngest Esther who hadn't reached her fourth birthday. By then I'd had a further baby girl, Leah, who was born on 6 September 1859.

---

[40] 1861 Census, Eliza Verral, born Henfield, 1816.

Chapter 5

The Family Grows Up

Soon after our move to Perching, Eli became concerned about the boys' future and how best to point them in the direction which suited them best. Richard loved farming, and so he could continue to learn this at Perching. John and Samuel were not so enthusiastic about working on the land, and so we needed to find positions where they could learn other trades.

John decided he would like to be a butcher. This is obviously a trade closely linked to farming, and although I always considered the slaughtering of our animals the more gruesome side of our work, John enjoyed his food, and I think this somehow attracted him to learn how to prepare meat for the housewife. Eli was able to find him a position as apprentice to a master butcher in Brighton by the name of Elisha Port, and John left home soon after our move to West Sussex. He was the first of the family to leave home, apart from little Ebenezer whom God had taken to be with himself! John was able to live in the household of his employer in Ship Street, Brighton.[41]

I hated seeing the family splitting up, but clearly it was the right thing to happen. The boys in particular needed to find their own way in the world. In our daily family devotions, Eli always prayed for

---

[41] 1861 Census, John Page, born 1840, Dicker.

the children who were missing from around the large kitchen table. Although we wanted them to get on in their chosen careers, our main concern was for their spiritual well-being. This above all meant, in the words of my own father, 'that they might experience God's grace in their hearts'. We longed to see them aware of their personal sinfulness and trusting Jesus alone for their eternal salvation.

The next child to leave home and venture into the outside world was Samuel.

Positioned on our South Downs at Clayton are two windmills. We would see them regularly as we drove our pony and trap into Brighton. They were never working on Sundays when we occasionally drove to one of the Brighton chapels, but if it was a working day, the children always wanted to see whether the windmill blades were turning, and it fascinated them. Eli was able to make an arrangement with James Mitchell, who was the miller in charge of the windmills, to grind our wheat to provide the flour we needed for our own use, and one day, he took Samuel along with him when he went to see Mr Mitchell. When Samuel came home, he could talk about nothing else than the windmills, and he was determined to be a miller.

Largely because of Samuel's interest, Eli arranged for the older children to go and see the mills in action. They came back in great excitement and wanted to tell me all about it.

'There's an old windmill and a new one,' said Samuel. 'The old one is called Duncton Mill, and the newer one is a lady windmill called Jill.'

'There's an interesting story about Jill,' added Ruth, butting in. 'She was originally built on the Dyke Road, but her wind shaft broke and her blades collapsed. They mended her, but then a few years ago, they decided there was more wind on the hill where she is today nearer Duncton Mill, so they moved her.'

'Did the man tell you how they moved her,' I asked. 'It must have been a big job.'

'They had a team of horses and oxen to pull her,' said Samuel. 'Dad says he can remember hearing about it. It was in 1852, and he says everyone was saying how clever it was it to be able to move Jill without dismantling her.'

'Jill has four big sails at the front and a fantail with five blades at the back,' said Orpha. 'The man explained to us that it's the big sails turning that grind the corn, and the fantail balances the whole windmill, helping to ensure it's facing the right way to get the wind.'

'Yes, we saw how it turns,' said Ruth. 'The man said Jill is a post mill, which means she is anchored to the ground on a big post and then the whole windmill turns on this post to face the wind.'

'He explained that the more recent windmills are often now tower mills,' said Samuel. 'I think that means all the inner working parts of the mill are in a tower, which doesn't move, and the blades are built into a sort of cap that sits on top of the windmill and turns to make the blades face the wind. I'd like to see one of those,' he added.

'Did you see how the windmill grinds the corn?' I asked.

'Oh yes, that was great,' said Samuel. 'Everything is powered by the four big blades turning. When there's no wind, nothing happens, but once the blades turn, then the miller can connect the gear mechanism and the process can start. Sacks of grain are hauled up to the top of the windmill and emptied into a chute which channels the corn down to the big stone millstones. They turn and grind it all up. The miller can set the gap between the upper and lower millstones so as to control how fine the grain is ground. It's all very clever, and I can't wait to be a miller.'

Sussex Windmills
Jack and Jill by Henry Miller,
(used with permission) www.sussexprints.co.uk.

After this visit, all the children took a great deal of interest in our local windmills. Some years later, the Duncton Mill was dismantled. It had been built in 1765 and leased out by the owner on a ninety-nine-year lease. When this expired, it was decided it had had its life, and so a new windmill was built close by and the roundhouse of the old mill kept as a storage shed. There was great excitement when the new one was built in 1866, and it was called Jack. Samuel got his wish to see a tower mill as this was the design used for Jack. Our two windmills, Jack and Jill, attracted a lot of attention and became a well-known landmark on the Clayton hill above the Brighton road. [42]

Eli was able to find Samuel a position as miller's assistant in Brighton in the household of Thomas Brazier in Cheapside.[43] However,

---

[42] See appendix 3—Sussex Windmills.
[43] 1871 Census, Samuel Page, born 1842, Ticehurst.

working in Cheapside, Brighton, wasn't as romantic as being a miller in a windmill, and from the comments he made, I rather gather Samuel also struggled to get on with his boss. After a year or so, he decided he'd rather be a butcher. He moved to East Grinstead where he really found his niche and not only completed his apprenticeship to become a master butcher but also found a delightful wife, Mary Ann. Whilst living in East Grinstead, they gave us two granddaughters, Kate and Naomi, and then after Samuel qualified, we were able to help set him up with his own business as a master butcher in Croydon.

Chapter 6

Man Shall Not Live by Bread Alone

Life was very busy for us all in Perching and in general very positive, but I soon began to be concerned about my spiritual life and that of the children. Eli led us all in family prayers every morning and evening when he was at home. It was his custom to give a short exposition of the Bible passage he read and to apply this to the practical things in our lives as well as to our souls' needs in regard to personal sin and God's grace in Jesus Christ. Perhaps this was all we should need? To have our own pastor in the household is far more than most families have! But I really missed having a chapel locally where we could have fellowship with evangelical believers outside the family. I had so much enjoyed this privilege at the Dicker when we were first married and then at Burwash.

Most Sundays, Eli was away preaching, so it was left to me to organise any outings to church. We tried the Anglican Church in Fulking, but although it helped us to get to know some of our neighbours, from a spiritual point of view, it left me feeling dry and frustrated. I used to come away saying to myself, 'The Bible reading was great, much of the content of the prayerbook touched my soul, but why, oh why can't the vicar preach Christ crucified and tell us the old, old story of Jesus and his love?'

Occasionally, when circumstances on the farm allowed it, I took our pony and trap into Brighton. Ruth encouraged me in this and helped to get the younger children ready. The boys often found reasons not to come, but when the weather was good, they could sometimes be enticed by a suggestion of taking some food and eating it by the sea once we had attended the morning service at the chapel in West Street.

The situation changed once the younger girls were boarding with their school mistress Eliza Verrall. As often as possible, I would send Ruth to pick them up on Friday afternoon, and then there was the need to run them back to Brighton on Sunday. We would either go to the morning service at the chapel in West Street, take our lunch, and drop the girls off in the afternoon, or take them down to Brighton later in the day and stay there for an evening service. Although the distance meant we couldn't join fully into fellowship life at the chapel in Brighton, I benefited tremendously from the contact we had with the believers there and from the preaching of Mr John Grace, who was pastor at the Tabernacle as the chapel in West Street called itself, until his death in 1865.

We had been at Perching Manor Farm for about a year when one Sunday evening as Eli and I went upstairs to bed, having not seen each other all day, he took a printed booklet out of his pocket.

'Seli,' he said, 'old Jabeth Gurr passed this on to me this morning as I was shaking hands with him at the door of the chapel. You'll never guess what he said to me, "Mr Page, here's a *good* sermon for you."

'Maybe he wasn't implying mine was not a good sermon, but at the time it seemed like it, and I really had to fight against my pride and humble myself to read this booklet. After lunch, Mr and Mrs White who were entertaining me for the day left me alone to prepare myself for the evening session, and I sat down and read it. It really blessed me.'

'What is it, Eli?' I asked.

'It's a penny sermon by a young preacher in London, Charles Haddon Spurgeon. He's apparently creating quite a stir in the city, and reading this sermon, I can understand why. I thanked old Jabeth in the evening, and he told me the sermons are published every week. I'm arranging to have them posted to us. There's food there for our souls, and I can well foresee that God will use them to bless you at home and me in my preaching.'

It was well into Monday before I managed to get a few moments to myself to read the little sixteen-page booklet. It was the first of many sermons by Spurgeon that I read, and I shall never forget it. In fact, I've kept it as one of my treasures and have it in front of me as I write. It's entitled *The Work of the Holy Spirit* and states that it's a sermon by the Rev. C. H. Spurgeon preached at Park Street Chapel, Southwark, on Thursday evening, 5 November 1857. The text he's preaching from is Galatians 3:3: 'Are ye so foolish? having begun in the Spirit are ye now made perfect by the flesh?'

The sermon deals with the necessity of the work of God's Spirit to make us genuine Christians and then to keep us living as his children. I thought about this a lot over the next few days, and it helped me to turn my dependence away from myself and other Christians to God himself. I was concerned for the salvation of our children, most particularly at that time our older boys, and the sermon reminded me that spiritual regeneration was the work of the Holy Spirit. This realisation gave me a good degree of peace in trusting God to bring them to faith in his time. I regretted our distance from other like-minded Christians and was feeling a sense of bereavement from the loss of my friends at Limden and Burwash. My meditation on the text and sermon enabled me to see that it was God himself I needed most, and he was always with me, only a prayer away. Also as I analysed other feelings, I realised I was jealous of all the people Eli was spending more and more time with in the course of his increasing preaching ministry. Once again, God helped me to see the privilege of spiritual work and that my part at the moment was to keep things running at home to enable Eli to spend time away.

The printed sermons by C. H. Spurgeon were soon being delivered by the postman every Thursday morning and became a solid source of spiritual food for both Eli and me at that stage in our lives. Sometimes when Eli was away, I used them in our family prayer times, reading extracts to the children and servants as I considered appropriate to the scripture passage we had read.

Later Eli became more cautious in recommending these sermons. His denomination began to criticise Spurgeon's clear open offer of the gospel, and the accusation was made that this young preacher was straying from true Calvinistic theology. I must say that for myself, I was always much blessed by what I read and looked forward to receiving these sermons each week.

One little town that Eli visited a lot during our earlier years in Perching was Henfield. There was a small group of believers there who were dissatisfied with the Anglican Church in the small town, and Eli offered to come regularly on a week evening to preach for them. They met in the home of one of the group, and Eli would go across to Henfield during the afternoon and have tea with one or other of the families to encourage them and give some pastoral guidance and then stay and lead a service.[44] One day Ruth asked me whether I thought her dad would mind her going with him.

'I'm sure he would be delighted,' I said. 'It will be good for you too,' I added. 'You'll meet new people and probably see your father in a different light.'

I was very pleased that Ruth wanted to go with her father, but at the same time, part of me was quite envious. I would have loved to have been able to share more in Eli's preaching ministry but knew that our circumstances made this impossible. In fact, although it was very rarely voiced, I knew that without my presence at home with the family and farm, it would have been impossible for Eli to spend the time he did in travelling around preaching.

One thing that did disturb me somewhat as I thought about Ruth accompanying Eli was the fact that he was mostly very late home. He encouraged his congregation to talk with him after he had preached,

---

[44] Ralph Chambers, 'Henfield', op. cit., vol. 2, 41.

and I had heard indirectly how many were finding his advice and sympathy so helpful.

I suggested that Ruth should ask her father herself about going with him to Henfield as I wanted it to come across to him as her own idea. Eli was very pleased with Ruth's request, and when we later talked about it together, he expressed the same hope that I had had, namely that it indicated a genuine concern in Ruth for spiritual things and the needs of her soul.

My concern about the late return was solved when Eli discovered that there was a post coach running between Henfield and Brighton each evening which came via Edburton.

'It will mean that Ruth would need to leave the meeting promptly in order the catch it,' I warned Eli. 'Which will also mean that you will have to restrict the length of your sermon!'

'My dear,' answered Eli, 'when I'm in full flow, I'm not going to be stopped by the departure of a post coach!'

In the event, I heard that Eli did keep a watch on the time as the meeting progressed and, to the amusement of his congregation, would interrupt his remarks at the appropriate moment and say, 'Right, girl, it's time you were leaving to catch your coach home!'[45]

Eli always had a soft spot for his eldest daughter, and I'm sure it was these regular times out together which gave them this special relationship.

---

[45] John Richard Thomas, 'Oral history', op. cit.

Chapter 7
Sheep Washing and Shearing

After the lambing season in early spring, the next busy time in the sheep farmer's year is May to June. This is when the animals are sheared. However, the first stage in harvesting the sheep's wool is to wash it thoroughly. It's surprising how much dust and grit accumulate in a sheep's woolly coat, and to bring in the most money for its fleece and also to avoid quick blunting of the cutting shears, as much of this grit as possible needs to be removed.

The village of Fulking has a natural spring. Fresh clear water bubbles out of the side of the hill, and over the years, the resulting stream has cut its way through rising ground to form a bank on either side. This has provided an ideal location for a natural sheep dip. When the time comes to give the animals their annual bath, the stream is easily dammed at the appropriate point to cause the water to build up within the two banks to give an approximately three-foot-deep pool. Pens are then constructed on both sides of the raised stream, the animals herded into one of these, and thrown one by one into the water. Two or three men stand in the stream up to their waists in the water and ensure the sheep are well washed before being pushed up the bank and out of the stream into the pen on the far side.[46]

---

[46] Nathaniel P. Blaker, 'Sheep washing', op. cit.

Although summer sunshine is usually providing a reasonable air temperature by the time we need to dip the sheep, the water bubbling straight out of the hillside is still extremely cold. To stand for several hours up to their waists in icy cold water is not particularly healthy for the men involved, and when the work is finished, they were often hardly able to stagger down the lane to the Shepherd and Dog through stiffness and cold. I'm told that in the earlier 1800s, the parish of Fulking, of which Perching is part, boasted 2,600 sheep and 258 humans. Although there are now slightly fewer sheep, it is nevertheless several day's work to dip them all, and prolonged exposure to this icy water by the men involved has shown to bring on early rheumatism. After we had been in Perching two or three years, a method was found to protect the men somewhat. Waterproof barrels were somehow anchored into the bottom of the stream at appropriate intervals, and the men could then stand in these and still manhandle the sheep as necessary. I'm pretty certain it was Eli who came up with this idea just as it was he who later financed the fixture of a text of scripture at the village fountain:

'He sendeth springs into the valley which run among the hills
  Oh that men would praise the Lord for his goodness.'

When we first came to Perching, there was very little traffic along the road running between the villages, just a few carts a day. This made the sheep washing easier as the stream ran alongside the road, and the sheep pen into which the washed animals scrambled, being pushed from behind by the men in the stream, included the road itself. If and when a cart approached, it had to wait at the constructed barrier for a suitable moment until it could conveniently be let through. This has very rarely proved a problem, and the drivers are usually more than happy to watch the procedure for a while from the vantage point of their carts, throwing the occasional derogatory comment or cheering a particularly cheeky sheep.

Soon after the sheep washing came the shearing. As with most farmers, Eli was content to let this work be carried out by a gang of experts. These were local Sussex men trained and experienced in sheep shearing who came together each year under the command of a captain and his lieutenant. As with many aspects of country life, there are certain traditions linked with shearing. Although this was all new to us when we first took over Perching Manor Farm, we soon learnt the procedure as it had developed over many years and were glad to cooperate in the way that was expected of us.

Before the shearing can begin, the band of merry men meet in the home of the captain to plan their itinerary. This meeting is referred to as the White Ram, and at the end of it, the captain, or no doubt his wife, provides the supper.

The gang which arrived on the appointed day to us was made up of about a dozen men, the captain and his lieutenant who were easily distinguishable as they wore special hats bearing gold and silver braid, and a tar boy. The farmer they were working for was always referred to as master, so this was Eli's privileged title. We were expected to lay on plenty of mild beer to satisfy the men's thirst during their day's work, to give a substantial meal at midday, and more food and drink at the end of the day.

Sheep shearing at Perching Manor Farm
See page 357; *Anthony R. Brooks (2008) The Changing Times of Fulking & Edburton: 1900 to 2007. Chichester: RPM Print & Design.*

It was interesting to watch how things were done. After he had completed shearing a sheep and before releasing it, the shearer would inspect the animal carefully, and if he had nicked the skin at all, he would shout out, 'Tar boy!' and the answer would be heard 'Coming, sir'. This young lad, whose job it was to move around amongst the men with a tin of tar in his hand, would then run up and dipping his finger in the tar would smear some over any abrasion in the sheep's skin. This was an important job as the tar prevented any worries from flies or infection in the wound. When I saw the state of the tar boy at the end of the day, with smears of black tar all over his clothes and often on his face as well as his hands, I was very thankful none of our boys ever had this job. However, I understand it was much coveted amongst the boys of the village!

It was expected that each man would shear at least twenty sheep in a day, and when the day's work was over, the men would spent the evening singing, drinking, and smoking their long clay pipes.[47]

When all the farms had been dealt with and the shearing finished for the season, the gang would meet in the Shepherd and Dog and their captain would share out the money earned and make arrangements for the following year. This gathering was referred to as the Black Ram, and I understand it was a very merry time.[48]

I was intrigued to watch the sheep being sheared. Their coats seemed to come off so easily, and then they appeared so naked as they ran off, having been dabbed with tar if necessary.

I remember saying to Eli the first year of our sheep farming experience at Perching that I was amazed how quietly the sheep accepted what they were going through. Pigs would have been quite different. They squeal loudly at the slightest provocation. It reminded me of the prophetic

---

[47] Nathaniel P. Blaker, 'Sheep shearing', op. cit.
[48] See appendix 4—A traditional Sussex sheep shearing song.

passage about Jesus in the book of Isaiah[49] that as a sheep before its shearer is dumb, so he opened not his mouth. I had felt so humbled to think that the Son of God had come willingly to die as an atonement for my sins. He had shown no resistance as he was mocked, tortured, and nailed to a cross.

'You know, Seli,' said Eli, 'I feel I need to use this opportunity to speak to the shearing gang about Jesus. In the evenings, they are eating and drinking at our expense on our land, and although it's unusual, they can hardly object if I give them an appreciative word of thanks and conclude with a few spiritual thoughts directing them to the Good Shepherd who laid down his life for his sheep.'

'Much like you did for our hop pickers,' I said. 'We must do that next year and pray hard that God will speak to their hearts.'

So in the following years, this is exactly what Eli did. We found that most of the men had a great respect for religion but were not used to it being mixed with their everyday life. It was normally confined to church and not talked about otherwise. They seemed quite pleased, however, to listen to what Eli had to say. It was well known that he was a nonconformist preacher, and since he was well respected as a fair and capable employer and an enterprising farmer, he had their respect.

---

[49] Isaiah 53:6.

Chapter 8

Marriages

In the early 1860s Richard introduced us to a young lady he was walking out with. I'm not sure how they first met, but we first became aware that he must have a rather special girlfriend when at every opportunity, he would saddle his favourite horse and disappear in the direction of Poynings and Ditchling. By this time, Richard was taking a good bit of responsibility for running the farm and managing the farmworkers as Eli was spending an increasing amount of time travelling around the villages preaching. This of course meant that Richard's free time was limited; however, he usually managed to get away on a Saturday or Sunday afternoon.

One afternoon, he returned earlier than usual. We heard his horse on the cobblestones in the yard, and then Ruth called out, 'Mum, Richard's got someone with him! There are two horses ridden into the yard.'

After a few minutes Richard pushed open the door from the yard, which opened directly into the kitchen, and ushered in a well-dressed young lady. Her entrance made a good impression. She was dressed for riding but had taken off her riding helmet, and her long fair hair was neatly tied into plaits around the back of her head and framed a very pleasant cheerful face. She displayed confidence, interest, and friendliness, and her eyes sparkled as she looked to Richard to be introduced.

'This is Elizabeth,' stammered Richard, 'Elizabeth Payne Heaver. She's a school mistress, and her father farms Chapel Farm in East Chiltington.'

'You are very welcome, Elizabeth,' I said and proceeded to introduce Ruth, Naomi, and Orpha, who were with me in the kitchen.

Elizabeth showed great interest in our manor house and was eager to have a look around during which time Richard revealed increasing impatience as he obviously wanted to show her around the farm.

'We also have a fine old house,' she said. 'Chapel Farm House dates back to the first half of the sixteenth century. It was earlier a far larger house than we have today and belonged to the Chaloner family. Even though we are just farmers, there's something rather special about living in a house with history.'

All this gave me quite an affinity with Elizabeth, and I was interested to learn that she was the eldest child of William and Elizabeth Heaver and was born the same year as Richard, 1838.

Elizabeth's relationship with our Richard developed, and both Eli and I were pleased with the match. They married in the spring of 1863 in the fine old church in East Chiltingdon. At that time, I was nursing baby Naphthali, our fourteenth and final child, who had been born on 20 December 1862. Eli drove me and the younger children the thirteen miles to East Chiltingdon in the pony and trap, and we were all well entertained after the wedding by Elizabeth's parents at Chapel Farm.

Richard and Elizabeth lived with us for a few months, and then in what seemed a miracle, Eli was able to get them a neighbouring farm at Edburton. Although Eli missed having Richard working with him, it was clearly better for Richard to be his own master and to make and learn from his own mistakes without his father breathing down his neck!

Unfortunately, John's love life ran less smoothly, and I maintain that the main reason for this is the fact he wasn't living at home.

One Sunday, sometime before Richard and Elizabeth were married, John was home for the weekend, and as we were all eating together around our large kitchen table, he informed us he had a girlfriend. As you might imagine, this created a lot of interest. John wouldn't say much about her, merely that her name was Mary Ann and that she was working and living in the same household as himself. Eli was away preaching as he often was at weekends, and I felt very much the responsibility of reacting wisely to John's news.

I was greatly relieved when, after we had all left the table and the girls were clearing away the dishes and washing up, John followed me into the garden where I had gone to shake the crumbs off the tablecloth for the birds and asked me what I thought. I had gathered from the fact that John had wanted to announce this friendship to the family that it was serious, and this helped me to formulate my thoughts.

'I'm very pleased for you, John,' I said. 'Tell me about Mary Ann.'

'She's wonderful, Mum,' said John. 'She's a serious girl, not very tall, with darkish hair and lovely brown eyes which seem to sparkle when we chat. We really get on well together, but the problem is we have to see each other secretly. Mary Ann is the maid in the same household as I'm living, and when Mrs Port thought we were getting a bit too friendly, she spoke to her husband, my boss, about it, and he warned me that they wouldn't allow a relationship developing in their house.'

'I was afraid that would happen when you said she worked in the same house,' I responded. 'Are you and Mary Ann so important to each other that you are prepared for the risk of one or both of you losing your job because of your friendship? How do you manage to see each other now then?'

John was silent for a bit, then he said, 'I'd better tell you, Mum, but I'm not sure how I'm going to tell Dad. The only way we can see each other is for me to creep into her bedroom at nights, and yes, Mary Ann thinks there's a baby on the way.'

'Oh, John!' I said. 'That's serious. What do you think you are going to do? How old is Mary Ann?'

'I want to marry her, Mum, and she's just one year younger than me. I'm now twenty-two, and Mary Ann has just had her twenty-first birthday.'

'Well, that's something to be thankful for,' I said. 'At least you are both adults even if you aren't very morally responsible.'

'We've talked and talked about it,' added John, 'and Mary Ann daren't tell her mother until we have some definite plan. What I was wondering was whether we couldn't both come back here and I could help on the farm for a bit until the baby is born, and we can then make a life of our own together.'

'We'll obviously have to talk to your father about it,' I said, 'and it's probably best if I tell him the situation first. He's not going to be too happy with you!'

John had to leave to get back to Brighton before Eli was home, and anyway, I was sure it would be best for me to tell him about the situation that had developed.

Eli was even more angry than I had anticipated. I think in regard to the children, he always had in his mind the example of his namesake, Eli the priest in the Old Testament. The Bible shows us that the biblical Eli had been a very godly man and a good conscientious priest, but his sons had brought disgrace on the priesthood through their sinful behaviour, and God had laid the responsibility for this on Eli's weakness in not restraining them.

Eli spoke of thrashing John and then, rather contradictorily, said he never wanted to see him again and certainly never wanted to see this Mary Ann girl with whom he had sinned.

I had thankfully had more time to think the situation through and now could quietly share with Eli my thoughts.

'Eli,' I said, 'John is now an adult. We have brought him up well, and he is essentially a kind and considerate young man. I think that if John had been living in a more open situation, this wouldn't have happened. He and Mary Ann were forced to see each other in the secret of her bedroom because they saw no other way. Their behaviour was wrong both before God and the society in which we live, but they are two young, warm-blooded human beings in love. I once heard my father say that if the temptation and the opportunity come together, it takes God's special grace and strength to resist it.'

'There's another thing, Eli,' I added. 'Although it seems a long time ago, remember that Richard was born less than seven months after our marriage!'

Eli was quiet for several minutes and then put his arms round me and kissed me.

'Thank you, Seli dear,' he said. 'What a blessing you are to me, and how wise God was in giving us men female helpmeets to complement our wilder natures!'

Then he added, 'But, Seli, what are we going to do? Have you thought that through too?'

I told him John's wish to get married as quickly as possible and then his suggestion that he could help on the farm and they could both live with us until the baby was born.

'And what do you think about that yourself, Seli?' he asked.

'What do you think, Eli?' I answered.

Eli was quiet for a moment or two and then commented, 'I'm not so sure it's a good idea. I know we have in mind for Richard and Elizabeth to live here until we can find a farm for them and I know we have a big house, but in principle, God's way is for a man to leave his father and mother and cleave to his wife. Mary Ann might not feel comfortable being here with us, and the two need the opportunity to spend time together, a thing which has been denied them up to now. Perhaps we could help them rent a small house or apartment in Brighton from where, if his boss allows it, John could continue with his work and training as a butcher.'

I was very positive about Eli's suggestion, and we agreed we would talk to John about it at the earliest opportunity. In fact, because it wasn't so easy for John to get away, Eli decided he would ride into Brighton the next evening and discuss his offer with John.

When Eli got to Brighton, he was able to take John to a local inn and talk about the situation. Although John was at first hesitant to say much, once he realised as his parents we were not going to condemn him but rather help, it was obviously a great relief to him, and he poured out his heart to his father. The situation was more urgent than John had felt able to tell me the day before.

As far as she could estimate, Mary Ann was at least seven months pregnant, and Mrs Port had that very day realised that she was with child as this could no longer be hidden. Mary Ann had refused to say who the father was, and Mrs Port had then told her she no longer had a job and should return home to her family. The problem was Mary Ann no longer had a home as her father had died and the family scattered. Without either a family home or a husband to care for her, there was really little choice for Mary Ann but to go voluntarily into a workhouse to have the baby, and this was far from ideal.

Eli put his suggestion to John that he was willing to rent a small house for them in Brighton. He told John bluntly that he should talk to his boss and confess he was the father of Mary Ann's baby. Then to say they intended to get married as soon as possible and that although his parents were shocked at what had happened, they were prepared to support them in the situation by finding them suitable accommodation in the area. John should apologise for abusing the privilege of being part of the Port household and to express the hope he would be allowed to continue with his job.

'Act humbly, John,' Eli said. 'You have no rights in this situation. You need the forgiveness of God and the forgiveness and understanding of Elisha Port and his wife.'

The next day John spoke with his boss, and Mr Port's immediate reaction was to fire him. Later, however, because he had found John a very satisfactory worker, he relented and allowed John to stay on. We were all very relieved at this.

'That's more than John deserves,' Eli said, 'but God is merciful, and he can move the hearts of all men.'

It was clear that there was no time for a wedding before the baby arrived, but John and Mary Ann assured us that they were determined to put this matter right at the earliest opportunity.

Mary Ann came to us for a couple of weeks until Eli could find them an apartment close to John's work, and they were then able to be there together in Brighton for the birth of their baby.

We wanted to get to know Mary Ann, and her stay with us gave this opportunity. Although at first she was rather shy, I was able to get quite close to her.

She was a Hampshire girl born in the village of Lyndhurst in the New Forest where her father had been a farm labourer. Sadly, her family home had broken up before she was in her teens, through the death of her father, and I quite think this had made her a very insecure young lady. Having found love with John and acceptance with our family was very precious to her.

Emily was born in the summer of 1862 and, being born out of wedlock, was christened Emily Page Blake.

I had quite expected the couple to get married soon after this, but time slipped by and it wasn't until Mary Ann found herself pregnant a second time that they settled on a date for a wedding. They were married in the summer of 1863, and their second daughter, Ruth, was born that same autumn.

So though the circumstances were quite different, we had two family weddings in 1863, Richard's in the spring and John's in the summer, and we welcomed two new daughters-in-law into the Page family.

I must say it concerned me a lot that John and Mary Ann were living together as man and wife whilst unmarried. I found it very difficult to visit them or to look them in the eyes when they visited us. I just felt they were disgracing the family and was fearful that God would punish them for living in sin.

I asked Eli about it, and his thoughts helped me a lot.

'Seli,' Eli said, 'John and Mary Ann's situation has forced me to think through a number of issues. Firstly, what does God's Word tell us about marriage? Essentially, it tells us that a man should leave his father and mother and cling to his wife and the two should become one flesh.[50]

---

[50] Genesis 2:24; Matthew 19:4–6.

'God's Word lays down no specific form or ceremony for marriage. The church and society has done that. I believe a public service in which the two partners commit themselves together by vows is right and proper, but remember it's not something laid down by God in his Word. In the case of Isaac, we read simply that he took Rebecca into his tent and she became his wife.[51] This would seem to indicate that in God's eyes, it's a man and woman coming together in the sexual act which makes them one flesh and that this is the essence of marriage. Remember too God's warning through Paul to the Corinthians, that they were to avoid casual sex because a sexual relationship with a prostitute makes them one flesh with that prostitute.[52] As believers, God tells us we are indwelt by the Holy Spirit, so we need to keep ourselves holy. The sin of adultery is condemned in one of the ten commands God's Word gives us for our own happiness and well-being.'

'So how does that apply to John?' I asked.

'John and Mary Ann need to be married in a formal and legal way. There's no question about that,' said Eli. 'But I've come to believe that in God's eyes, they are already married. I've told John this and that because of his sexual relationship with Mary Ann, he needs to consider his union with her as binding as if they had had a formal ceremony. For the sake of society, they need to have a wedding ceremony as soon as possible, but in God's eyes, they are already one flesh.'

'Oh, Eli,' I said, 'that helps me so much. I love them both, but up to now, I haven't been able to think of Mary Ann as really one of the family. Now I can. I shall keep praying for them and long that they will both really experience God's love and grace and will also very quickly be able to legalise their marriage.'

While all this was happening, my own mother was needing more and more care, and she was eventually called to her heavenly home in the late autumn of 1862.

---

[51] Genesis 24:67.
[52] 1 Corinthians 6:15–16.

Chapter 9

Eli as Itinerant Preacher

Looking back over the years, it's remarkable to me that Eli's vision of enlarging his farming activities in order to give himself more time for his preaching ministry actually came to fruition. I'm the first to acknowledge that Eli's thoughts must have been God-inspired and that in seeking to honour his divine Master, God's blessing was upon us.

By the mid 1860s at Perching Farm, Edburton, we had nearly 500 acres of land, a very adequate-sized home for our large family, and more than twenty farmworkers. Ruth, under her father's direction, was managing the accounts, and I had eight further daughters who, in addition to helping me run the home, could also help look after the dairy, the hens, and our large kitchen garden. Although I felt the responsibility for everything in Eli's absence, I had Richard and his very capable wife nearby to turn to in an emergency. God is good and so worthy of our humble faith, trust, and committed service.

Although now preaching most Sundays and several weekday evenings as well, Eli was still overseeing the farm. He had men who managed the everyday running of things, but he still held the reins firmly in his own hands. He planned each week's activities and ensured his foremen knew what was required of them. He rode regularly around the farm to keep the men on their toes and was happy to roll up his sleeves and assist when the pressure was on. He negotiated prices for the purchase and sale of livestock and the purchase of seed and sale of produce. He visited the markets regularly and kept himself informed of the views and activities of other local farmers and was not averse to providing a round of beers to our villagers in the Shepherd and Dog. He used to tell me that this grass-roots contact with the world around him kept his preaching practical and relevant.

Eli had no time for theological theorising. I remember one evening, when he returned from preaching at a certain chapel, he told me he had been challenged after the sermon by a young man who had resented his reference to Jesus as the eternal Son of God.

'He tried to lecture me on the subject,' said Eli. 'He maintained that Jesus only became the Son of God at the time of his human birth and that prior to that, he could be called the Word of God but not the Son of God. I was aware that there has recently been a controversy about this theological point, and I guess I need to think about it a bit more. I told the young man I would write to him as I needed just then to encourage other members of the congregation who were waiting to speak to me and not discuss theology with him.'

It was late that evening and I knew Eli was tired, so I didn't want to prolong the discussion then, but I was very interested to know how Eli would reply to the young man and was determined to raise the matter again. However, I couldn't resist one more comment.

'But surely, Eli,' I said, 'it's contrary to all we've ever been taught to say that God didn't have a Son through all eternity. We talk about Father, Son, and Holy Spirit as the triune god who had no beginning and will have no end!'

'Yes, you're right, Seli. I thought about the whole subject on the way home, and it's a good job Jehu knows his way back here through these dark lanes as I wasn't really directing him at all! In itself, it's not a bad thing to think through some of these points of doctrine, however, we need to be very careful if we find our conclusions differ from the traditional theological statements expressed in the historical confessions of faith. Obviously, it's the Holy Scriptures themselves which are the ultimate truth and must be the basis of our faith, not the confessions of faith formulated by mere men, however godly they may have been. When I answer this young man, I need to quote the scriptures not the Westminster Confession.'

'Have you any scriptures in mind?' I asked.

'Yes,' answered Eli, 'I remember now reading an article by J. C. Philpot on this subject in the *Gospel Standard*, and although I read it quite fleetingly, I do remember he quoted several scriptures in support of the traditional view of the Trinity. One was the well-known verse John 3:16: "God so loved the world that He gave his only begotten Son." He then rightly raised the question, How could God give us his Son if he wasn't his Son until he was conceived by the Virgin Mary? The other thought is that Jesus more often referred to himself as the Son of man than the Son of God. He had always been the Son of God, but only through his incarnation did he become the Son of man.'

I thanked Eli for sharing his thoughts with me. I often felt that the preaching side of his life was something I couldn't share in, so it pleased me a lot when he talked to me like this.

Eli was to have many more theological issues to think through as his preaching took over more and more of his life. I was generally aware when he had spiritual things on his mind, and I think it helped him to talk to me about them. I'll be telling you about some of them later.

In the autumn of 1865, there was a major development for Eli in his role as an independent Christian minister.

Up to that point, Eli had been an itinerant preacher, that is, he had merely responded to invitations to preach, and these had come from village chapels and groups of believers all over Sussex. There were many village chapels without a regular minister, and these depended on men like Eli to lead their Sunday services and preach God's Word to them. Eli's favourite stallion, Jehu, had plenty of exercise carrying his master mile after mile each week around the Sussex lanes and villages as his rider in turn was seeking to be obedient to his heavenly Master. Knowing the sort of person Eli was, I'm sure he would sometimes urge Jehu home by shortcuts across fields by jumping hedges and ditches, and it was common knowledge that in going to Brighton, he would often ride straight up Perching Hill across the Downs to the Devil's Dyke and down the other side.

Then in 1865 this changed. I remember well the evening when my husband said to me, 'Seli, my darling, the friends in Mayfield want me to be their pastor.'

'Mayfield!' I gasped. 'That must be thirty miles away. How could we stay here and you be pastor at Mayfield?'

'I'm still praying and thinking about it,' answered Eli, 'but it wouldn't be impossible to do. I would have to leave here Saturday afternoon at the latest and then return Monday, which is not a lot different from what I have to do some weekends now.'

'But wouldn't being pastor at Mayfield involve more than just preaching twice on a Sunday?' I asked.

'I would have to try to fit in pastoral visits and any necessary meetings either on a Saturday or a Monday, which might mean sometimes leaving here on a Friday or perhaps occasionally returning on a Tuesday,' explained Eli. 'I can't see that it would be possible to leave the farm here and move to Mayfield. We've the children and grandchildren to think about. We are essentially a farming family, and they are all very much involved in the work here. I shall explain this to the friends at Mayfield, and they would have to accept me on this basis.'

'What's happening in Mayfield now?' I asked. 'I thought the chapel building had been closed.'

'It's all been very complicated,' said Eli frowning. 'You may remember old Jack Sawyer, who helped us with the charcoal burning at Limden, telling us about Mr Burch. Well, Mr Burch had a good Christian friend, a certain Mr Stone, who helped finance his ministry, and he built a small chapel for the group of believers in Mayfield who were coming together under Mr Burch's preaching. As is often the case, however, the ownership of a chapel building can be a problem. The nonconformist believers in Mayfield had no official organisation, and so there was no one to own the building. It was officially owned by Mr Stone, and in his will, he stipulated that it was to be used by the Mayfield believers as long as Mr Burch needed it. Well, Mr Burch died a few years ago, and the descendant of the original Mr Stone to whom the chapel then belonged wasn't particularly sympathetic to our Christian friends and demanded the key to the building and closed it. This meant that the believers then had no building to meet in.'

'I know you've been going regularly to preach and encourage them,' I said with interest. 'Where have they been meeting then?'

'Mostly in the farm cottage of one of the group,' answered Eli. 'They've stayed together and have actually grown in numbers and have been praying for a suitable building. Well, God has wonderfully heard their prayers. The owner of the chapel himself died some months ago, and his executors decided to offer the building for sale. This took place at an auction in Tunbridge Wells at the end of June this year. Unknown to our Mayfield friends, God put it in the heart of a sympathetic Christian believer, a certain Mr Miles, to buy the building. He was able to purchase it for £85 and has now given it back to the group with the advice that they step out in faith and call a minister to lead them.'[53]

'Isn't God wonderful?' I exclaimed. 'So that's where you come into the picture.'

'Yes,' said Eli smiling. 'They had a meeting and unanimously agreed they should invite me to be their pastor. It will be a real challenge, but I can't help feeling it's from God and should now be my life's work. Things are running well here, and under your watchful eye and the work of our capable employees, it doesn't need a lot of practical help from me. I believe I could be away an extra night or two each week without losing my grip on the business.'

'Is old Jack Sawyer still alive?' I asked. 'It must be twenty years ago or more since he helped us at Limden Farm.'

'No, old Jack is long gone,' said Eli, 'but I tell you who is there, and that's George and Sarah Fuller, from the Burwash fellowship. Sarah

---

[53] Ralph Chambers, 'Mayfield', op. cit., vol. 2, 63.

never stops reminding me how you befriended her and advised them to foster children when they couldn't have any of their own.'

'Oh, bless her,' I said smiling. 'It really seemed to help both Sarah personally and also her marriage relationship to George to have those little children to look after.'

As we settled down to sleep, I couldn't get my mind off all Eli had said. I found the news about Mayfield worrying. I was already feeling that I had the brunt of the responsibility of bringing up the children. Little Nap was not yet three, Leah was only five, and Dorcas just eight. Also the older children found me a good sounding board for airing their views and grievances. Eli was away a lot already, and I could see that this commitment at Mayfield would keep him away from Perching even more.

Chapter 10

More Changes

Family life doesn't stand still! As I experienced the boys finding themselves girlfriends and getting married, I began to look at our girls and wonder how long it would be before young men would begin to arrive on the scene requesting to walk out with Ruth, Orpha, and Naomi. What sort of young men would they be? And also, thinking seriously, how would Eli cope with this? As it worked out, all three were married within a year of each other.

Eli had a very special relationship with Ruth. She handled the farm accounts efficiently, understood the business side of farming, and I know Eli could also talk to her about spiritual things. I know he felt she would make a very valuable wife to someone, and through something he once said, I think he hoped she would marry a minister or pastor.

Because Ruth accompanied Eli on some of his preaching engagements, she had the opportunity to meet a range of young men, and I know she turned down several dating requests.

Not infrequently, farm machinery needed attention, and through his preaching, Eli knew a blacksmith in the village of Albourne, which was about five miles north of us, to whom he sometimes gave business. Mostly the father, Josias, would come to the farm to deal with things, occasionally taking parts back to his workshop to be welded or remade, but one day the younger son of the family came in his father's place. Our farm foreman dealt with him first and then sent him to the house to speak to Ruth about the account. Obviously something clicked between them because soon after this I noticed when horses needed new shoes, instead of sending one of her sisters to the blacksmith, Ruth took the horses herself. I also realised she was using the blacksmith at Albourne which wasn't actually the closest.

One evening I said to Eli, 'How would you feel about having a blacksmith for a son-in-law?'

'I suppose it's that Holder lad,' Eli answered. 'He's recently been coming along to my Henfield meetings, and although they've been very discreet about it, I know he and Ruth have been chatting a little before the service begins.'

A few weeks later, Ruth announced to the family that she was walking out with Dan Holder from Albourne. She would occasionally bring him home to tea, and one evening Dan asked Eli whether he could talk to him. Eli told me later that he was quite impressed with Dan. He had asked to marry Ruth and had explained that his father, Josias, was selling up in Albourne and was negotiating to buy a blacksmith business in the village of Patcham where he would make Dan his legal partner. His father was now coming up to sixty and planned to retire shortly once the new business was up and running. Dan and Ruth would then have the business themselves.

'Hasn't Dan got an older brother?' I questioned. 'Where does he fit into this?'

'Yes,' Eli answered. 'Benjamin is about five years older than Dan but is the son of Josias's first wife, Philadelphia, who died in 1841. Dan said Benjamin had learnt the wheelwright side of the business, and when he got married a few years ago, Josias set him up with his own wheelwright shop in the village of Keymer.'

'That all sounds very satisfactory then,' I said smiling.

'Josias is a good man and a devout Christian believer, and I have a great respect for him,' said Eli. 'I told Dan he had my permission to marry Ruth if she is in agreement. Now that Dan has formally asked for her hand in marriage, I suggest it would be good if you could find an opportunity to talk to Ruth intimately, just to be sure she is happy about it and realises what's she's doing.'

Chapter 11

Ruth's Wedding

It was Easter Monday 1868. Over the weekend, we had remembered firstly on Good Friday our Lord's death and then on Easter morning his glorious resurrection. Each Easter is important to me as these historical events behind our Easter celebrations are the very core of our faith. In our Saviour's death, we recognise and accept in humble trust a holy god's gracious provision for the full forgiveness of all our sins, and he has done this in a way which not only wonderfully displays his love but at the same time satisfies his holy justice. Then through our Saviour's return to life in his new resurrection body, we see the guarantee of our own resurrection into eternal life and have a living hope beyond our few years here on earth.

Coming as it does in springtime, Easter speaks of new life in every sense, and on this particular Easter Monday, it brought a new beginning for Ruth's earthly life. It was her wedding day to Dan Holder.

I remember the day well. When we first woke, there was a light mist hanging over the fields, but soon the rays of the rising sun melted this away, and we knew it was going to be a lovely spring day.

We had borrowed a carriage with two horses for the day, and the family adorned it with the fresh green of sprouting hazel twigs and bunches of yellow primroses from the hedgerows. We had appointed two of our workmen as chauffeurs, and Eli together with Ruth in her white bridal gown and Orpha and Naomi in light yellow dresses rode into Brighton ahead of the rest of the family. I and the younger children followed next in our own trap which was also adorned with spring growth. The horses too were decorated with sprigs of spring flowers. Richard and Elizabeth followed in their own pony and trap with our grandchildren, William and Mercy, Elizabeth herself being heavy with her third expected child. The procession attracted a lot of attention. If Eli had had his way, none of this elaborate procedure would have happened, but I was thankful that Ruth's sisters had initiative and imagination.

The wedding took place at the Tabernacle, West Street, Brighton, and Pastor William Harbour took the service.

It was an emotional occasion for all of us and, strangely enough, for Eli in particular. It was his duty to give Ruth away to her new husband, and this he found very difficult. Ruth, as our eldest daughter, was very special to us. She had been such an essential part of Perching Manor Farm and so intimately and spiritually close to Eli that, as he later confided to me, to give her up was almost more than he could bear. The thought suddenly came to him that God had given up his Son in love for him, Eli Page, and in a fresh way, he had a small inkling of the sacrifice this must been for our heavenly Father. Struggling with this emotion, he declined to walk up the aisle with Ruth but gave her to Orpha and Naomi to deliver to Dan, her husband to be, and joined them at the front of the chapel just in time to formally respond to William Harbour's question, 'Who giveth this women to this man?' with the answer 'I do!'

Charles Mitchell was Dan's best man, whom, as you will hear, we got to know quite well in the next few months and years.

After the service, all the Page family and the Holder family and a good number of invited friends returned to Perching for a celebratory meal. The procession of carriages, traps, horses, and ponies taking the gentler route, up the London Road out of Brighton, through Preston, and then Patcham, where Ruth and Dan would be living, on through

Pyecombe and Poynings and thus through Fulking and home, was a sight to behold and created quite a stir.

A few of our friends on horses and ponies took the shorter but steeper track across the top of the Devil's Dyke and were waiting for us when we arrived.

God favoured us with warm spring weather and all felt comfortable eating outside on the long trestle tables we had set up for the occasion. Dan's parents had been very insistent that they play their part in the arrangements, so we had suggested that they should bring the tables and benches and we as the farmers would provide the food. A fatted pig had been killed a few days earlier, and we had roasted it on a spit in readiness for carving. Vegetables had already been prepared, and while our guests chatted and quenched their thirst after the journey, these were cooked on our kitchen stove. The meal went well, and we were so thankful that our family and guests mixed and communicated in a relaxed way. Eli had invited friends he knew well from the different chapels around and several from the congregation in Mayfield.

Of course the day really belonged to Ruth and Dan, and as the time together drew to a close, Eli gave them a blessing and encouragement from the scriptures, and at Ruth's request, we sang a new hymn we had recently learned. It had been written by William Gadsby and gave honour and praise to the Lord Jesus and wonderfully expressed hers and Dan's confidence in him and his grace for the future:

> Immortal honours rest on Jesus' head;
> My God, my portion, and my Living Bread;
> In Him I live, upon Him cast my care;
> He saves from death, destruction, and despair.
> He is my Refuge in each deep distress;
> The Lord my strength and glorious righteousness;
> Through floods and flames He leads me safely on,
> And daily makes His sovereign goodness known.
> My every need He richly will supply;
> Nor will His mercy ever let me die;

> In Him there dwells a treasure all divine,
> And matchless grace has made that treasure mine.
> O that my soul could love and praise Him more,
> His beauties trace, His majesty adore;
> Live near His heart, upon His bosom lean;
> Obey His voice, and all His will esteem.[54]

We then committed them both to God afresh, and our chauffeur for the day drove them back to Patcham to their new home.

As Eli said, once everyone had departed and we had a few minutes to ourselves, 'It's difficult to let Ruth go, but she goes with our blessing, and as far as inner spiritual life is concerned, I'm happier about her and Dan than any other of our children at the moment.'

Arising out of Ruth's wedding came the engagement of our second oldest daughter.

Charles Mitchell, Dan's best man, had met Orpha before that Easter weekend, but the wedding ceremony drew them together and obviously something clicked between them.

Charles was the fourth child of Mary Mitchell, and sadly, she had died at his birth. His father, Henry Mitchell, was a master carpenter with his own business, and thankfully for the children, Henry's mother had been able to come and live with them as housekeeper and substitute mother.[55] Together with his older brother, also named Henry, Charles did an apprenticeship in his father's firm as a carpenter, but his heart wasn't really in this. His home was in the hamlet of Blackstone just outside Woodmancote, and not far from Dan's home village of Albourne, a few miles north of us. Orpha and Charles were soon officially engaged, and when the village store in Fulking became vacant, Eli suggested to the couple that they might do worse than take it over. This rather appealed

---

[54] Gadsby's Hymns, No. 667. The Gospel Standard Publications.
[55] 1851 Census, Charles Mitchell, born 1845, Woodmancote.

to Charles and Orpha, and so the two fathers talked it over together and agreed to help them get started.

With their future fixed, there was no need to delay a wedding, and this was another lovely occasion in the autumn of the same year as Ruth's. Our local Anglican vicar married them in the beautiful old Edburton Church, five minutes' walk up the road, and as you can guess, having them near at hand running our village grocery and draper's store thrilled me greatly.

The third marriage within those twelve months, in the early spring of 1869, was Naomi's, and she married a farmer from West Grinstead, William Rufus Wells. William was the oldest son of a farming family near West Grinstead, he was the same age as Naomi, and soon after their marriage, they were able to take on a 120-acre farm at Slaugham.[56]

---

[56] 1871 Census, William Wells, born 1847, West Grinstead.

Chapter 12

John and Mary Ann

One morning Richard's wife, Elizabeth, called in to see me. She did this fairly frequently, and I was always pleased to have an excuse to sit down and make a pot of tea to share with her. That morning she had little Ada with her, who was then just about two, and we gave her some wooden blocks to play with on the floor while we chatted. I could sense Elizabeth had something on her mind and very soon it came out.

'Mum,' she said in a serious tone, 'Richard is very worried about John and Mary Ann. Yesterday he had business to do in Brighton and called in to see them. John hadn't then arrived back from work, so Richard could chat to Mary Ann alone. He thinks she is very ill. Babies keep on coming, and she is never able to regain her strength properly before she falls pregnant again. I know this is a fairly common problem, but Richard thinks there is something deeper which is affecting her. While he was there, she hardly had the strength to deal with the children, and when he showed sympathy, she burst into tears and sobbed and sobbed. She already has Emily, Ruth, Harry, and Ellen, she lost the last baby, and now she's pregnant again.'

Elizabeth looked at me anxiously. I think she knew her own mother would probably simply comment, 'Well, that's married life, we've all had days like that, and one must simply brace oneself and get on with living!'

I was rather more sympathetic. I had got to know Mary Ann somewhat when she had lived with us for a few weeks after she had lost her position in the Port household, and I had witnessed her sudden mood swings. One day she seemed to have all the strength in the world and was full of enthusiasm about her life, and then shortly afterwards, she appeared illogically negative and could hardly get out of bed.

'Of course another problem is that she's isolated there in Brighton with very few friends and no family of her own to turn to,' I commented.

'Yes, that must be part of it,' answered Elizabeth, obviously relieved that I wasn't simply dismissing the situation.

'Richard feels we should do something to help them,' continued Elizabeth. 'Lying in bed last night, he had an idea. He wonders whether Dad would consider asking John to come and help him run the farm. He's recently lost William Saunders and Briar Cottage is empty. What do you think, Mum?'

'Do you think John would want to do that?' I asked thoughtfully. 'But it's true, if he agreed, it would bring the family closer and enable us to help Mary Ann with the children.'

I must say I was thrilled that Richard and Elizabeth were thinking like this. Richard and John had grown up together and had always been close mates even though they were quite different in temperament. Although Richard has a lot of Eli in him, he also had my more passive nature. John had more of a 'jump and think later' temperament which has tended to get him into trouble. Although I felt it would be good if he could finish his training as a butcher, I could see that if he was prepared to bring his family to Edburton, it could really benefit Mary Ann and the children.

I talked to Eli about the suggestion, explaining that it had come from Richard because of his concern for Mary Ann. In principle he was happy about the idea of having John with us on the farm, particularly as he saw himself being away more and more, but was a little concerned that since farming wasn't John's first choice of career, he wouldn't put his whole mind to it.

'Put the idea to him,' I said. 'Say we are concerned about Mary Ann and the children and think that with William Saunders moving on, for them to come to Edburton could be mutually beneficial to all of us and see what he thinks.'

I was pleased that after some thought, John welcomed his father's offer. He had of course been brought up with farming and spent his teenage years learning from his father, so Eli had no hesitation in appointing him farm foreman. However, as Mary Ann pointed out, their next child was expected within less than two months, and it would be wiser to wait and have the baby in Brighton where medical attention was nearer at hand if necessary. All arrangements were therefore made for the move, and as soon as the baby was born, they moved into Briar Cottage.

Although the birth went well, in the following few weeks, Mary Ann had some severe bouts of depression; however, she seemed to settle down, and the older children obviously enjoyed being with their cousins, William and Mercy. For several weeks, she seemed really happy and sociable, although I sensed sometimes overmuch so. Knowing a little of the pattern of things in her life, this caused me to watch anxiously for any indication of a swing in the opposite direction. I'm sorry to say it came sooner than I had expected.

One morning John put a worried head around my kitchen door, and I could see something was wrong.

'Mum,' he said, 'Mary Ann is having a really bad day, have you got time to call and see her?'

I knew I had to make time, and when I called into Briar Cottage, I was so glad I had. Mary Ann was sitting at the kitchen table in a lifeless manner with a faraway look in her eyes. Emily, who was then seven, was trying to spoon-feed two-year-old Ellen with what looked like porridge, little Harry was screaming on the floor, and I could hear Kate, their new baby, also crying somewhere in the house. I tried to speak to Mary Ann and, getting no response, quickly saw that I needed to take control of the situation. I picked up Harry and sat him on my knee, and he stopped crying at once.

'He hasn't had any breakfast yet,' explained Emily, 'I thought I ought to feed Ellen first.'

'Where's Ruth?' I asked.

'We both usually have lessons at Uncle Richard's house with Miss Andrews,' answered Emily, 'but I thought I ought to stay and help Mummy this morning.'

Once I'd made sure that the older three children had had some nourishment, I rocked little Kate gently in my arms and sent Emily off to her lessons. Then I made a pot of tea for Mary Ann and myself. At first it seemed that poor Mary was beyond even tears. She appeared completely listless and vacant. However, a cup of tea eventually revived her a little, and she began to sob.

'I'm so frightened, Mum,' she wept. 'I don't understand why I feel like this, and I'm afraid I'll do something dreadful to the children. I feel to be swamped with a great wave of depression. I force myself out of bed and try to begin my jobs, but I just can't cope with the thought of the day ahead. The children cry, and in the end, I just don't care anymore. I love it here in the country; sometimes in Brighton it was awful, and I hate towns. I'm so grateful to you and Dad for letting us come here. It's the best home I've had since I was a child in the New Forest. I ought to be happy and on top of the world, but I feel so wretched and miserable. Why is it, Mum?'

Sadly, I didn't know the answer to that question, and I really didn't know what to say to Mary Ann. I knew what it was to have bad mornings, I guess everyone does, but I'd never experienced what Mary Ann was describing. I realised it wasn't just laziness. This was an illness.

I told Mary Ann I would send one or other of my girls round to help her in the mornings until she felt better, and I would find her an herbal drink that might help. I had in mind balm tea, which I had always found helped me when I was feeling a bit down. I also thought about tincture of gentian, which you can buy at some specialised shops. My own mother always recommended this to aid recovery after an illness or after a depressing winter. A few drops taken regularly in hot water is supposed to do a world of good!

We continued to do what we could to help Mary Ann. Her mood swings were drastic, and at times we feared for both her and the children's safety. One day John came in very worried and asked me whether I thought the family would understand if he and Mary Ann let Orpha and Charles look after baby Kate for them. He said his sister had offered to help with Kate if they needed this, and now Mary Ann was sometimes feeling so wretched that she didn't feel able to cope with the baby at all.

I don't think even this made me realise how desperate the situation was, but knowing how much Orpha would love a baby to care for, I agreed it could be a way of helping Mary Ann.

During the next couple of years, Mary Ann seemed to get worse rather than better, and we all took turns in having the children for shorter and longer periods. Then John announced in despair that Mary Ann was again pregnant. The thought of another child drove her into a deeper depression, and after the baby was born, she was so bad that the authorities said she must go into an asylum. We had all feared this might happen, and I doubted whether the family would ever be able to become a unit together again. Sadly, my doubts proved to be the reality. The younger children came to me in Perching Manor, and after a while, John went back to his chosen profession as a butcher working in Western Road, Hove, as an assistant to his brother-in-law John Combridge, Elizabeth's husband, whom she married in 1875.

Eli never quite came to terms with John's situation. He didn't understand depression and at first told John he needed to take a firmer line with Mary Ann. He later realised it wasn't as simple as that although he still tended to blame John for the breakup of his family. To me, John's understanding of his wife's condition was something very positive, and I was proud of him for it, but having said that, I'm not sure we all made right decisions in regard to Mary Ann. I pray for her regularly along with all our children and grandchildren and long to see her out of the asylum.

Chapter 13

Mayfield

Eli accepted the call to be the regular minister and pastor at the independent 'cause' in Mayfield in 1865.

I had often wondered why the chapels in the villages around us were referred to as 'causes', and one day in conversation with Eli when he was using the term, I asked him about it. Eli explained that these congregations of Christian believers had come into existence because the mainstream churches had strayed from the teaching of the Bible. The eighteenth century evangelical awakening had resulted in a good number of new Christians hungry for the Word of God, and when their spiritual needs were not met by the clergy and traditional practises of the Anglican Churches, they formed their own gatherings for fellowship and spiritual food. They soon realised, however, that these new chapels had a greater reason for their existence than purely the needs of their congregations. Their main calling was to be lights in the spiritual darkness of the world around them in maintaining and proclaiming God's truth in its pure biblical form. Of course we all fail in this, but at least that's the grand objective. With this in mind, they began to refer to each other as 'causes of truth', or as time went by, simply 'causes'.

Mayfield is an ancient Sussex town about thirty miles from us in Perching, and as a family, we all soon got used to Eli leaving us on a

Saturday afternoon and returning midday Monday. From my point of view, it is far from an ideal arrangement as neither myself nor any of the family can share in the fellowship of the believers in Mayfield or benefit from Eli's Sunday preaching. I know Eli himself was aware of this, and it concerned him at times. When he was home, he led family devotions each evening, and as often as possible he also had a Bible reading and prayer with those of us available at breakfast. For the main devotional time, Eli would read a passage of scripture, working steadily through one book of the Bible at a time, give a short comment on it to help the children and grandchildren understand what was read, and often apply it in some way to make its meaning relevant to ourselves. He would then pray, bringing praise to God for his love to us in Jesus and beseeching him for his mercy and help in the work of the day. When Eli was away, I led the evening devotions but felt very much my inadequacy in doing this. As I think I mentioned earlier, I would from time to time read a paragraph or two from one of the penny sermons by C. H. Spurgeon, which came in the post each week. I found these extremely helpful, and by selecting paragraphs which I felt to be relevant to the spiritual condition of members of the family and staff, I could preach to them in an indirect way.

However, despite the disadvantages of Eli's involvement at Mayfield, I found in time that it brought a new and interesting dimension to my own life. Because his ministry in Mayfield was so important to him, Eli wanted to share all sorts of things with me, and I found that I soon began to feel part of the fellowship there although I could very rarely be there in person.

The fellowship of believers in Mayfield weren't at that time part of any denomination. It didn't practise baptism in any form or have any formal church membership, and the friends there considered themselves an independent cause. Many of the chapels in Sussex were like this. They were places where the gospel was preached, where the Bible had a central place, and where the need for a personal experience of God's grace was emphasised. Eli was known at that time to be an independent minister, and it was on this basis that he had been invited to be the regular minister at Mayfield.

However, as Eli discovered, and confided in me, there is a tremendous difference between moving around to different congregations each week and the new responsibility he had now taken on of preaching regularly to the same group of people. Even whilst involved in the former, he had realised the need for continuity, hence his willingness to preach to the small group in Henfield most Thursday evenings, a practise he is still continuing as I write.

Eli had the temperament which saw the big picture, and he had less patience with details. He saw the purpose of his preaching to communicate God's grace through proclaiming the Word of God. As he said to me on several occasions, 'Seli, if I didn't believe that the Bible was the Word of God and that it's a sword, a hammer, and a fire as it declares of itself, then I would give up preaching. In the hands of the Holy Spirit, it is all these and can convince men of sin, humble them before God, and bring them to faith in Christ. My calling is to read and explain texts from the Bible, humbly depending on God to use his own Word as the seed of faith and as light to lighten our lives.'

Now, however, as the minister of Mayfield, he was being challenged to think through theological issues in a little more detail.

One of the first of these theological challenges arose through a question from one of his congregation, 'Pastor, are we antinomians?'

'Obviously,' he told me with a grin on, 'one of this person's friends had accused me of being one of these theological creatures!'

'Am I an antinomian, Seli?'

'I know you're anti a lot of things, Eli,' I answered, 'but I am not so sure I know what an antinomian is.'

'The term really means someone who is against law, but I've decided that to use the term as a Christian is very misleading. I've had to think about it somewhat,' said Eli, 'and I don't really know how to answer that question.

'I think one reason the subject has arisen is that William Huntington used to proclaim boldly that as New Testament believers we need not have a conscience about keeping God's law. He made a big thing of this, and I guess many people hearing him understood him to mean Christians can do what they like. I can't believe he meant this at all but was trying to explain, perhaps rather clumsily, the passages in Romans and Galatians where the apostle Paul writes, "We are not under law but under grace." Anyway the reaction of most orthodox ministers to William Huntington was to condemn him as a heretic, an antinomian heretic.

'Now as I see it,' Eli continued, 'every truly born-again believer knows he's not saved by keeping God's law. It's impossible to gain salvation that way. Our salvation is God's free gift through Jesus Christ, who kept the law on our behalf and died to forgive our transgression of it. The question really is, as believing Christians, saved through faith in Christ, are we duty-bound to keep God's law or not? Most sensible Christians would answer this by saying of course we must keep God's law, we mustn't steal, we mustn't kill, we mustn't commit adultery, of course, we aren't anti-law. They might well add with the sentiment of King David of old, "We love God's law, it's right and good and holy, it's an honour for us to keep it."

'All well and good. We aren't antinomians! But then another respected minister, William Gadsby, comes along and says, "Hi, old William Huntington wasn't wrong, you know. In these New Testament days, we aren't under God's law any more, we are under the gospel." Wonderful sounding words, but what do they mean to the down-to-earth farm labourers of Sussex? I heard it reported that one housewife commented that she wouldn't allow William Gadsby in her house as he would most likely run off with the silver!

'Seli, I think the answer lies in the fact that we have been adopted into God's family as his children. God is no longer our Judge, he's our Father. His law tells us how he wants us to behave. It brings him sorrow when we transgress it, but he will never condemn us for these failures. As the apostle John tells us, if any man sin, we have an advocate with the Father, Jesus Christ, whose precious blood goes on cleansing us from all sin. This must surely be the meaning of being under grace or, as William Gadsby called it, being under the gospel. I've decided to refuse to say whether I'm antinomian or not. I think either way, I would be misunderstood. I shall just ask the person concerned to listen to my preaching and decide for himself.'

Mayfield is a delightful little village in the north-eastern corner of Sussex, much nearer to our previous farm at Ticehurst than here in Perching. I'm told that its original Saxon name was Maghefeld, or maid's field, and the village sign shows young women and children in a flower-covered meadow. It's a village with a history and, at one stage, belonged to the kings of Wessex. In the early ninth century, the then king gave it to Canterbury Cathedral and later one of the archbishop's palaces was built there, Mayfield Palace.

I have memories still of my first visit to Mayfield long before Eli was minister there. Several large prosperous-looking houses with a cluster of smaller houses beyond them are visible across the fields from quite a distance away, the village being situated on slightly higher ground than the surrounding countryside. The approach is up a very straight driveway known as the Level. As is true of many of our Sussex lanes this is not easy to negotiate, being well-rutted and pitted by the wheels of wagons and carriages and the hoof prints of oxen and horses. What impressed me was a raised walkway to the left of the lane, which Eli later told me had been constructed by the owner of the fields to enable the ladies of Mayfield to take a comfortable walk even in winter. At the end of the walkway was a gate which was locally referred to as the 'turn back' gate.[57]

Eli had always been interested in local history and thought the children should know about it too, so I picked up a good deal of information from conversations over the meal table.

The prosperity of Mayfield dates back to the boom of the iron industry in the Sussex Weald in the sixteenth century. Ironstone was found in the underlining clay, and the furnaces were fired by charcoal from the surrounding forests. The industry declined when iron-making

---

[57] Eva Margaretta Bell-Irving, *Mayfield: The Story of an Old Wealden Village*, 1903, 1.

began to be fuelled by coke made from coal, as there wasn't suitable coal to be mined in the area.

In the 1700s Mayfield was also a notorious centre for smuggling, and perhaps understandably, this illegal trading increased with the decline of income from iron-making.

Wool was a plentiful commodity from the large population of sheep on the South Downs, and Europe across the channel wanted wool. However, as far back as 1300 an export duty had been placed on wool, and over the following centuries wool traders had found ways of shipping bundles of sheep's wool across to the continent illegally from a number of the small south-coast ports. In return they brought back wines, spirits, tobacco, and other goods. There was good money to be made, and port officials could be bribed!

It appears that most of the population was involved in the smuggling in one way or another, but in the early 1700s the main wool smugglers were the Mayfield Gang under their leader Gabriel Tomkins. They were referred to as Owlers, since they used an owl call to warn one another of danger. The Mayfield Gang actually had widespread respect, as unlike other gangs after them, such as the Hawkhurst Gang and the Groombridge Gang, they refrained from using violence unless in self-defence and poured much of their profits back into the local community. Gabriel, however, was captured in 1724, and the Mayfield Gang broke up. Other known gang members were Jacob Walter and Thomas Bigg, and it's interesting that all these family names are still around and belong to very respectable members of the community.

(If Selina had known the following poem written by Rudyard Kipling, who lived in Burwash, after her death, between 1902 and 1936, she may well have included it in her diary. It's added here for interest.)

> If you wake at midnight, and hear a horse's feet,
> Don't go drawing back the blind, or looking in the street,
> Them that asks no questions isn't told a lie.
> Watch the wall, my darling, while the Gentlemen go by!

Five-and-twenty ponies,
Trotting through the dark—Brandy for the Parson,
'Baccy for the Clerk;
Laces for a lady; letters for a spy,
And watch the wall, my darling, while the Gentlemen go by!

Running round the woodlump if you chance to find
Little barrels, roped and tarred, all full of brandy-wine;
Don't you shout to come and look, nor take 'em for your play;
Put the brushwood back again—and they'll be gone next day!

If you see the stable-door setting open wide;
If you see a tired horse lying down inside;
If your mother mends a coat cut about and tore;
If the lining's wet and warm—don't you ask no more!

If you meet King George's men, dressed in blue and red,
You be careful what you say, and mindful what is said.
If they call you 'pretty maid,' and chuck you 'neath the chin,
Don't you tell where no one is, nor yet where no one's been!

Knocks and footsteps round the house—whistles after dark—
You've no call for running out till the house—dogs bark.
Trusty's here, and Pincher's here, and see how dumb they lie—
They don't fret to follow when the Gentlemen go by!

If you do as you've been told, likely there's a chance
You'll be give a dainty doll, all the way from France,
With a cap of Valenciennes, and a velvet hood—
A present from the Gentlemen, along o' being good!

Five-and-twenty ponies,
Trotting through the dark—Brandy for the Parson,
'Baccy for the Clerk.
Them that asks no questions isn't told a lie—
Watch the wall, my darling, while the Gentlemen go by!

But Eli loved best the historical events which showed that God was at work. He loved to find evidence that God had had his true believing children in Mayfield in past centuries, and he has sometimes commented that it was encouraging to believe that it was the prayers and faithful witness of true Christian believers in the past that was still bearing fruit in this Sussex village in our day.

In the sixteenth century, when the Roman Catholic Queen Mary was on the throne, six fearless protestant Christians from Mayfield were burnt at the stake. The Bible had recently been published in the English language and authorised by Mary's father, Henry VIII, and these worthy Christians having discovered that salvation is through faith in Jesus Christ alone and not through an adherence to Catholic rituals, refused to give up their newfound faith and were prepared to die for it. Four were burnt in Mayfield itself on 24 September 1556 and a further two in the county town of Lewis the following year.

One of those who suffered and died in the county town of Lewis for his faith was William Maynard, who stemmed from one of the well-established families in Mayfield. Within fifty years of his martyrdom in the year 1600, another member of the Maynard family was baptised in the village and given the name John. By this time, there was again freedom for protestants in Britain with Mary's sister Elizabeth I on the throne. John studied at Oxford and, taking holy orders, became minister in Mayfield in 1624. His learning and extraordinary ability were recognised, and in 1643 he was appointed a member of the Westminster Assembly of Divines. This assembly was set up by parliament with the approval of the House of Lords in an attempt to establish a basis of theology and practise for the Anglican Church acceptable to the various strains of protestant thought within Britain. On two separate occasions, John Maynard also preached before parliament, which was obviously another honour for the little village of Mayfield where he was the ordained minister. He confessed his belief as a puritan and, because of this, was forced in 1662 to relinquish his position in the church, being unable to agree with the conditions of the Act of Uniformity. He continued to live in Mayfield and died in 1665. On his tombstone in the Mayfield cemetery, it's recorded: 'For forty years he shone as a light and glory to his Mayfield flock.'

God blessed Eli's preaching in Mayfield. More and more people were attracted to him, and the small group very soon grew too big for the small chapel. Within a few years, Eli suggested building a balcony to accommodate the growing congregation, and this was taken up with enthusiasm. But then even this was too small, and when it was recognised that the building was unsafe, it was decided to build a new bigger and more substantial chapel, and this was opened in 1873.[58]

But before the new chapel was built, the Mayfield fellowship had moved in a new direction. Eli had been very exercised about the position of independents in regard to baptism. In theory, like the Anglican Church, they believed in infant baptism, but in rejecting the belief that children were made regenerate through baptism, many independent pastors were simply putting their hands on the babies of their members and praying for them. No water was used, and they called this dedication and not baptism. This meant that many members of these churches weren't baptised at all. This became a concern, and several of the independent chapels around us in Sussex were becoming Baptist and practising adult baptism by immersion on a personal confession of faith. Eli confided in me one evening that the whole question of baptism was becoming a challenge to him.

'Selina,' he said, 'as you know, the emphasis in my spiritual thinking, and therefore my preaching, has always been centred on the need for the new birth and a living, personal faith in the Lord Jesus Christ. God has blessed my preaching in Mayfield, and I now have a largish congregation that is learning how to live out the Christian life. Some have been asking me if they need to be baptised now they are believers. I have tended to avoid this subject, and since many of them were baptised in the Anglican Church as infants, I have hesitated to encourage a second baptism. However, I'm now having second thoughts about this.'

---

[58] Ralph Chambers, 'Mayfield', op. cit., vol. 2, 63f.

'My parents used to tell us,' I said, 'that we children were baptised into the fold of the Christian church on the basis of their faith. I've always wondered though how this could apply when the parents weren't believers.'

'That's just the point,' answered Eli. 'In the New Testament, baptism is always linked with faith and the command is "believe and be baptised". I'm really coming to think that our Baptist friends have got it right and that any form of baptism before there is personal faith is a mere ceremony without meaning.'

'So what are you going to do about it?' I asked. 'And remember that if you become Baptist, you will have to be baptised by immersion yourself!'

'It's all a bit delicate,' answered Eli. 'I don't want to split up my congregation, but on the other hand, I sense they are ready for this, and there can be some advantage in me leading the way and being baptised myself.'

Eli was baptised by immersion on the 9 May 1871. It was a very spiritual and emotional experience for him. For many Christians, the full significance of their immersion in water in the name of the Father, the Son, and the Holy Spirit only comes later, but Eli was fully aware of what he was publically confessing. He knew he was identifying himself with the death and resurrection of Jesus Christ. He was showing that he had died with Christ and just as Christ had risen from the dead so he, Eli Page, as he came up out of the water, had been raised to a holy life of service for his Master.

The devil really attacked Eli for his act of obedience in following his Master, and that evening and the next morning, my husband was in a terrible state. He confessed to me with sighs and groans that he was a complete hypocrite. It was presumption for him to make that public stand. The Lord had forsaken him, and how on earth was he going to preach later that day? I prayed for him earnestly after he left for his preaching engagement and felt so burdened for him. However, God is so good and far greater than our fears, and Eli came home to tell me of a wonderful experience. As he had begun to preach, the Holy Spirit blessed him with such an overwhelming sense of God's love for him that as he wrote years later to his daughter Ruth:

But oh, I shall never forget it. The dear Lord broke in with His love, in such a way, that I thought I must stop from preaching and shout aloud for joy.[59]

I guess most preachers, if not all Christians, have someone whose example they greatly respect and whose Christian life and ministry they seek to emulate.

If asked, I would say for me, such a person living in my own lifetime would be the Rev. Charles Spurgeon. I read his penny sermons avidly each week and, in my rather isolated position at Edburton, gain most of my spiritual food from them. I was thrilled when in 1865 Charles Spurgeon began to publish a monthly newsletter called *The Sword and Trowel*. This gave me a deeper insight into his life and the various aspects of his ministry, all of which interests me enormously.

However, enough of me, what I really intended to say was that if Eli were to own to having a mentor, I would suggest it would be William Gadsby. Of course he denies that he thinks that highly of any man, and I know he doesn't agree with everything that Gadsby taught. However Eli often refers to Gadsby, and this prompted me to read a short biography he had about him.

I soon began to see what had attracted Eli to this late preacher from Manchester (William Gadsby had died in 1844 at the age of seventy-one) and could recognise certain similarities with Eli himself. William had stemmed from a poor family and had had little or no education. After running wild as a teenager, he had been aroused to think about the solemn fact of eternity at the age of seventeen after watching a public hanging. He was converted and began to preach at the age of twenty-five. His preaching came from his heart, which as Eli himself knew, is the type of preaching that holds people's attention and will often move their hearts too. He became pastor of a church in Manchester in 1805 but, in a sense, merely used this as his base for extensive preaching

---

[59] Extract from Eli Page's letter to Ruth Holder of 27 November 1877.

over a wide area. He walked miles each week preaching in villages and towns around Manchester and was said to have travelled more than 60,000 miles and to have preached more than 12,000 sermons. He would regularly walk back to Manchester for a week evening meeting and then again to preach to his home congregation on Sundays. The people loved him, and he was influential in establishing about forty new chapels. He was also very socially minded and was not only ready to give his last penny to someone in need but was ready to use his influence as a popular preacher to promote social justice politically.[60]

William Gadsby was a Strict and Particular Baptist. This had become a specific denomination in England by the early nineteenth century to distinguish those Baptist chapels which maintained their hold on Calvinistic theology and required baptism by immersion as a prerequisite to taking part in their communion services and sharing the bread and the wine. It followed then quite naturally that, following Eli's own baptism, the chapel at Mayfield should join themselves to the Strict Baptist denomination and introduced formal church membership. Church members were required to give testimony of genuine repentance from a former way of life, and to confess a personal faith in Jesus Christ as their Lord and Saviour.

A new and more substantial chapel building was completed in 1873, and the plaque built into the front of the building states 'Particular Baptist Chapel' with the date. The word 'particular' refers to the biblical doctrine of 'particular redemption' which understands Jesus' statement 'I am the good Shepherd and I know my sheep . . . I lay down my life for the sheep'[61] to mean that he died for his sheep as particular and individual people whom he foreknew from eternity past. It was felt necessary to include this word 'particular' in the title of the denomination to distinguish it from general Baptists, many of whom believed that Jesus died for the world in general and not for individuals in particular.

---

[60] William Gadsby, www.strictbaptisthistory.org.uk.
[61] John 10:14–15.

Chapter 14

A Sunday Evening Service at Mayfield Chapel

In 1873, my birthday, the 17 August, happened to fall on a Sunday, and on the evening before, Richard called by and offered to run me across to Mayfield for the evening service the next day as a birthday treat! In general I was very much tied to the house and farm, so this was a real treat for me. Eli had already left for the weekend, so it would be a surprise for him to see me in the congregation, although at the back of my mind I did wonder whether he had in fact suggested this idea to Richard. As I thought about the offer, I realised that it couldn't have been a nicer birthday treat. I would be able to leave my youngest, Nap, who was then ten, under the care of his older sisters, would have my oldest son to myself for the duration of the journey in the pony and trap, and then experience a worship service as one of my husband's congregation and hear him preach. I went to bed thanking God for putting this idea into my family's mind!

We knew the journey would take us about two hours, so we left in the middle of the afternoon and took some bread and cheese and some light ale to sustain us. It was a lovely journey. Richard took us through the delightful village of Ditchling and then the rather narrow lanes to Uckfield and thus on to Mayfield. There were signs that the summer was coming to a close. Many of the fields had already been harvested, but beyond the hedgerows along some of the lanes, beautiful yellow corn was waving in the light breeze. The hedges were laden with berries, dark-red hawthorn, lighter-red rosehips, and black, juicy-looking blackberries. The hazelnuts were more hidden, but there to be seen by the observant eye. I would have loved to have stopped and picked some of these blackberries and nuts but knew it wasn't the day or time to do that, so I relaxed and simply enjoyed all I saw. A jay flew across the lane in front of us, and I was fairly sure it had a nut in its beak. Something was stopping it screeching in that familiar jay manner.

Richard was pleased to see how other farmers were coping with their harvesting, and we chatted about his farm and the family.

I suggested we should stop and eat our tea before reaching Mayfield, and Richard found a very pleasant spot and guided the pony off the lane on to the edge of a grass field which had been freshly mowed for a second crop of hay. There was a delightful view across open countryside, and I enjoyed this very simple birthday tea tremendously. Somehow the light breeze and scent from the cut grass took me back to childhood picnics in the hayfields of Ripe. I found it difficult to believe that I was now fifty-five and the mother of fourteen children! Getting old is a strange experience. I knew very well my body was past its best. For instance, I wouldn't be able to have any more children. But on the other hand, inside I'm still the same Selina, or Silly, as my brothers used to call me, and I was thrilled to find I could so enjoy eating bread and cheese in a hayfield just like a little girl.

We arrived in Mayfield in good time for the evening service, but already there were a good number of people in the chapel. Richard and I found a seat halfway back in the balcony, and I was interested to watch as more and more people come in and, apart from a few odd seats, fill up the whole chapel. At the front, under the pulpit, was a desk facing the congregation and around it a large semicircular pew facing the pulpit. Three men dressed in their best smock coats came forward and sat in this honoured front pew. As the service was due to start, three more men emerged from the vestry door at the front of the chapel led by my husband. Eli ascended the stairs into the pulpit, two of the men sat with the others in the semicircular pew, and the third took his place at the desk.

'Friends, we shall begin our service to the glory of God by singing John Newton's time-honoured hymn, "Amazing Grace" which, for those of you who have our Gadsby's hymnbook, is number 198.' The gentleman at the front desk, whom I assumed was Eli's head deacon, Mr Lusted, spoke in a good clear voice which carried well around the chapel. He proceeded to read the first and second verses of the hymn and then one of the gentlemen in the front pew called out, 'Tune Leicester Abbey' and blow the opening note on a small whistle. The gentleman next to him then struck the same note in a good baritone voice, and we all stood and joined in singing 'which saved a wretch like me'. I could hear a good bass voice and also a clear tenor coming from the 'singing seat' at the front and most, if not all the congregation, were singing lustily but solemnly in parts that best suited their level of voice. A good half of the congregation had hymnbooks, and I quite imagine that, for the others, the deacon would read the verses one by one for hymns which were less well known. This had always been the procedure in the Burwash chapel and also earlier when we worshipped in the chapel at Lower Dicker.

Eli read a longish chapter from John's Gospel in what I call his Sunday voice, much more precise and clear than the Sussex drawl I was used to hearing on the farm. He then led the congregation in a fairly long prayer which humbled me. I felt he was really communicating with God and was leading all of us to the 'throne of grace'. After a further congregational hymn, Eli then announced his text: the words of Jesus to the Jews in Capernaum who were sceptical about his authority, 'No man can come to me, except the Father which hath sent me draw him', from St John's Gospel chapter 6, verse 44.

'Well, that's an encouraging text for my birthday, I don't think,' I muttered to myself.

Yet soon I began to enter into Jesus' words as Eli explained the background, mentioning that in an earlier verse Jesus had assured his hearers that 'him that cometh to me I will in no wise cast out'. And then a little later, 'Verily, verily, I say unto you, He that believeth on me hath everlasting life.'

'Jesus nowhere discouraged his hearers to come to him and follow him,' explained Eli. 'In fact, he invited them warmly and exhorted with intense feeling, all who were tired with the circumstances of their lives and weary with the problems and suffering of being fallen human beings to come to him and find rest and peace.'

Eli then explained what it meant to come to Jesus. It meant to accept him for all he claimed to be, to believe in him and trust him, and to love him and to follow his commands and teachings.

'But,' he added, 'our text shows us that it's all of God's grace. "No man can come to me, except the Father which hath sent me draw him."'

He then proceeded to show, firstly, wherein this inability lay and then, secondly, the ways in which the Father draws us to Jesus.

I loved one of my husband's illustrations which he drew from his other life as a farmer. Having made the point that there was rarely any physical inabilities in us to stop us coming to church, singing gospel hymns, being baptised, and living a Christian life, 'Neither,' said he, 'is there normally any mental disability which could stop us studying, understanding, and applying Jesus' words to ourselves. Yet there is a fundamental disability. It lies in our very natures. We are all fallen human beings, and as such, it is completely unnatural for us and, in fact, impossible for us to love an unseen God and his Son Jesus Christ without a miracle of his grace. This miracle is here described as the Father drawing us. In another place, it's described as being born again of the Spirit. Without this, no man can come to Jesus and enter into the relationship of love and trust to which he invites us.'

Then came the illustration.

'At home, in Edburton,' he said, 'we have any number of sheep. My shepherd knows how many. We also have two dogs. Now these are all animals. The sheep wander across the hillside eating grass. They do it all day and every day. My dogs have the physical ability to wander slowly across the Downs. They have mouths and teeth, but can they live like the sheep? It's impossible for them because, by nature, they are fundamentally different. It would take a miracle to make a dog behave like a sheep. They don't want to, and they can't. Now Jesus knew that for a fallen human being like you and me to behave like a child of God is just as impossible without a miracle of God's grace.

'This miracle happened to John Newton,' continued Eli, 'and we sang the hymn he wrote to express this change. "Amazing grace how sweet the sound that saved a wretch like me. I once was lost but now I'm found was blind but now I see." God the Father, through the Holy Spirit, drew John Newton to faith in Jesus. If you read his biography, you'll see it took many years, and when the change came, he had so many regrets for the evil of his past life. God did it for John Newton, and he's done it for many of us here tonight.'

Eli then continued and showed the different means the Father uses to draw us to Jesus and then ended by quoting the promise given through Isaiah. 'Seek the Lord while He may be found, call upon Him while he is near.' He concluded with the encouragement that if tonight we feel the prompting to come to Jesus, then this is the Father drawing us.

'You can be sure,' he said, 'it's not the devil prompting you to do this. It's also not your own fallen nature. My dogs don't look at the sheep and want to be like them. In fact, I rather think they despise them. "Whoever will, may come," said Jesus. Come and trust him tonight, and you will experience all the blessing which John Newton expressed in his wonderful hymn.'

The sky was beautiful as we jogged steadily back to Edburton, and I thanked Richard so much for a really wonderful birthday treat.

'Mum,' he answered, 'Dad's sermon spoke to me tonight. I think it's given me what I needed. The thing that has tortured me over the years is the fact that I felt I could do nothing about my salvation. I was either one of God's elect or I wasn't. That illustration of a dog having no wish to become a sheep made me see that as I very much want to belong to Jesus, then the Father is drawing me and Jesus welcomes all who come to him. It's wonderful, Mum. I've always envied the faith that you and Dad have, and now I believe I can think positively and begin to thank the Lord for dying for me and seek to grow as a Christian. Pray for me, Mum.'

'Oh, Richard!' I said beaming with delight. 'What a birthday this is. I shall certainly be praying for you and for Elizabeth too as you share this with her.'

Chapter 15

Spiritual Conversation

Eli would occasionally use me as a sounding board for his thoughts, and one evening after prayers when most of the family had left the room to finish their jobs before bed, he put to me a rather interesting question.

'Do you think everyone has a duty to believe in Jesus, Seli,' he asked with the sort of look that showed he'd already had his own ideas about this.

I had to think about his question for a moment or two before giving my preacher husband an answer.

'To use the word "duty", about faith, is rather a strange way of thinking in my opinion,' I said.

Eli didn't respond immediately, so I felt he wanted a bit more of an answer.

'We've tried to teach our children their duty in regard to a whole manner of things, haven't we?' I added. 'But I've never heard you say they must believe in Jesus or you would cane them! Duty to me is something that needs to be enforced as an obligation.'

'Yet,' responded Eli, 'didn't Jesus say that light is come into the world but men loved their darkness and that this rejection of the light is their condemnation? Doesn't that imply that it was their duty to accept the light, namely accept him, and they would be punished eternally if they didn't?'

'I think "duty" is the wrong word,' I answered. 'If a man is drowning and someone throws him a rope, he wouldn't shout, "Young man, it's your duty to catch hold of the rope or you will be punished by drowning." He's more likely to shout, "Catch hold, catch hold!" and then be terribly upset if the drowning man couldn't or wouldn't.'

Eli thought for a moment and bent across and kissed me. 'Selina Page,' he said. 'I believe you've got more sense than many of our so-called theologians. There have been debates for years on this question of duty–faith and its implications for the preaching of the gospel. I'm sure these learned men wouldn't accept your explanation. It's too simple and doesn't deal with the complications they've thought up by accepting one side or the other. But I believe it's a good way for a simple village pastor to think.

'Tell me something else, Seli. You have this rope in your hand and the man is drowning, but you know he's not got the power in him to grasp the rope if you throw it. Do you throw the rope or not?'

'Of course I would,' I answered. 'I'd throw it and shout and then pray that somehow God would give him the strength to grasp hold of it.'

'But don't you think that by throwing it and calling to him to catch hold of it you would be implying to him he had the ability in himself to save himself? And then if God gave him that ability, he would congratulate himself and not give God the glory.'

'Oh, Eli,' I gasped, 'is that really the way you preachers think? You can't leave a man to drown just in case he doesn't thank you for saving him! Surely you can trust God to make a person aware of his total dependence on his Saviour?'

Eli was quiet for a moment then added, 'The thing is, Seli, we know we are saved by God's grace. The verses we love to quote from Ephesians chapter 2 say, "For by grace are ye saved through faith; and that not of yourselves: it is the gift of God: Not of works, lest any man should boast." It appears that more and more Christian ministers today are either overlooking this verse and others like it, or deliberately rejecting their obvious meaning. These preachers are teaching that men have the ability in themselves to believe or not believe as and when they will. Some of our Strict Baptist leaders have reacted against this by saying we shouldn't exhort people to do what they can't do. So we shouldn't call on them to repent and believe.'

'But, Eli,' I interrupted, 'isn't that being as bad as the other side? It's surely overlooking or reinterpreting such verses as "Go ye into all the world and preach the Gospel to every creature".'

'It's all a question of what the gospel is,' answered Eli. 'At the moment, I'm trying the preach Jesus without actually calling people to believe in him. Am I right in doing that? I ask myself. I'm having doubts. I was challenged recently when reading how the apostle Peter preached on the day of Pentecost. Mr Spurgeon at the Metropolitan Tabernacle has no qualms in following the apostles' example and is using all sorts of arguments in his sermons to persuade his hearers they need to repent and trust Jesus alone for their salvation.'

I enjoyed these talks with Eli, and it helped me to pray for him and his ministry at Mayfield. What was wonderfully clear was that God was using him and the church was growing and people were being baptised. That thrilled me and made me see more and more that salvation is of all God's grace and power and he can use uneducated men like my husband who were fully committed to serve him.

These theological discussions occurred every now and then over the next few years, but there was one other I must tell you about as its outcome was very significant for Eli's spiritual life and his ministry.

'I preach that the only way of salvation is through the death of Jesus for our sins on the cross at Calvary,' Eli said to me one evening. 'This is the gospel, and it's wonderful. There's nothing we can do to merit salvation from our sins, but Jesus has done everything that's necessary on our behalf. I've recently been meditating on this, Seli, and thinking firstly about the sufficiency of Jesus' death and then how it is applied to us. My thoughts have really both challenged me and encouraged me. Have you got time for me to share them with you?'

'Oh, yes please, Eli,' I said. 'I love to know what you're thinking. Because you are waiting on God to hear what you should preach, when you tell me first, it's like me getting my own personal sermon.'

'It's interesting you say that, Seli, but the act of preaching is an amazing experience in itself, and I rarely feel my thoughts are complete until I'm preaching them. This means that you need to be careful in thinking I'm giving you God's message when I'm just sharing my thoughts.'

'I don't think I understand, Eli,' I said frowning. 'What is different about actually preaching?'

'I can only say what I experience,' answered Eli. 'It might be different for other people because I know some preachers write out their sermon in full before preaching it. I can't do that, and in fact, I don't want to do that, because I find my sermon only really comes together as I preach it. Of course the thoughts I have about a text as I prepare are important, and I will mostly try and jot down the various points I feel I should make in the sermon. It doesn't always happen, yet I'm happiest when the content from the text warms my heart and becomes a message I have a burden to share with my congregation. Even then, often new thoughts come as I preach, and the whole comes together in a wonderful way. Sometimes my own sermon affects me so emotionally that I have difficulty in continuing. I'm sure this is what is meant by unction. It's certainly nothing that I can work up myself. I believe it must be the Holy Spirit. It's very humbling.'

'Thank you for telling me that, Eli,' I said quietly.

There was a moment's silence, then Eli added, 'But I was telling you about the new realisation I've had about the direction and object of saving faith.'

'Yes,' I said. 'You were talking about the sufficiency of Christ's death before I distracted you.'

'That's it,' responded Eli stretching out his hand to me. 'We know God has his elect people. The Bible makes this very clear, and Jesus refers to God's elect as "those whom my father has given me". It's logical that these who were chosen and loved before the foundation of the world were those on Jesus' heart and mind when he died. In fact, shortly before his death, he said to his Father, "I pray not for the world but for them which thou hast given me; for they are thine" and "Neither pray I for these alone, but for them also which shall believe on me through their word".[62] That to me is a remarkable description of the elect: those who will believe in Jesus through the preaching of firstly the apostles and then of all those who have continued to preach the message of Jesus up until today. No one need worry about being or not being the elect, the challenge is to believe.

'Now at one stage, I tended to consider that the value of the atonement was only sufficient for those who will be actually saved. I still believe the intent of it was, but the more I have thought about Jesus as the eternal Son of God, infinite in holiness and righteousness, I have become convinced that the value of Christ's death for man's sin must be as infinite as his righteousness. Somehow that has stirred me to preach with greater fervency. I'm convinced now that the worst possible sinner who sits under my preaching in Mayfield can become as holy as Jesus himself. Isn't that amazing!

'Then I've also been moved to think about the faith that saves us. When I've tried to analyse my view of my own faith, I find that I have tended to look within me in order to see whether I see my faith. If I can, then I have peace and a degree of assurance that Jesus died for me. If I can't, and some days it's like that, then I feel desperate and wonder how I can dare claim to be a child of God and a preacher.'

I said nothing because I knew very well there were days when Eli was at peace with God and other days when he appeared very depressed.

'Seli,' continued Eli, 'God has shown me I mustn't look at myself for peace and assurance. It's both wrong and dangerous. I must always look at Jesus. To see him dying for me and rising again from the tomb for me, that's the source of my peace. Peter could walk on the waves when he had his eyes on Jesus. Paul exhorts us to run the race set before us looking unto Jesus. To take our eyes off Jesus and look within ourselves

---

[62] John 17:9, 20.

is a temptation from Satan. If we are a true child of God, we shall never find any comfort by looking at ourselves and we shall live our lives in misery.'

Darkness had fallen during our conversation, and I got up and lit the lamp.

'Eli,' I said, returning to the table, 'is this going to change your preaching?'

'I think it might well do, Seli,' Eli answered. 'It will certainly encourage me to preach Jesus. I shall try to see him in every text, and I'm already realising that the Old Testament is just as full of Christ as the New. My encouragement is in the words of Jesus himself: "And I, if I be lifted up from the earth will draw all men to me."'[63]

Not everything Eli shared with me about his weekends in Mayfield was spiritual. Knowing I was safe to confide in, he would often tell me of some of the pastoral problems that arose amongst his congregation. When he knew that particular issues were troubling people, he tried to bring out biblical principles in his sermons which he considered would help to clarify the answer to these problems.

One Monday evening, Eli made a confession. 'You know probably better than anyone, Seli,' he said, 'that I'm not a very patient man. I'm not proud of this, and I pray to have more patience when dealing with people and things that annoy me. Well, yesterday evening in the service there was an old man at the back of the chapel snoring. He has been coming Sunday evenings off and on for some time and tells me his name is William. It's true that I had been preaching for nearly an hour, but I'm afraid when his snoring got louder and louder, I lost my patience and threw a hymnbook at him.'[64]

'You did what, Eli?' I said in alarm. 'You threw a hymnbook at him!'

'I'm afraid so, Seli. I realise now that I would have done better to have asked one of the deacons to go and wake him, but you know what

---

[63] John 12:32.
[64] John Richard Thomas, 'Oral History', op. cit.

it is, on the spur of the moment you don't always think clearly, and he was distracting me so much.'

'Did it hit him?' I asked.

'No, it hit the wall behind him and dropped onto his lap,' answered Eli. 'He woke up with a start, and I'm afraid I then shouted "If God's Word doesn't keep you awake, perhaps this will!"'

'Oh, Eli,' I said in a worried way, 'I hope there won't be repercussions.'

'He apologised to me at the end of the service, and I also said I hope it wasn't too much of a shock to his system to be woken up like that. We parted as friends, or at least it seemed so, but I guess the news will get around the churches that Eli Page throws Gadsby hymnbooks at sleeping parishioners!'

Chapter 16

The Lord Gives and the Lord Takes Away

Quiet moments were rare for me at Perching Manor, and with Eli now away so much with his preaching, both family and staff problems mostly seemed to fall onto my lap. I'm of the impression that, compared with many folk around me, our gracious Creator must have blessed me with above average patience and common sense for which I never cease to thank him! More often than not, with sensitivity to the particular character of the person concerned and with patience and prayer, I'm able to defuse potentially explosive situations and pour oil on troubled waters.

Some years were more eventful than others, and 1875 was certainly one such. As the year began, we already had nineteen grandchildren, and a further three were born that year! God had really blessed us in regard to our children. I had given birth to fourteen babies, and we had only lost one, little Ebenezer, who died before his first birthday. So now with thirteen grown children, seven of which were then married and producing children themselves, we were becoming quite a clan!

Although our children and grandchildren brought us much joy, they were also a source of worry and heartache. Sadly, we lost Ruth and Dan's third child. Little John Eli Holder died shortly before his third birthday. My diary tells me that the date of his funeral was 13 May 1873. Eli and I were able to attend his burial in the Patcham Parish churchyard. Mercy, his older sister, was then four years old, and although we could talk to her about heaven, she was quite heartbroken with the thought that she wouldn't have John to play with any more. Grace, Ruth's youngest at that time, was only thirteen months old and thankfully unaware of what was happening.

Richard's oldest child was William, named after his wife's father, William Heaver. Because Richard and Elizabeth had had the opportunity to rent a neighbouring farm and were consequently living close by in Edburton, little William was a very frequent visitor to Perching Manor. He was a great little chap and loved the countryside and farming. In good Page tradition, Elizabeth continued to provide a new addition to the growing clan every two years, so very quickly, little William acquired two sisters, Mary Kate and Ada Louisa, and then when he was six, a little brother, Walter. It was a happy family, and Richard was able to hire a governess, Fanny Andrews, who lived-in with the family and gave the children lessons every morning. Once John and Mary Ann had moved into Briar Cottage in the village, their older children, Emily, Ruth, and Harry Eli were able to join these lessons for a while too.

William was a special grandson to both Eli and me. He was the oldest child of our oldest offspring, and his love for the countryside gave Eli the joy of foreseeing another Page taking forward the family's tradition of farming into another generation. He loved going around our farm with Eli, and although Eli didn't show his feelings towards his family openly, I know he enjoyed these times too. As well as talking about the farm, 'Granddad' explained a lot about the countryside to little William. I remember one spring day William came back from a walk very excited about cuckoos. They had heard one calling across the fields, and Eli had explained how the cuckoo is such a cheeky and lazy bird. That mother cuckoo laid her eggs one at a time, singly, in the nests of other birds so that they had the responsibility of hatching them and then feeding the young cuckoo youngster.

After thinking a bit, William commented, 'That's a bit like Uncle John and Auntie Mary. They've given baby Kate to Auntie Orpha to look after, and you are looking after cousin Ruth.'

'No, William,' I answered. 'It's not the same at all. Auntie Mary isn't very well, so we are helping her.'

I knew from things he said that Eli also told William Bible stories and talked to him about Jesus coming to save us from our sins. As I think back now, it's such a comfort to me to remember William saying how kind Jesus must have been to sit little children on his knee and then to die to forgive their sins so that they could go to heaven where everything is wonderful.

Then the blow came! In the early months of 1875, William caught diphtheria. I remember the day a very worried Elizabeth came round to talk to me. William was in bed with a very high temperature, a nasty sore throat, and she was keeping the other children away from him. Several other children in the village caught the disease, but it seemed to affect William the most. His throat got really nasty with a horrible grey coating and the poor little fellow was really ill. We prayed so much for him.

One day Eli said to me, 'I think we are going to lose William, Seli. I've been so burdened for him in prayer, and I believe God has given me peace in knowing there is a place reserved for him in glory.'

I could say nothing. It was going to be so hard not to have his cheerful call as he ran to find me in the parlour. But if God wanted him with him, who was I to rebel? The words of Job came to my mind. 'The Lord gave and the Lord hath taken away, blessed be the name of the Lord.'[65] I realised that it would need special grace to be able to say this from my heart, and I prayed that when, as it seemed most likely, William was taken from us, I might really be able to praise God with the acceptance that he knows best.

After about a month of suffering, William was really very little better, and then suddenly, his whole body seemed to fail. He was struggling to

---

[65] Job 1:21.

breathe, and as Elizabeth expressed it later, it was as though the disease was sapping his life away. Richard was sitting with him when he died, and the doctor said that the diphtheria had affected his heart.

William was the first member of the Page family to be buried in the Edburton Parish Church cemetery. It was a sad occasion for all of us. Although we tried to give thanks to God for the eleven years we had enjoyed William with us, it was very difficult not to think of his death from a human point of view and regret with tears the potential life that had been taken from us. Richard, in particular, was badly shaken by William's death. He had placed great hopes on his firstborn son working with him on the farm and eventually taking over from him. Thankfully, Walter, who was then just five years old, also loved helping his dad, so I began to pray specifically that he would very quickly replace William both in Richard's affections and his hopes for the future.

Chapter 17

Two Contrasting Weddings

Later that same year, we had a much happier event in our parish church when at the end of September, Elizabeth, our sixth daughter, married John Combridge.

Interestingly, although we very quickly got used to calling them Combridge when Elizabeth married John, his surname was Martin! The explanation for the change of name is fairly simple. John Martin had served his apprenticeship as a butcher with his uncle, Daniel Combridge, in Western Road, Brighton, and after John's marriage, his uncle decided to retire and offered to leave the business to John on the understanding he took the family name. It was a wonderful opportunity for John and Elizabeth, and after some thought, they agreed to this stipulation.

As Elizabeth explained to me, 'Mum, it's far easier for me as I've already given up my name of Page, and whether I'm Martin or Combridge, it doesn't really matter. It's John I've married not his name! But John is fighting a sense of betrayal to his father, who as you know died some years ago.'

'How does John's mother feel about it?' I asked.

'It doesn't seem to be a problem to her,' said Elizabeth smiling, 'probably because Combridge was her maiden name anyway. But in a silly sort of way, this upsets John more because he thinks she should mind!'

Elizabeth and John decided they wanted a proper church wedding, and the Rev. Christopher Wilkie, curate at St Andrew's, Edburton, agreed to tie the knot for them. Because of the need to talk over details for the wedding, Elizabeth got to know Christopher Wilkie and his wife Melian quite well.

One evening after a talk at the rectory, Elizabeth came home full of enthusiasm about the village of Edburton and its church.

'Did you know, Mum, that the village is named after the granddaughter of King Alfred the Great, Edburga of Winchester? And she founded the church here around the year 940?'

'I thought the building dated back to eleven hundred and something,' I answered. 'There's a plaque somewhere saying that.'

'Apparently the original building collapsed, and the origin of the present one dates back to the twelfth century,' responded Elizabeth. 'Rev. Wilkie says much of the stone they used to build it was brought over from Normandy. He showed me round the church and pointed out the font, where they baptise babies. He says it's made of lead and is quite rare. Apparently, Cromwell's men would often raid the churches and lead was valuable for their weapons, but this font was used as a water trough for their horses so it was never stolen.

'Another interesting story the Rev. Wilkie told me was about one of the earlier ministers, George Keith. He was a Scot but went across to America and became a Quaker. This was during the late 1600s. Because of his strong-minded views, on slavery for instance, he was expelled from the Quakers and came back to Britain and became an Anglican. His heart was on mission, and in 1700 he went back to America as an Anglican missionary. He was the first missionary for the Society for the Propagation of the Gospel in Foreign Parts and became quite famous as a travelling theologian and preacher. When he eventually came back to Britain, he was made vicar of our village church. Isn't that amazing! He was quite old and weak by then, and Rev. Wilkie said he often had to be carried into the church to conduct the services.

'I feel quite proud that I can be married in a church with this sort of history,' added Elizabeth.

While Elizabeth and John were planning their wedding, Mary suddenly announced that she and James Peacock wanted to get married too.

'Do you mean you want to have a double wedding here at St Andrew's?' I asked.

'I don't think so,' said Mary. 'James and I want something much simpler and have decided we would like, if possible, to be married in the little independent chapel at Bolney, where we first met. You'll remember, Mum, that time I went with Dad when he was preaching there.'

'That will please your dad,' I answered. 'Have you thought who you want to marry you? Bolney Chapel doesn't have a regular minister, does it?'

'We wondered about asking Eli Ashdown,' said Mary rather shyly. 'He has been very involved with the meetings at Burgess Hill and Scaynes Hill, and James looks to him as his pastor. I like him very much too.'

Eli was very pleased about Mary's wish to be married by Eli Ashdown at Bolney, as I was sure he would be. Anglican Church weddings were not really his cup of tea, as we say.

'You know Eli Ashdown quite well, don't you, Eli?' I asked him when I had him to myself that evening. 'Didn't you baptise him at Mayfield?'

'Yes, my dear,' answered Eli, smiling. 'Our stories are rather similar. Eli Ashdown was a member at the Jireh Chapel, Lewis, when I first knew him, which as you know is a Huntingtonian cause and doesn't practise baptism. Old William Huntington did a great deal of good in Sussex, but it's a pity he wasn't a Baptist. The Bolney Chapel originated through his preaching, you know. The story goes that he preached there in an orchard belonging to a Mr Blaker around the turn of the century. About 600 people came to hear him, and God really blessed that sermon and a good number were converted and began to meet together for fellowship and worship in a barn at Gassons Farm. Then later, they turned two cottages in Twineham Lane into a meeting hall. I remember preaching there myself. It was really just two low-ceilinged living rooms joined together. The present chapel building was only built in 1859, after we came here to Perching.[66] I'm quite thrilled that Mary wants to be married there. It's much more the Page way of doing things than an Anglican wedding.'

'But what about Eli Ashdown? You began to tell me about him.'

'Oh, yes,' continued Eli, 'Eli Ashdown. Well, he was sent out to preach from Jireh Chapel, Lewis, which you might almost call the cathedral of the Independent Chapels in Sussex. William Huntington's grave is there, and he is still greatly respected. Anyway, after a while, Eli began to see that baptism by immersion on confession of a personal faith in Christ is the most obvious interpretation of New Testament teaching on baptism. In the same way as I did, he then found it embarrassing to be an unbaptised preacher, and in 1872 he asked me to baptise him at Mayfield. His parents are members with us, and Eli was actually born in Mayfield. They love his preaching at Burgess Hill, Scaynes Hill, and Bolney, which are three closely related meetings, and I understand the friends at Burgess Hill are now forming a definite church membership and have asked Eli to be their pastor. He has accepted on the understanding they become a Baptist church affiliated to the Strict Baptists. At present, of the three meetings, Bolney is the only one with its own building, but the friends at Burgess Hill have plans to build a chapel once they get themselves established with Eli Ashdown as pastor.'

It fascinates me to hear how these nonconformist gatherings of Christians originated and are developing in our Sussex villages. My Eli has become a very significant part of this development. He is well known and loved, and although now based as the pastor at Mayfield, he still preaches regularly around the villages on weekday evenings. Many village nonconformist fellowships have been able to build

---

[66] Ralph Chambers, 'Bolney', op. cit., vol. 2, 123.

themselves chapels, but some still meet in barns, cottages, farmhouses, or schoolrooms.

'Do you know the history of the Burgess Hill meeting?' I asked, not wanting to close the subject.

'Well, yes,' said Eli, 'the friends there were telling me about it a few months ago. It's all happened quite recently.

'About ten years ago, in the mid 1860s, William Philpott, who is now farming at Awbrook Farm, near Scaynes Hill, became dissatisfied with St John's Church, Burgess Hill, where he was a lay reader, and began to attend the chapel at Bolney. Through his influence, a few others from Burgess Hill soon began to travel across to Bolney for the Sunday services, and William felt the time had come to start a meeting where he was then living. He was then an enthusiastic young man of about twenty-five and had just set up home with a young wife. Although they only had a farm cottage, they opened it up as a meeting place for like-minded believers and invited local preachers to lead services. Often ministers who had preached at Bolney in the morning and afternoon were prepared to come across to the cottage meeting at Burgess Hill to lead an evening service. This continued for about three years until William Philpott and his wife were able to get a farm of their own nearer Scaynes Hill and so moved away from Burgess Hill. Thankfully, there was then enough interest and enthusiasm for the work to continue and the remaining small group was able to use a large schoolroom for their services. I've preached there for them, and that's where they still meet Sunday by Sunday. But wonderfully having taken the important step of covenanting together and inviting Eli Ashdown as pastor, God has honoured this step of faith and a friend has given them a plot of land in Park Road where they are now building themselves a chapel.'[67]

'Do you know what has happened to William Philpott?' I asked. 'It seems everything that has developed in Burgess Hill came about through his initiative.'

---

[67] Ralph Chambers, 'Burgess Hill', op. cit., vol. 2, 114f.

'From what I hear,' answered Eli, 'William is continuing to promote God's kingdom wonderfully in Sussex.

'About the same time as he was initiating the Burgess Hill meeting, a grocer from Dane Hill, George Wickham, was led by God to begin a ministry in Scaynes Hill. George saw the need and was able to gather a small group together who were hungry for God's Word, and they met together regularly in a small room. God had obviously given George gifts in preaching, and he was able to provide spiritual nourishment for these dear folk and establish a small fellowship. Then the church at Salem, Portsmouth, recognised his gifts and called him to be their pastor. The small group in Scaynes Hill struggled as best they could without an obvious spiritual leader for about a year, and this was the situation when God provided William Philpott with Awbrook Farm. They welcomed his leadership, and after a while, he was able to rent a small chapel for them to meet in. However, the latest news is less encouraging, the owner of the chapel has recently died, and the group are being turned out of their meeting place.'[68]

'I'll be praying for them,' I said. 'I'm sure God won't forsake them. William Philpott sounds a thoroughly good man and I'm sure must be God's shepherd to care for the flock there in Scaynes Hill. Do you know him personally, Eli?'

'It's interesting you say that,' answered Eli. 'I've spoken to him a number of times, and he told me his early training in farming was as a shepherd on his grandfather's farm in Surrey.'

'That's wonderful,' I answered. 'There's a likeness to King David there. But in William's case, God took him from his grandfather's flock in Surrey to care for his spiritual flock of believing farmworkers in Sussex!'

'Yes, he's a good spiritual man and a good farmer too,' said Eli smiling. 'I called in at Awbrook Farm once and was very impressed with his wife, Elizabeth, too. She is the eldest daughter of Peter Agate,

---

[68] Ralph Chambers, 'Scaynes Hill', op. cit., vol. 2, 114ff.

a good Christian farmworker in the parish of Slaugham, near to where Naomi and William are farming.'

'That's really wonderful to hear,' I answered. 'It thrills me to learn how God is working in our Sussex villages, thank you, Eli. We don't get time to talk enough. Sometimes I feel your ministry and church work is taking you further and further away from me.' I gave my husband a gentle smile and touched his arm lovingly.

'I hope not, Seli,' responded Eli with a sigh. 'I couldn't be doing all I'm doing without you keeping the family and farm together here at home.'

In the event Mary and James's wedding took place a couple of weeks before that of Elizabeth and John. It was a quiet and simple affair in the Bolney Chapel on Wednesday afternoon, 8 September. Eli and I were the witnesses, and Eli Ashdown heard their vows and gave them a lovely, encouraging Bible-based message to start them off in their new life together.

Twelve days later, on Monday, 20 September, the curate at Edburton married Elizabeth and John at St Andrew's Church. Our John, Elizabeth's brother, together with our Dorcas were the official witnesses, and we had a celebratory meal at Perching Manor Farm to send the happy couple off with God's blessing.

Chapter 18

'A Faithful God' — But Is He?

For a number of years after their wedding in 1868, Orpha and Charles ran the draper's shop in Fulking. It was good to have them in the village particularly as our other married daughters were living further away, Ruth in Patcham, Naomi in Slaugham.

Orpha was our second daughter and fifth child, and after having named our first daughter Ruth, it seemed fitting to name our second after her sister by marriage in the biblical story. But without really believing that a name can affect a child's destiny, more than once I said to Eli that it would have been better not to name one of our children after a biblical character who had turned away her allegiance to the god of Israel.

Our Orpha was a serious child and was often burdened by circumstances and never really appeared to be carefree and happy. As far as we could judge, she had a good relationship with her husband, but they never managed to have children, and I know this was a sorrow to her. She didn't talk about it much, but I remember one day when we heard that John's wife, Mary Ann, was once more with child, despite struggling with severe depression, she burst out in a way that revealed a deep inner bitterness.

'God's so unfair,' she exclaimed. 'He's not allowing me a baby but doesn't stop Mary Ann having them one after another.'

It was partly this that prompted me to wholeheartedly agree to the suggestion that Orpha and Charles look after Mary Ann's little daughter Kate when another baby was proving just too much for her. Although they never legally adopted Kate, she is still with Charles today even though now he has another wife. But that's the story I'm coming to.

After a few years running the village store in Fulking, Charles looked for the opportunity for a change. Orpha was frequently ill, and without her by his side, shopkeeping was not really what he wanted to be doing. We knew this and tried to help him.

About that time, Eli was spending time encouraging a small group of believers in the village of Hurstpierpoint, the village where Charles had been brought up, about five miles north of us. For lack of leadership, they were no longer meeting regularly for fellowship and worship, and Eli tried to remedy this by arranging Sunday preachers for them and, when he could, leading a week evening service. This resulted in a few of them asking Eli to baptise them, and in 1875 under his guidance, they formed themselves into a definite church with Strict Baptist principles. The following year, they were able to build themselves a small chapel in Chinese Lane together with an adjoining chapel house and, with Eli's encouragement, they called Henry Miles to be their pastor.[69]

During the time Eli was regularly visiting the friends at Hurstpierpoint, he got to hear about a small farm of about forty acres to rent, and Charles and Orpha took it over and moved there with Kate in the autumn of 1874.

However, Orpha's health continued to deteriorate, and by the end of 1876 we were all very concerned for her. Eli would often call in to see Orpha on his way home from Mayfield on a Monday, and one evening he came home looking particularly anxious and later confided in me that he was extremely worried about her.

'Seli,' he said, 'if I knew she was right with God, I would be less anxious. She and Charles meet with the friends at Hope Chapel most Sundays, but Orpha seems to have a complete blank about spiritual

---

[69] Ralph Chambers, 'Hurstpierpoint', op.cit., vol. 2, 39f.

things. She doesn't disagree with what I say when I talk to her about her soul, and she is happy for me to read the scriptures and pray with her, but I can sense none of that inner response that I've come to recognise from someone who has the life of God's Spirit in them.'

'I pray for her and Charles and little Kate so often,' I added, looking anxiously at Eli.

A few weeks later, Eli shared an experience with me that really lifted my spirit.

'My dear,' he said, 'Orpha has been so much on my heart. I love all our children, but somehow I feel a greater sense of responsibility for the girls and, at the moment, for Orpha in particular. I've been wrestling with God for her soul, and this morning as I was praying with such a burden for her eternal welfare, I sensed a wonderful release. I believe God has assured me she is his.'

'That's wonderful, Eli,' I cried. 'Wonderful,' and tears came into my eyes, partly for Orpha and partly for my husband as I saw what this meant to him.

'I'm now able to pray in an entirely different way, Seli,' Eli added. 'I'm taking back to God his own promise, that all things that we ask of him believing we shall receive. He's given me the faith to believe that Orpha will experience God's grace and trust herself to Christ before she dies. Faith is God's gift, and in giving me this faith, I believe it's the assurance that my prayer is answered and he will give her saving faith too.'

For some weeks Eli had a much more cheerful attitude about Orpha. He visited her regularly, talked with her, and prayed with her.

One beautiful spring morning, I took the pony and trap and drove up to Horns Farm, Hurstpierpoint, myself to see Orpha. I took her a jar of honey from our bees and some plum jam. I was shocked at her appearance, and although I tried not to show it, I think she could sense my reaction.

'Mum, I'm getting weaker and weaker,' she said, 'and some nights the pain is almost unbearable. They say it's my kidneys.'

I took the bull by the horns, as the saying goes, and with an overwhelming love for my daughter, I blurted out the one thing that was on my heart.

'Orpha, my dear, are you ready to die? Are you ready to face God?'

'No, Mum, I'm not, and I'm not going to die. I'm thirty-two, I've got a husband and adopted daughter to look after. God can't let me die yet. I don't want to know. I don't want to think about it.'

I gave her a hug and a kiss and sat down to talk about other things, but deep within me, I felt despair. I had little doubt that Orpha had only a short while to live, and she was refusing to make her peace with God, refusing to acknowledge sin and her need of a Saviour.

Eli too became increasingly perturbed. He was sure God had given him assurance that his prayer for Orpha had been heard and his understanding of this was that she would show evidence of repentance and faith in Jesus. Yet we could both see that her physical life was ebbing away and there remained no acceptance of this or obvious concern for her never-dying soul.

It was a tremendous test of Eli's faith. The burden had started as a father's loving concern for his daughter's salvation, but for Eli, it had now developed into something even more fundamental to his whole existence, namely God's faithfulness and the reality of his own acceptance by God.

How fundamental this was to Eli is expressed in a letter he wrote to a minister friend, Wilfred Hoadley. He showed me the letter, and when I realised the significance of what he said, he allowed me to make a copy of it.

Edburton, March 27, 1877

My dear friend,

I found yours when I came home today and have booked you for the 21st May. But it is a solemn question as to whether I shall not have to give up preaching before then, my poor daughter is almost if not quite gone, and should she depart and bear no evidence of her salvation, I cannot see how it is possible for me to go on preaching. For to preach a faithful God, and myself shut out, I cannot. My dear friend I do indeed have to travel in deep waters.

You may say 'You have been mistaken in the promise, many a one has.' I know it, and if the dear Lord is pleased to open up wherein I have been mistaken then it would well, but I am not my own, I cannot believe and let go the promise just as I please. Sometimes it is all well for a few minutes, and never did I so feelingly plead the dear name and Person of Jesus before, but something says 'what of that, if you get no answer, for the Word says whatsoever you ask in my name it shall be done or given to you.' The Lord only knows where this will end, I feel to hang between hope and fear; it will be one of two things, either my tongue will shout aloud to his praise or I shall have to sit down in dumb silence.

Yours sincerely,

Eli Page[70]

Orpha died on the 18 April, just three weeks after Eli's letter to his friend. On the Monday afternoon of that last week of her life, Eli had called in to see her as usual. He had begun to feel encouraged in his confidence of her salvation as during his several visits the previous week, Orpha had begun to allow herself to believe she was dying and had wanted to talk about eternity. Eli told me that he had shared with her some of the wonderful scripture texts about the hereafter and, in particular, the verse in the Corinthian letter which states that 'eye hath not see, nor ear heard what God hath prepared for those who love Him.'[71] He left her with the challenge as to whether she loved him and

---

[70] John Richard Thomas, op. cit.
[71] 1 Corinthians 2:9.

gave her the biggest reason for loving him, namely that he had sent his Son Jesus to die for the sins of all who receive him.

When he returned that Monday afternoon, he found Orpha very weak but looking very much brighter.

'Dad,' she said, 'I love him. He died for me. I feel the assurance of that in my heart. After you left me last Friday, I felt desperate. All sorts of wrong things that I had said and done came into my mind, and I tossed and turned in bed for hours. Then I cried to God for mercy, and I suddenly realised, I think really for the first time, what it means that Jesus died for sinners. At first I couldn't believe it could mean me. It was just for the elect, wasn't it? But then suddenly, and it must have been God, I remembered the verse you often read to us, "God so loved the world that he sent His only begotten Son, that whosoever believeth in Him shall not perish but have eternal life."[72] I had such a sense of happiness and peace. Dad, I can die now!'

Eli was in tears when he told me, and the next day we both drove up to Hurstpierpoint to see Orpha. She was in a lot of pain and very weak, but there was a new look in her eyes. We read the scriptures to her and prayed and had much peace in leaving her to God's mercy. It was more difficult to comfort Charles and Kate. The latter having just had her seventh birthday. Eli tried to explain to them what had happed to Orpha and that now the one we all loved was going to see Jesus and we would meet again if we too trusted God for his mercy in his Son Jesus.

That was the Tuesday, and Orpha died early the next morning.

To take the story further, Charles found life very difficult without Orpha. We helped him as much as we could, and one way of doing this was to have Kate to stay from time to time. One evening about a year after Orpha's passing, when he was calling by to pick up Kate, he asked whether he could speak to Eli and me together. It was a good moment as Eli had just come in, so I made us all a cup of tea, and we sat down together around the kitchen table.

'So what is it, son?' asked Eli encouragingly.

---

[72] John 3:16.

Charles hesitated for a moment and then rather diffidently blurted out what was on his heart. 'I'm walking out with Emily Walker,' he said. 'You will know her family from Hope Chapel.'

'That's good, Charles,' said Eli, after a moment's hesitation. 'A man needs a wife, and we know life has been very lonely for you. We don't have any problem with that, do we, Seli?'

'You've both been so good to me,' added Charles, 'and I don't want you to think I've forgotten Orpha. She was my first love, and being with her and part of your family has been very important to me.'

'I can assure you,' said Eli, 'that we won't think any the worse of you if you remarry. Orpha is in glory and doesn't need you anymore, but you need a wife.'

'How will this affect Kate?' I asked. 'Have you talked to Emily about that or is it too soon?'

'It's still early days,' answered Charles, now looking very much more at ease. 'I wanted you to know before it was talked about publically. I've had Kate since she was a few months old, and although John comes to see her occasionally, she really doesn't know him as a father figure. I'm the father she knows, I love her and hope very much that if things proceed with Emily, she will accept us both.'

'How old is Emily?' I asked.

'She's just two years older than me,' responded Charles. 'We've known each other since we were children together in the village.'

'William Walker is also a farmer, isn't he?' said Eli. 'That's good, Emily will be used to farm life and should be a great help to you.'

After Charles was gone, I tried to get my thoughts together. Life had to go on and a man needs a wife, but somehow I knew it would take time for me to accept another woman in Orpha's place. 'I wonder how Kate will accept it,' I asked myself.

Charles and Emily were married in the autumn of 1878, and thankfully, Emily was pleased to accept Kate as part of the package of her marriage.[73]

---

[73] 1881 Census, Charles Mitchell, born 1845, Hurstpierpoint.

Chapter 19

Page in History

I must bring my ramblings to a close, but there's one other incident I'd like to share for which some family members have criticised Eli strongly.

One morning when Eli was opening the post, he turned to me with a wide smile and exclaimed, 'This is interesting, Seli.'

I waited while he perused what looked to me to be an official notification of something or other.

'Is it serious, Eli?' I asked anxiously.

'No, nothing serious,' he answered passing me the letter, 'but quite extraordinary and unexpected.'

The letter heading showed that it was from the Metropolitan Board of Works in London, and although the language of the letter was difficult to understand, I gathered it referred to land in the Edgeware area of Middlesex.

'What's this all about, Eli?' I asked. 'Your family has never had farmland in Middlesex, have they?'

'Well, according to this, we might have,' responded Eli. 'It seems that during the reign of Henry VIII, grazing land in the Edgeware area was granted to someone in the Page family for services rendered to the king and country. Then later, during the civil war in Cromwell's time, when I guess everything was in confusion and maybe that particular ancestor of mine, if he was such, was killed in battle, the family lost sight of their ownership of it. Or maybe the land was even confiscated, if Sir Page of the seventeenth century happened to be one of Cromwell's Roundheads fighting against the king, which was more than likely!'

'Wow, that's really fascinating,' I answered excitedly. 'It brings history to life to realise our own family played a part in it. But what is the letter saying? Why are they writing to you now?'

'Well, it seems that the land in question has been used as common land, available for all to use for grazing, but the letter states that under the Metropolitan Commons Act 1878 the Metropolitan Board of Works, which controls all public facilities in the London area, has the right to purchase common land to ensure its continuity. With that in mind, they are trying to ascertain who legally owns this fairly substantial acreage of land in Edgeware. Since records show it was bequeathed to the Page family in the sixteenth century, they have written to me.'

Looking somewhat amazed, I blurted out, 'But does it belong to you, Eli?'

'I've absolutely no idea, Seli,' my husband answered. 'I've never heard about it before. Obviously I would need to prove my ownership of it to the Metropolitan Board of Works, and this is really what this letter is offering me the chance to do. I shall need to think and pray about the whole thing.

'For the moment, my dear,' added Eli, 'I'd rather we keep this to ourselves. That land will be worth a lot of money, and I don't want the family getting ideas of grandeur.'

Several days went by, and Eli said no more to me about the letter or how he was thinking about it. He was away a lot with his preaching and was busy with farming things when he was at home. At last my curiosity got the better of me, and one evening I asked him point-blank whether he had decided how he was going to react to it.

'I very nearly put the situation in the hands of a solicitor to try and establish any rights we had to this land,' Eli answered, 'but then felt so convicted by a passage of God's Word from which I had felt directed to preach last Sunday evening, that I realised that I just had to let the matter rest.'

'What was the scripture?' I asked my husband with interest.

'It's a passage in the prophecy of Jeremiah,' answered Eli. 'The prophet was given a word from God for his servant Baruch which included these words: "Seekest thou great things for thyself? Seek them not."[74] In my sermon, I compared that warning in the Old Testament with Jesus' promise in Matthew's Gospel: "Seek ye first the Kingdom of God and his righteousness and all these things shall be added unto you."[75]

'It was quite amazing, Seli,' added Eli, 'once I'd made up my mind not to proceed with any attempt to claim a right to the land in Edgeware, I began to see things from a more sensible point of view. We have all that we need. God's been wonderfully good to us in really blessing us with temporal things. I'm a minister of Jesus Christ, who himself lived a very simple life, making no demands for any material possessions in this world. It's probably unlikely that I could establish ownership of that valuable common land anyway, so to seek it is akin to coveting it, which also is wrong. Then thinking further, if we were to get the money for it, would that really help our children? I believe it's right that a man should work for his living, and this is the way we have brought up our children. We see evidence so often that excessive wealth becomes a curse rather than a blessing. No, I'm happy to let this pass. In fact, I've already written a reply to the letter saying I doubt whether I'm the rightful owner of the land and I'm making no attempt to prove otherwise. If after all this someone else brings up the evidence that it belongs to me, I shall take this as coming from God, but I'm not expecting this to happen.'

Sometime later Eli did mention the Edgeware land to the family and explained his reasons for declining to pursue any claim to the

---

[74] Jeremiah 45:5.
[75] Matthew 6:33.

ownership of it. I think at the time, most of the children respected their father's point of view, but I was aware that from time to time later, the comment was made, 'If only we had had the money for that land in Edgeware!'[76]

---

[76] John Richard Thomas, 'The Lost Page Millions'.

Chapter 20

Ebenezer Dan Holder

It's now summer 1883, and in a few weeks, I shall be celebrating my sixty-fifth birthday. Where have the years gone? In some ways, it seems only yesterday that I was a small girl walking the fields of Ripe with my dear father. On the other hand, so much has happened to me as a wife and mother that I find it extremely difficult to believe there was a life before my marriage to Eli! Truly the human mind is a strange and remarkable creation.

Eli continues to be away a great deal with his preaching, but I'm so thankful for my children and grandchildren who are all a great comfort to me. Ruth comes across from Patcham to see me regularly, and I recently felt I should share with her the fact that I'm writing this diary. I suggested to her she might like to continue the story into the next generation. We shall see whether she takes this up, or rather you will see, as it will most certainly be after my Lord has taken me to glory to be with him forever.

Ruth now has five children. She and Dan lost little John Eli some years ago, and very sadly a few weeks ago, their little Joseph died—he was just sixteen months. We can't understand God's ways in allowing these things to happen. As believers we certainly aren't exempt from the illnesses that beset all mankind, but we do have the promise of our heavenly Father's grace and help in time of need. One of his names is the 'God of all comfort', and we do believe too that he makes all things work together for our good, although we don't often see this at the time.

Following little Joseph's death, we had two of Ruth's younger children to stay with us for a while to help relieve the pressure at home. Mary is coming up to her eighth birthday, and Ebenezer is now six. Living on the farm here is a lot different from the smithy in Patcham, and with Auntie Esther here to look after them, they seemed to really enjoy their holiday. Eb is a quiet, sensitive little lad, and I was a bit worried that Eli's often abrupt manner might frighten him, but I needn't have feared. I think the fact that he is named after the little son we lost gives Eli a special affinity to Eb, and the latter has really got to love his granddad. Eli introduced him to the farm and the countryside, and Eb would come back from their walks together very excited at all they had seen and done.

Uncle Nap was also a great hit with the children. It was the beginning of haymaking, and Nap took Eb with him to help turn the cut grass in the fields. One day in particular, the sun was really hot, and Eb came back complaining of a headache. My mind went to the story of the son of the Shunammite woman in the book of Kings who had also come home from the fields crying, 'My head, my head.' You will remember that this lad died, but in a wonderful way, Elisha restored him to life again.[77]

'Oh dear,' I said to myself, 'I trust and pray Eb's reaction to the hot sun is not so serious, we don't have Elisha the prophet here to raise him back to life again.'

Then it struck me that this wasn't the point, for although we don't have Elisha with us, we have his god. This led me to simply pray that Eb would be well after a good night's sleep, and thankfully, it was so.

---

[77] 2 Kings 4:18ff.

Chapter 21

My Epilogue

There's one other experience I'd like to add which occurred earlier this year and spoke to me very clearly. It gave me fresh light on my whole life, and I'd like to share this with you as a conclusion to these personal reminiscences.

Each week I've continued to receive Spurgeon's printed sermons, and there was one which particularly aroused my interest as it was entitled 'Hands Full of Honey',[78] which is a subject with which I'm very familiar! The text of the sermon is from Judges chapter 14 which is recounting the experience and exploits of Samson.

As a young man Samson had come face-to-face with a lion, and Spurgeon makes the point that God brings all kinds of dangers and difficult experiences into our lives both to test us and train us. Thinking about my own life, I decided that my 'lions' have been due firstly to my frequent pregnancies and bearing children and then secondly to the frequent absence of my husband and often having to bear the ultimate responsibility for the family and staff and emergencies which cropped up on the farm.

---

[78] *Metropolitan Tabernacle Pulpit*, 78ff. Sermon 1703 preached 28 January 1883.

The devil has tempted me in regard to these things. I have at times sensed myself becoming angry and bitter, thinking that neither God nor my husband really loved me or cared for my well-being. Samson had no weapon with which to defend himself against the lion and was, naturally speaking, helpless to cope with the situation. I felt I could sympathise with this. However, the Spirit of God came mightily on Samson, and he slew the lion with his bare hands. Looking back, I too can praise God for the supernatural ways he has strengthened me, given me contentment to accept these things as part of the all things which work together for my ultimate good[79] and helped me to cope reasonably adequately with every situation that has occurred in my life.

But the text proceeds further. Returning to the spot later, Samson discovers that a swarm of bees had settled in the carcass of the lion, probably by then just the skeleton, and had produced honey which he was able to extract both for himself and his parents.

The Rev. Spurgeon makes the point that this is exactly what God will often do for us. Out of our victories over those difficult situations come sweetness. The essence of this sweetness, this honey to feed our souls, is a closer relationship with the Lord Jesus. I know this has happened to me. An awareness of my own inadequacies to cope with the difficulties in my life has driven me to prayer, and then experiencing God's help has caused me to trust him and love him in a deeper way. Through my understanding of the Bible, I know that I have only been able to experience this love of God because Jesus died for me. My Saviour has become very precious to me.

But we read that Samson walked on his way eating the honey from the honeycomb in his hand, which he had taken from the carcass of the lion, and also that there was enough to share with his parents.

Life has gone on, but the sweetness and preciousness of my relationship with the Lord Jesus, which I sense has to a large degree come out of the carcass of the victories he gave me over self-pity and despair, have remained with me. I have fed on him through his Word,

---

[79] Romans 6:28.

and I believe he has slowly been changing my character to make me more like him. Thus, just as Samson shared the honey with his parents, my blessing has in turn been a benefit to my husband and children.

Wanting to give all the glory to God, I really believe that my family have benefited from my faith in Christ and my walk with him. Having Jesus with me has, I'm sure, made me more patient, given me more understanding of others, and more wisdom in what I say and what I don't say. My prayer is that each of my children and grandchildren will truly eat of the 'honey' of a personal relationship with my Jesus and that, like Selina of the last century, my life might bear much fruit for eternity.

Postscript

Selina died on 8 February 1886, and her funeral took place on what would have been Eli and her forty-eighth wedding anniversary, 12 February.

Her husband and family missed her terribly. She had been the focal point around which her large family had existed, and they all loved her dearly. Her patience and wisdom had, in an unobtrusive way, exerted a tremendous influence in the home, often defusing potential conflicts between her more volatile husband and the family and staff. This influence was graciously acknowledged by her husband in the scripture text chosen for her and engraved on her tombstone. It is still there for all to read, close to the back of the church in the graveyard of St Andrew's Church, Edburton: 'Blessed are the peacemakers, for they shall be called the children of God.'

The influence of Selina's life and prayers has without doubt benefited not only her immediate family but also the following generations down through into the twenty-first century.

SELINA,
THE BELOVED WIFE OF
ELI PACE,
OF PERCHING MANOR,
DIED FEBRUARY 8TH 1886,
AGED 68 YEARS.

"Blessed are the peacemakers for they shall be called the children of God." Matt. v. 9.

Appendix 1

Eli's Own Testimony of His Conversion

Extracts from a sermon preached by Eli Page at the Dicker on the afternoon of 22 September 1887 celebrating the Dicker Chapel's fiftieth anniversary and published in the *Gospel Standard*.

'What hath God wrought!' Num 23:23.

I stand before you this afternoon under very peculiar circumstances, having known your former place of worship from my childhood, and this one ever since it was built. When asked to come and preach on this occasion I at first demurred, but having known the rise of this congregation from the commencement, I felt I should not do right to refuse. My fellow-sinners, we are exhorted to acknowledge God in all our ways, and he has promised to direct our steps.

This fiftieth year is so interwoven with my life that I cannot refrain from mentioning it.

Fifty years ago the seventh of last February I was left an orphan in the world, and then God took me up; as the Word says: *'When my father and my mother forsake me, then the Lord will take me up.'* (Ps. xxvii. 10.).

Again: Fifty years ago the Lord put a cry into my soul, which he heard and answered, as surely as the sun now shines. He stopped me, a wild, profligate youth, in my mad career. Shall this be hid in darkness and obscurity? Shall I not exclaim, *'What hath God wrought!'* After this I felt the holy law of God in my conscience.

Now I have a little statement to make with regard to this place, for we wish to acknowledge God's hand. When a wild, ungodly youth I used to meet in the room in this village in old Mr. Reed's time, and the cause, after Mr. R. gave up speaking, was carried on by supply ministers until the time that Mr. Cowper was settled here as the pastor, which was in the year 1837.

I come now to something that more deeply concerns us. Where shall I commence upon the words of my text? I might speak of Balaam, but I have not time. These words were spoken by an ungodly man, but he was compelled to speak them by the Spirit of God.

You read that the Lord met Balaam, and that he put words into his mouth. It is one thing to have the light of the Spirit and another thing to have the grace of God. Balaam had light, but no grace. He had light to see the blessedness of God's people in death, and consequently he said, *'Let me die the death of the righteous, and let my last end be like his.'* But Balaam had no desire to live their life. Now, poor tried soul, you have what Balaam had not, for you want to live the life of a child of God as well as die his death. You know if you have the life you will have the death of a child of God.

There is something in divine life that craves the presence of God. I remember forty-nine years ago, when I came to this chapel how desirous I was for the dear old man to come to the evidences of a child of God, and when I heard them described I inwardly exclaimed, 'That is it! I have it here in my breast.'

On one particular occasion I felt I was doomed to destruction. It was a solemn time. You who knew Mr. Cowper will remember his solemn way of beginning, as if he would cut up everything root and branch. I felt I should surely be found on the wrong side. But after cutting as if he would cut everything to pieces, he would then describe the movements of life in the soul; and on that particular occasion I could say, 'Bless God I possess it.' I left the chapel assured I should go to heaven, and longed and prayed for the grave; but here I am, spared to speak to you here this afternoon, and what for God only knows; but he knows my aim would be your good and his glory.

Appendix 2

Newspaper account of a significant incident in Eli's childhood

Sussex Advertiser (15 December 1823)

At about 8 o'clock on last Friday evening, as Mr Page, a farmer of Hellingly was crossing the Dicker on his way home from Horsebridge, where he had been to a tithe feast, he received a bludgeon blow on his temple from some villain who contrived to get unheard behind him, (Mr P being deaf) and after repeating his blows robbed him of a Check on the Hailsham Bank for Thirty Six pounds, a sovereign, and some silver and made off with his booty. Mr Page on recovering from his surprise and the immediate effect of the blows contrived to get home where he had the best assistance the neighbourhood afforded. Suspicion, we hear, points strongly at a doubtful character, residing in the parish. The Horsebridge Prosecuting Society offer a reward of Five Pounds for the apprehension and conviction of the robber.

Sussex Advertiser (22 December 1823)

James Bennett, the man suspected of robbing Mr Page of Hellingly on his way home from a tithe feast at Horsebridge on Friday se'night, as stated in our last Journal, has been since taken into custody and charged with the offence, in consequence of which he on Wednesday last underwent a long examination before a sitting of Magistrate, at Hailsham, where Mr Page, (the hurt he received requiring great care) previously arrived in a post-chaise. The prisoner was, by I. Thomas, Esq. fully committed for trial on strong circumstantial evidence, an account of which we have received in detail, but after the recent observations of Mr Justice Park, at Hertford, we feel no disposition to give it early publicity. The accused is only 18 years of age, a good looking young man, by trade a carpenter, and considered an excellent workman. The check on the Hailsham Bank, for £36, taken from the prosecutor, has been found; it was discovered lying in a sort of dry ditch, not far from the spot whereon the robbery was committed.

Sussex Advertiser (29 December 1823)

James Bennett, the younger, aged 18, stood indicted for having, on the 12th day of December instant, feloniously assaulted on the King's highway, in the parish of Hellingly, Richard Page, and stealing from his person one sovereign, 13 shillings, and a check on a Banker of the value of £36, the property of him, the said Richard Page.

It appeared in evidence, that the prosecutor, on the day mentioned in the indictment, had been to a tithe-feast, at an inn, in the neighbourhood, and on his return home was attacked by the prisoner, who felled him to the ground with a large stick, and then committed the robbery, after which the prisoner went to his father's house.

Several witnesses proved having seen the stick, (which was produced in Court) in the prisoner's possession on the evening of the robbery, which he endeavoured to conceal beneath his round-frock and that he followed the Prosecutor out of the public-house. The prisoner was also traced by his footsteps across a ploughed field leading to the house where he lived, the impressions exactly corresponding with his nailed half-boots. It likewise appeared that the habits of the prisoner were so abandoned, that he was a terror to his own father, who was afraid to live with him.

The learned Judge summed up the evidence with his usual perspicuity and impartiality, and the Jury, after some consultation, returned a verdict of Guilty, but recommended the Prisoner to mercy, on account of his youth, in which recommendation the prosecutor joined.

His Lordship proceeded in the most solemn and impressive terms, to point out to the prisoner the enormity of his offence, and pronounced the awful sentence of Death, The prisoner appeared absorbed in grief, and was removed from the bar greatly affected.

Much praise was due to Mr Paris, the Constable, on this occasion, who made an accurate drawing of the boot-impressions by which Bennett was traced, and which when compared with the half-boots he had on when he committed the robbery, exactly corresponded, and gave great weight to the evidence on which the prisoner was convicted.

Appendix 3

Sussex Windmills

In summer 1973, Jack and Jill became cinema stars when Universal Pictures made the film *The Black Windmill*. Actors featured in the film included Michael Caine, Janet Suzman, Donald Pleasence and Joss Ackland.

The windmills stand atop the scenic South Downs with spectacular views of the Sussex Weald. They are seven miles north of the city of Brighton and Hove. As well as *Jack* and *Jill*, the roundhouse of *Duncton Mill* survives, located a short distance east of *Jack*.

The mills are easily accessible by road at the end of Mill Lane from the A273 road where it crosses the South Downs. There is ample free parking in the car park beside the mills.

The working life of the mills ended in 1906 and in 1908 *Jill* was damaged in a storm. She lost her fantail and sails over the years until in 1953 restoration was carried out by E Hole and Son, the Burgess Hill millwrights, funded by Cuckfield Rural District Council. In 1978, restoration of *Jill* to working order was commenced. *Jill* ground flour again in 1986. During the Great Storm of 1987, the mill's sails were set in motion with the brake on, setting fire to the mill. Some members of the Windmill Society were able to get to the mill and save her.[80]

---

[80] *Wikipedia*, 'The Clayton Windmills'

Today, *Jill* is in working order and open to the public most Sundays between May and September. She produces stoneground wholemeal flour on an occasional basis. The vast majority of her flour is sold to visitors. It is ground from organic wheat, grown locally in Sussex. On the occasions when the wind is blowing and *Jill* is in operation, a guide is available to explain the process of milling. *Jill* Windmill is owned by Mid Sussex District Council.

Jack is now privately owned and all machinery below windshaft level has been removed. In 1966, however, Jack was fitted with new sails in order to appear in the film mentioned above.

Appendix 4

A traditional Sussex sheep shearing song quoted by Dr Blaker
in his reminiscences entitled *Sussex in Bygone Days*.

Come all my jolly boys and we'll together go
    Abroad with our Captain, to shear the lamb and ewe,
    All in the merry month of June, of all times in the year,
It always comes in season the ewes and lambs to shear;
And there we must work hard, boys, until our backs do ache,
And our master, he will bring us beer whenever we do lack.
Our master he comes round to see his work done well,
He says, 'Boys, shear them close, for there is but little wool!'
'O yes, Master,' then we reply, 'we'll do it well if we can,'
When our Captain calls, 'Shear close, boys,' to each and every man;
And at some places still we have this story all day long,
'Shear them well and close, boys,' and this is all their song.
And then our noble Captain doth unto our master say,
'Come, let us have one bucket of your good ale I pray';
He turns unto our Captain, and makes him this reply,
'You shall have the best of beer, I promise, presently,'
Then out with the bucket pretty Betsy she doth come,
And Master says, 'Maid, mind and see that every man have some.'
This is some of our pastime as we the sheep do shear,
And though we are such merry boys, we work hard I declare;
And when 'tis night and we are done, our master is more free,

And fills us well with good strong beer. And pipes and tobaccee;
And so we sit and drink and smoke and sing and roar,
Till we become more merry far than we had been before.
When all our work is done, and all our sheep are shorn,
Then home with our Captain, to drink the ale that's strong;
'Tis a barrel then of hum-cup, which we call the 'black ram.'
And we do sit and swagger, and think that we are men,
And yet before 'tis night, I'll stand you half-a-crown,
That if you haven't especial care this ram will knock you down.

Index

A

Albourne   241-2, 248
antinomians   259-61
Arlington   52, 56-7, 59, 72, 90, 101, 124
Ashdown, Eli   289-91, 293
atonement, extent and sufficiency of Christ's   279
Australia   95
Awbrook Farm, Scaynes Hill   291-2

B

beekeeping   161, 177-9
believer's baptism   136, 258, 265-6, 268, 289-90
Bennett, James   94-5, 319-20
Bexhill   32
birds' eggs, collecting   175
Blaker, Nathaniel   186
Bolney, Gassons Farm   289
Bolney, Twineham Lane   290
Bowleys Farm   56, 61

Briar Cottage, Edburton   252-3, 284
Brighthelmstone   23
Brighton   23, 26, 28, 30, 33, 163, 175, 186-7, 207, 209-10, 212-13, 216, 230-3, 246, 251-4
Brighton, West Street Chapel   216
Burch, William   149
Burgess Hill   289-92, 323
Burton, David   90
butter making   64

C

Calvinism   124, 135-6, 218, 268
Camberlot Lane, Dicker   61, 93
causes of truth   137, 257
charcoal burning   140, 145, 150, 238
Clifton Farm, Arlington   56-7, 59, 61, 72, 97, 101, 116, 121-2, 125, 129, 171
Combridge, John   255, 287
Cowper, William   55, 316
Crowborough   32
Croydon   213

D

Devil's Dyke   186, 192, 199, 238, 247
Dicker Common   61-2, 93
diphtheria   285-6
duty faith   275-7

E

East Chiltington   228
East Grinstead   213
Edburton   192, 219, 228, 235, 249, 252-3, 267, 272-3, 284, 286, 288, 293, 298, 313
Edburton Church, St Andrew's   288-9
Edgeware   303-6
Elliott, General   30
eternal life   25, 154, 245, 300
eternal Sonship of Jesus   55, 236-7
evangelical awakening   41, 135, 257

F

Flimwell   124, 137
Ford, James   130, 142
Ford, Mary   131-3, 141, 143-4, 165
Fulking   186, 189, 191-2, 215, 221-2, 247-8, 295-6
Fuller, Elizabeth   186
Fuller, George   168-9
Fuller, Sarah   168, 239

G

Gadsby, William   247, 260, 267-8
Gilbert, George   29-30
Gospel, free offer   277
Gospel Standard   237, 315
Grace, John   216
Guy, Richard   68, 79-80

H

Hailsham   17, 94, 319-20
Harbour, William   246
Harman, Doris and Harold   17, 105-6
Harmer, Ann   165-7, 169
harvesting grain   153
harvesting hops   139, 157, 159
Heathfield   29-30, 32, 42, 136, 186
Heathfield Park   32
Hellingly   43, 51-2, 319-20
Henfield   207, 218-19, 242, 259
Henry VIII   264, 303
herbal medicine   112, 254
Hoadley, Wilfred   298
Holder, Benjamin   242
Holder, Dan   11, 242, 245, 307
Holder, Ebenezer Dan   11, 307
Holder, John Eli   283
Holder, Josias   241-2
hop-growing   116, 127
Huntington, William   46, 66, 135-6, 259-60, 289-90
Hurstpierpoint   296-7, 300-1

Hurstpierpoint, Hope Chapel 296, 301
Hurstpierpoint, Horns Farm 297

I

Ingram, Benjamin 23

J

Jenkins, Jenkins 43-4

K

Keith, George 288
Kipling, Rudyard 262

L

Lewis 17, 42-4, 46, 52, 67, 264, 289-90
Lewis, Jireh Chapel 46, 289-90
Limden Farm 116-17, 119, 121-3, 131, 137, 143, 147, 149, 153, 155, 158, 161-3, 165, 169, 171
Limden Lane 124, 137, 165, 171, 173, 205
Lower Dicker Chapel 42, 51, 67
lucifers 110-11

M

Mabbs Hill 124
Manchester 267-8
Mannington 42, 45
Martin, John 287

Mayfield 17, 146, 149, 169, 238-40, 247, 257-9, 261-2, 264-5, 268-70, 277, 279-80, 289-90, 296
Mayfield Chapel 269
Mayfield martyrs 264
Maynard, John 264
Metropolitan Board of Works 303-4
Miles, Henry 296
Mitchell, Charles 246, 248, 301

N

national schools 163-4, 171, 207
Newton, John 53, 68, 271, 273
North Street, Brighton 28

O

Ote Hall 30-1

P

Page, Dorcas 161, 191, 205, 240, 293
Page, Ebenezer 161-2, 209, 283
Page, Elizabeth 161, 205, 255, 287-9, 292-3
Page, Elizabeth (neé Payne-Heaver) 228-9, 231, 246, 251-2, 274, 284-6
Page, John 99, 110, 113, 131-3, 209, 228-34, 251-3, 255, 285, 301
Page, Kate 213, 253, 255, 296, 300-1

Page, Leah   207, 240
Page, Mary   137, 161, 197, 199,
    205, 289-90, 293
Page, Mary Ann (neé Blake)   213,
    229-34, 251-5, 284, 295-6
Page, Mercy   137, 161, 197, 199,
    205
Page, Naomi   161, 166-7, 169, 171,
    197-8, 213, 228, 241, 246,
    249, 293, 295
Page, Naphthali   228, 240, 308
Page, Orpha   161, 166, 171, 197-
    8, 211, 228, 241, 246, 248-9,
    255, 295-301
Page, Richard (junior)   90-2, 103-
    4, 110, 129-31, 133, 141, 163,
    173-4, 177-80, 194-5, 227-9,
    231, 251-2, 269-70, 284
Page, Richard (senior)   43, 45,
    51-2, 320
Page, Ruth   116, 122, 125, 129,
    162-3, 180-1, 197-9, 206, 210-
    11, 216, 218-19, 227-8, 241-3,
    245-9, 284
Page, Walter   284, 286
Page, William   246, 253, 284-6
Parris, Philadelphia (neé Page)   72,
    94, 163
Parris, Ruth   163-4
Parris, Trayton   72, 75, 79-80, 92,
    142
Patcham   242, 246, 248, 284, 295,
    307-8
Payne, George   194, 201-2
Pell Green   137

Perching Manor Farm   187, 189,
    191, 216, 223, 246, 293
Philpot, J. C.   237
Philpott, William   291-2
pig slaughtering   76-7, 80-1
Pilgrim's Progress   20
Pitcher, Thomas   43
Port, Elisha   209, 232
Portsmouth, Salem Chapel   292
Poynings   192, 227, 247

R

Ripe   17-18, 28-9, 36, 42-3, 49,
    51, 56
Ripe Independent Chapel   42-3,
    52, 67
Robertsbridge   137
Romaine, William   135
Rotherfield   30, 32
Rowlands, Daniel   135

S

Sawyer, Jack   145-7, 149, 238-9
Scaynes Hill   289-92
Selina, Countess of Huntingdon
    18, 21-31, 36, 41, 43, 135, 311
sheep shearing   223-4, 325
sheep washing   221-2
Shepherd and Dog, Fulking pub
    222, 224, 236
Shover's Green   124, 137
Slaugham   249, 293, 295
smuggling   262
snow   109-10, 112

South Downs   36, 89, 187, 192, 197-8, 201, 210, 262, 323
spiritual unction   82, 278
Spurgeon, Charles Haddon   216-18, 258, 267, 277, 309-10
Staplehurst   149
Stonegate   116, 124, 132, 137, 147, 162-5, 171, 178, 205
Stonegate Farm   163, 178
Stores Farm   130-1, 141-2
Strict and Particular Baptist   268, 277, 290, 296
Sussex Windmills   212, 323

T

Thirty-Nine Articles   22, 42
Ticehurst   32, 115-16, 123-4, 130, 132, 161, 171, 212, 261
tinderbox   111
tithe feast   94, 319

U

Uckfield   269
Upper Dicker   55, 57

V

Verrall, Eliza   207, 216
Verrall, Elizabeth   52
Vinall, John   44, 52, 55, 67

W

Wadhurst   123-4, 137
Walker, Emily   301
Watson, Joshua   163-4
Watts, Isaac   68
Weller, James   137, 149
Wells, William Rufus   249
Wenham, Eliza   72, 79-80, 92, 97-8, 116, 132, 146, 163, 207
Wesley, Charles   31, 68
Wesley, John   22, 27, 31, 136
West Grinstead   249
Westgate, Ann   18, 194
Westgate, Samuel   18
Westgate, Sarah   30
Whitefield, George   22, 27, 31, 135
Wickham, George   292
Wilkie, Christopher   288
Wivelsfield   30-1
woodland, coppicing   184
Woodmancote   248